Graph-Powered Analytics and Machine Learning with TigerGraph

Driving Business Outcomes with Connected Data

Victor Lee, Phuc Kien Nguyen, and Alexander Thomas

Beijing · Boston · Farnham · Sebastopol · Tokyo

Graph-Powered Analytics and Machine Learning with TigerGraph

by Victor Lee, Phuc Kien Nguyen, and Alexander Thomas

Copyright © 2023 O'Reilly Media. All rights reserved.

Published by O'Reilly Media, Inc., 1005 Gravenstein Highway North, Sebastopol, CA 95472.

O'Reilly books may be purchased for educational, business, or sales promotional use. Online editions are also available for most titles (*http://oreilly.com*). For more information, contact our corporate/institutional sales department: 800-998-9938 or *corporate@oreilly.com*.

Acquisitions Editor: Nicole Butterfield	**Indexer:** BIM Creatives, LLC
Development Editor: Gary O'Brien	**Interior Designer:** David Futato
Production Editor: Jonathon Owen	**Cover Designer:** Karen Montgomery
Copyeditor: nSight, Inc.	**Illustrator:** Kate Dullea
Proofreader: Shannon Turlington	

July 2023:   First Edition

Release History for the First Edition

2023-07-21:   First Release

See *http://oreilly.com/catalog/errata.csp?isbn=9781098106652* for release details.

978-1-098-10665-2

[LSI]

Table of Contents

Part II. Analyze

Preface

Objectives

The goal of this book is to introduce you to the concepts, techniques, and tools for graph data structures, graph analytics, and graph machine learning. When you've finished the book, we hope you'll understand how graph analytics can be used to address a range of real-world problems. We want you to be able to answer questions like the following: Is graph a good fit for this task? What tools and techniques should I use? What are the meaningful relationships in my data, and how do I formulate a task in terms of relationship analysis?

In our experience, we see that many people quickly grasp the general concept and structure of graphs, but it takes more effort and experience to "think graph," that is, to develop the intuition for how best to model your data as a graph and then to formulate an analytical task as a graph query. Each chapter begins with a list of its objectives. The objectives fall into three general areas: learning concepts about graph analytics and machine learning; solving particular problems with graph analytics; and understanding how to use the GSQL query language and the TigerGraph graph platform.

Audience and Prerequisites

We designed this book for anyone who has an interest in data analytics and wants to learn about graph analytics. You don't need to be a serious programmer or a data scientist, but some exposure to databases and programming concepts will definitely help you to follow the presentations. When we go into depth on a few graph algorithms and machine learning techniques, we present some mathematical equations involving sets, summation, and limits. Those equations, however, are a supplement to our explanations with words and figures.

In the use case chapters, we will be running prewritten GSQL code on the TigerGraph Cloud platform. You'll just need a computer and internet access. If you are familiar with the SQL database query language and any mainstream programming language, then you will be able to understand much of the GSQL code. If you are not, you can simply follow the instructions and run the prewritten use case examples while following along with the commentary in the book.

Approach and Roadmap

We aim to present the material as motivated by real-world data analytics needs, as opposed to theoretical principles. We always try to explain things in the simplest terms we can, using everyday concepts instead of technical jargon.

The GSQL language is introduced through complete examples. Early in the book, we provide line-by-line descriptions of the purpose and function of each line. We also highlight language structures, syntax, and semantics that are particularly important. For a comprehensive tutorial to GSQL, you can refer to additional resources beyond this book.

This book is structured as three parts: Part I: Connect; Part II: Analyze; and Part III: Learn. Each part has two types of chapters. The first is a concept chapter, followed by two or three chapters of use cases on TigerGraph Cloud and GSQL.

Chapter	Format	Title
1	Introduction	Connections Are Everything
Part I: Connect		
2	Concept	Connect and Explore Data
3	Use Case, Introduction to TigerGraph	See Your Customers and Business Better: 360 Graphs
4	Use Case	Studying Startup Investments
5	Use Case	Detecting Fraud and Money Laundering Patterns
Part II: Analyze		
6	Concept	Analyzing Connections for Deeper Insight
7	Use Case	Better Referrals and Recommendations
8	Use Case	Strengthening Cybersecurity
9	Use Case	Analyzing Airline Flight Routes
Part III: Learn		
10	Concept	Graph-Powered Machine Learning Methods
11	Use Case	Entity Resolution Revisited
12	Use Case, Introduction to Machine Learning Workbench	Improving Fraud Detection

Conventions Used in This Book

The following typographical conventions are used in this book:

Italic
> Indicates new terms, URLs, email addresses, filenames, and file extensions.

`Constant width`
> Used for program listings, as well as within paragraphs to refer to program elements such as variable or function names, databases, data types, environment variables, statements, and keywords.

`Constant width bold`
> Indicates vertex or edge types.

 This element signifies a tip or suggestion.

 This element signifies a general note.

 This element indicates a warning or caution.

Using Code Examples

This book has its own GitHub repository at *https://github.com/TigerGraph-DevLabs/Book-graph-powered-analytics*.

The initial content for this site will be copies of all the use case examples. We will also gather the book's GSQL tips into a single document as a primer. As we receive feedback from readers (and we hope to hear from you!), we'll post answers to frequently asked questions. We'll also add additional or modified GSQL examples or point out how you can take advantage of new capabilities in the TigerGraph platform.

For additional resources on TigerGraph and the GSQL language, the most comprehensive material will be found through TigerGraph's main website (*https://www.tiger graph.com*), its documentation site (*https://docs.tigergraph.com*), or its YouTube channel (*https://www.youtube.com/@TigerGraph*).

You can contact the authors at *gpaml.book@gmail.com*.

O'Reilly Online Learning

O'REILLY® For more than 40 years, *O'Reilly Media* has provided technology and business training, knowledge, and insight to help companies succeed.

Our unique network of experts and innovators share their knowledge and expertise through books, articles, and our online learning platform. O'Reilly's online learning platform gives you on-demand access to live training courses, in-depth learning paths, interactive coding environments, and a vast collection of text and video from O'Reilly and 200+ other publishers. For more information, visit *https://oreilly.com*.

How to Contact Us

Please address comments and questions concerning this book to the publisher:

> O'Reilly Media, Inc.
> 1005 Gravenstein Highway North
> Sebastopol, CA 95472
> 800-889-8969 (in the United States or Canada)
> 707-829-7019 (international or local)
> 707-829-0104 (fax)
> *support@oreilly.com*
> *https://www.oreilly.com/about/contact.html*

We have a web page for this book, where we list errata, examples, and any additional information. You can access this page at *https://oreil.ly/gpaml*.

For news and information about our books and courses, visit *https://oreilly.com*.

Find us on LinkedIn: *https://linkedin.com/company/oreilly-media*

Follow us on Twitter: *https://twitter.com/oreillymedia*

Watch us on YouTube: *https://youtube.com/oreillymedia*

Acknowledgments

This book would not exist without Gaurav Deshpande, TigerGraph's VP of marketing, who proposed that we should and could write it. He wrote the original proposal and chapter outline; the three-part structure is his idea. Thank you to TigerGraph's CEO and Founder Dr. Yu Xu, who supported our effort and who granted us the flexibility to work on this project. Dr. Xu also envisioned GraphStudio and its Starter Kits. Mingxi Wu and Alin Deutsch developed the GSQL language with efficient graph analytics in mind.

Besides the official authors, several others contributed to the material in this book. Tom Reeve applied his professional writing skills and knowledge of graph concepts to help us write Chapter 2, when writer's block and procrastination seemed to be our biggest foe. Emily McAuliffe and Amanda Morris designed several of the figures in the Early Release edition of the book. We needed some data scientists to review our chapters on machine learning. We turned to Parker Erickson and Bill Shi, who not only are experts in graph machine learning but developed the TigerGraph ML Workbench.

We are indebted to Xinyu Chang, TigerGraph's original GSQL query and solutions expert, for developing or overseeing the development of many of the use case starter kits and graph algorithm implementations in this book. Yiming Pan also wrote or optimized several graph algorithms and queries. Many of the book's examples are based on designs that they developed for TigerGraph's customers. The schemas, queries, and output displays in those starter kits are just as much a part of the content of this book as are the English paragraphs. We made several improvements to the starter kits to adapt them for this book. A number of people helped with reviewing and standardizing the starter kits: Jon Herke, head of developer relations; and several TigerGraph interns: Abudula Aisikaer, Shreya Chaudhary, McKenzie Steenson, and Kristine Zheng. Renchu Song and Duc Le, who lead the design and development of TigerGraph Cloud and GraphStudio, made sure that our revised starter kits were released into the product.

A million thanks to our two development editors at O'Reilly. Nicole Taché showed us the ropes and got us to our first early release of two chapters, with insightful comments, advice, and encouragement for this project. Gary O'Brien steered us from there to completion, through thick and thin. Both are wonderful editors, who were a pleasure and an honor to work with. Thank you also to our production editor Jonathon Owen and copyeditor Adam Lawrence.

Victor would like to thank his parents George and Sylvia Lee for their tireless support of his academic and nonacademic pursuits. He would like to thank his wife Susan Haddox for always being there for him, for putting up with his writing late into the night, for watching any and all *Star Trek* with him, and for being his model for how a person can be wicked smart and kind and funny.

Kien would like to thank his mother, My Linh Ly, for being a constant source of inspiration and a driving force for his career. He is also thankful for his wife, Sammy Wai-lok Lee, who has always been there with him, giving color to his life and caring for him and their baby girl Liv Vy Ly Nguyen-Lee, who was born during the writing of this book.

Alex would like to thank his parents, Chris and Becky Thomas, and his sister, Ari, for their support and encouragement as discussion partners during the writing process. Special thanks goes to his wife Gloria Zhang for her incredible strength, her vast intelligence, and her limitless capability for inspiration.

CHAPTER 1

Connections Are Everything

In an extreme view, the world can be seen as only connections, nothing else. We think of a
dictionary as the repository of meaning, but it defines words only in terms of other words.
I liked the idea that a piece of information is really defined only by what it's related to, and
how it's related. There really is little else to meaning. The structure is everything.

—Tim Berners-Lee, *Weaving the Web: The Original Design and Ultimate Destiny of the*
World Wide Web (1999), p. 14

The 20th century demonstrated how much we could achieve with spreadsheets and
relational databases. Tabular data ruled. The 21st century has already shown us that
that isn't enough. Tables flatten our perspective, showing connections in only two
dimensions. In the real world, things are related to and connected to a myriad of
other things, and those relationships shape what is and what will happen. To gain full
understanding, we need to model these connections.

Personal computers were introduced in the 1970s, but they didn't take off until they
found their first killer apps: financial spreadsheets. VisiCalc on the Apple II and then
Lotus 1-2-3 on the IBM PC[1] automated the laborious and error-prone calculations
that bookkeepers had been doing by hand ever since the invention of writing and
arithmetic: adding up rows and columns of figures, and then perhaps performing
even more complex statistical calculations.

In 1970, E. F. Codd published his seminal paper on the relational database model.
In these early days of databases, a few models were bouncing around, including
the network database model. Codd's relational model was built on something that
everyone could identify with and was easy to program: the table.

---

1 "Killer Application," Wikipedia, last updated May 14, 2023, *https://en.wikipedia.org/wiki/Killer_application.*

Moreover, matrix algebra and many statistical methods are also ready-made to work with tables. Both physicists and business analysts used matrices to define and find the optimal solutions to everything from nuclear reactor design to supply chain management. Tables lend themselves to parallel processing; just partition the workload vertically or horizontally. Spreadsheets, relational databases, and matrix algebra: the tabular approach seemed to be the solution to everything.

Then the World Wide Web happened, and everything changed.

Connections Change Everything

The web is more than the internet. The internet began in the early 1970s as a data connection network between selected US research institutions. The World Wide Web, invented by CERN researcher Tim Berners-Lee in 1989, is a set of technologies running on top of the internet that make it much easier to publish, access, and connect data in a format easy for humans to consume and interact with. Browsers, hyperlinks, and web addresses are also hallmarks of the web. At the same time that the web was being developed, governments were loosening their controls on the internet and allowing private companies to expand it. We now have billions of interconnected web pages, connecting people, multimedia, facts, and opinions at a truly global scale. Having data isn't enough. How the data is structured matters.

What Is a Graph?

As the word "web" started to take on new connotations, so did the word "graph." For most people, "graph" was synonymous with a line chart that could show something such as a stock's price over time. Mathematicians had another meaning for the word, however, and as networks and connections started to matter to the business world, the mathematical meaning started to come to the fore.

A graph is an abstract data structure consisting of *vertices* (or *nodes*) and connections between vertices called *edges*. That's it. A graph is the idea of a network, constructed from these two types of elements. This abstraction allows us to study networks (or graphs) in general, to discover properties, and to devise algorithms to solve general tasks. Graph theory and graph analytics provided organizations with the tools they needed to leverage the sudden abundance of connected data.

In Figure 1-1, we can see the network of relationships between the actors and directors of *Star Wars* (1977) and *The Empire Strikes Back* (1980). This is easily modelable as a graph with different types of edges connecting the different types of vertices. Actors and movies can have an `acted_in` vertex connecting them, movies and other movies can be connected by an `is_sequel_of` vertex, and movies and directors can have a `directed_by` edge connection.

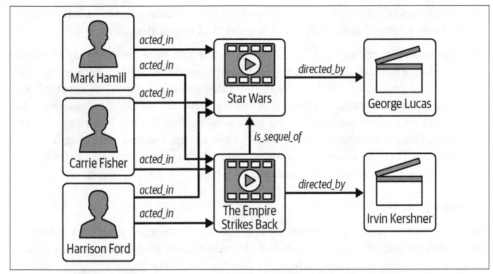

Figure 1-1. A graph showing some key players and connections in early Star Wars films

Why Graphs Matter

The web showed us that sometimes we accomplish more by having varied data that is linked together than by trying to merge it all into a few rigid tables. It also showed us that connections themselves are a form of information. We have a limitless number of types of relationships: parent–child, purchaser–product, friend–friend, and so on. As Berners-Lee observed, we get meaning from connections. When we know someone is a parent, we can infer that they have had certain life experiences and have certain concerns. We can also make informed guesses at how the parent and child will interact relative to each other.

The web, however, only highlighted what has always been true: data relationships matter when representing data and when analyzing data. Graphs can embody the informatiooonal content of relationships better than tables. This enriched data format is better at representing complex information, and when it comes to analytics, it produces more insightful results. Business-oriented data analysts appreciate the intuitive aspect of seeing relationships visualized as a graph, and data scientists find that the richer content yields more accurate machine learning models. As a bonus, graph databases often perform faster than relational databases when working on tasks involving searching multiple levels of connections (or multiple *hops*).

Structure matters

The founders of Google recognized that the web would become too large for anyone to grasp. We would need tools to help us search for and recommend pages. A key component of Google's early success was PageRank, an algorithm that models the internet as a set of interconnected pages and decides which are the most influential or authoritative pages—based solely on their pattern of interconnection.

Over the years, search engines have become better and better at inferring from our queries what we would really like to know and would find useful. One of Google's tools for that is its Knowledge Graph, an interconnected set of categorized and tagged facts and concepts, harvested from the broader web. After analyzing the user's query to understand not just the surface words but the implied categories and objectives, Google searches its Knowledge Graph to find the best matching facts and then presents them in a well-formatted sidebar. Only a graph has the flexibility and expressiveness to make sense of this universe of facts.

Communities matter

Facebook started as a social networking app for college students; it's grown to become the world's largest online social network. It's self-evident that Facebook cares about networks and graphs. From each user's perspective, there is oneself and one's set of friends. Though we act individually, people will naturally tend to gather into communities that evolve and have influence as though they were living entities themselves. Communities are powerful influences on what information we receive and how we form opinions. Businesses leverage community behavior for promoting their products. People also use social networks to promote political agendas. Detecting these communities is essential to understand the social dynamics, but you won't see the communities in a tabular view.

Patterns of connections matter

The same information can be presented either in tabular form or in graph form, but the graph form shows us things that the table obscures. Think of a family tree. We could list all the parent–child relationships in a table, but the table would miss important patterns that span multiple relationships: family, grandchildren, cousins.

A less obvious example is a graph of financial transactions. Financial institutions and vendors look for particular patterns of transactions that suggest possible fraudulent or money laundering activity. One pattern is a large amount of money being transferred from party to party, with a high percentage of the money coming back to the origin: a closed loop. Figure 1-2 shows such loops, extracted from a graph database containing millions of transactions, from our financial fraud example in Chapter 5. Other patterns can be linear or Y-shaped; anything is possible. The pattern depends on the nature of the data and the question of interest.

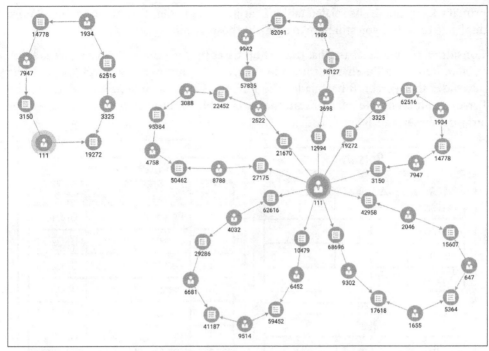

Figure 1-2. Graph search results showing sequences of transactions in a closed loop (see a larger version of this figure at https://oreil.ly/gpam0102)

Patterns can depend not only on the shape but on the type of vertex and type of edge. Figure 1-2 has two types of vertices: Accounts and Transactions (yes, the Transactions are vertices, not the edges). If we chose, we could separate Person and Account into separate entities. A person can be associated with multiple accounts. Breaking it up like this enables us to analyze the behavior of a Person, not just an Account. Modeling important concepts as vertex types enables richer search analytical capability, as we will see in later chapters.

Edges Outperform Table Joins

It's true that you can represent vertices as tables and edges as tables. What is actually different about a graph, and why do we claim it is faster for multihop operations? First of all, the graph is not just the visualization. We visualize data for human convenience, but the computer doesn't need this visual aspect at all.

The performance advantage of graphs comes down to the mechanics of how searching for and utilizing connections actually takes place in a relational database versus a graph database. In a relational database, there is no link between tables until you run a query. Yes, if you have declared and enforced a foreign key in one table to reference another table, then you know that the foreign key column's value will correspond to a primary key value in its related table. That just means that two different tables store duplicate data, but you still have to seek out those matching records.

Consider a simple database that tracks purchases by customers. We have three tables: Person, Item, and Purchases, shown in Figure 1-3. Suppose we want to know all the purchases that Person B has made. The Purchases table is organized by date, not by Person, so it seems we need to scan the entire table to find Person B's purchases. For large databases, this is very inefficient.

Person

PID	Details			
Person A				
Person B				
Person C				
Person D				

Item

IID	Details			
Item 1				
Item 2				
Item 3				
Item 4				
Item 5				

Purchases

TID	PID	IID	Date
1	Person A	Item 1	01-01-23
2	Person C	Item 4	01-02-23
3	Person D	Item 5	01-02-23
4	Person B	Item 2	01-04-23
5	Person C	Item 3	01-07-23
6	Person B	Item 1	01-07-23
7	Person D	Item 4	01-07-23
8	Person B	Item 4	01-08-23
9	Person C	Item 1	01-10-23
10	Person B	Item 3	01-12-23
11	Person D	Item 1	01-12-23

Figure 1-3. Relational table structure for Person-Purchases-Item database

This is a common problem, so relational databases have created a solution: secondary indexes. Just like a reference book's index can tell you the page numbers of where certain key topics appear, a table index tells you the row address where certain column values appear. Figure 1-4 sketches out the idea of indexes for the PID (Person ID) and IID (Item ID) columns of the Purchases table. Great, now we know Person B's purchases are listed in rows 4, 6, 8, and 10 of the table. There are still some trade-offs, however. It takes time and storage space to create an index and then to maintain it as the database evolves, and it is still an extra step to go to the index rather than going directly to the data rows that have what you want. The index itself is a table. How quickly can we find Person B among all the persons?

Without index:

1. Read each row in Purchases table (slow and not scalable).

With index:

1. Go to a secondary index for the Purchases table.
2. Find the row of interest (could be fast).
3. Use the index.

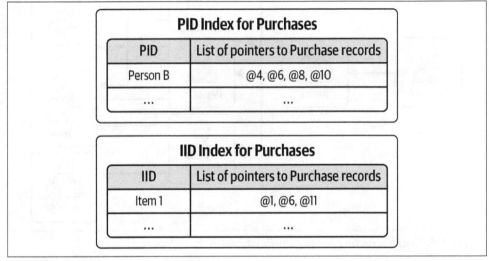

Figure 1-4. Secondary indexes for Purchases table

A graph database or graph analytics platform eliminates the problem of searching through tables and building indexes in order to find connections: the connections are already there.

In a graph, an edge points directly to its endpoint vertices. There is no need to read through a table, and there is no need to build an extra indexing structure. While the speed difference may be modest for one connection, a graph can be hundreds of times faster when you want to repeat this across a chain of connections and when you need to join many data records, such as entire tables. For example, suppose we want to answer this question: "Find the items that were purchased by persons who also bought the item that you just bought." Figure 1-5 displays exactly this, where "you" are Person A:

1. Person A bought Item 1.

2. Persons B, C, and D also bought Item 1.

3. Persons B, C, and D also bought Items 2, 3, 4, and 5.

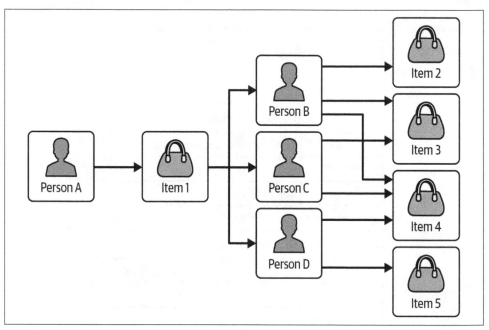

Figure 1-5. Graph structure for Person-Purchases-Item database

This is a three-hop query—pretty simple for a graph. We traverse a total of 9 vertices and 11 edges to answer this question.

In a table-based system, this would take three table joins. Good query optimization and indexing will reduce the amount of work so that it comes close to the very efficient graph model, but at the cost of going back and forth between the data tables and the indexes and performing the index lookups. The graph doesn't need indexes for this query because the connections are already built-in and optimized.

One cautionary note: the full performance benefit is only realized on "native" graphs, which are designed from the ground up to be graphs. It is possible to build a graph system on top of a tabular database. That combination will function like a graph but will not perform like one.

Graph Analytics and Machine Learning

Perhaps the biggest benefit of graph-structured data is how it can improve analytics results and performance. We gather and store data for many reasons. Sometimes all we want to do is to recall a particular bit of information exactly as it was recorded before. For example, a credit card company records each of your transactions. Each month, it sends you a statement that lists each of your transactions and payments. Data tables are sufficient for this simple listing and summing.

Businesses these days need to do more with the data than just these baseline tasks. They need to find and capture more revenue opportunities, cut losses from fraud and waste, and reduce risk. Seeing patterns in their data can help with all these needs. For example, what is your credit card spending pattern over time? Can they categorize you with other persons with similar patterns? How can the business use social network relationships to serve its interests, such as promoting business through recommendations or predicting behavior based on family connections? The business has customer information from multiple sources. Data differences such as typos, differences in allowed characters, name or address changes, and customers' intentional use of different online personae can make them seem like multiple different persons. Can the business use analytics to detect and integrate these records? Are you committing card fraud, or has someone stolen your card number?

Analysis is about seeing patterns. Patterns are collections of relationships structured in a certain way, which is also exactly what graphs are. A pattern can have both structural and quantitative aspects, such as "the average household has 1.4 pets." The structural part (the housing relationships that define a household, and the relationship between certain animals and households) can be encoded as a graph pattern query. Graph databases and graph analytics platforms can do quantitative analysis, too, of course. Part 2 of this book will help you to understand and apply graph analytics.

Graph-Enhanced Machine Learning

Machine learning is using past data to detect a pattern that might help us predict future activity. Since graphs are the natural way to represent, store, and analyze patterns, it stands to reason that graphs will help us make better predictions.

Conventional supervised machine learning makes some assumptions about the data that simplifies that analysis and that works well with tabular data. First, we assume that every data point exists in isolation: every record in our dataset is statistically independent of every other record. Second, we assume that the data points are identically distributed when creating supervised machine learning models. So we believe that every sample comes from the same distribution. The notion for these two assumptions is known as *independent and identically distributed (i.i.d.)*. However, real-life events do not always adhere to the phenomenon of i.i.d.

To get the most accurate machine learning models, we need to take into account the relationships between data points. For example, when we model a social network with people interacting with one another, people who share the same friends are more likely to get into contact with one another than with others who do not have common friends. Graphs allow us to explicitly leverage the relations between the data points between common friends because we model the relationships and not just the nodes independently.

There are several ways that graph data can improve machine learning. One way is to use selected graph algorithms or other graph queries to assess the relational characteristics of data points (vertices). For example, the PageRank scores of parties in a transactional graph have helped to predict fraudsters. You can use these graph-based features that embody the relationships between data points to enrich your existing feature sets while retaining your existing model training methods.

Instead of following this traditional machine learning approach, where features are designed and handpicked during the feature engineering phase, you can generate features from the graph automatically by learning the graph's structure. This so-called *graph representation learning* alleviates the need for feature engineering. It is less dependent on the analyst's domain knowledge to design meaningful features as it follows a data-driven approach. There are two flavors of graph representation learning: embedding and graph neutral networks. Embedding techniques produce vectors associated with each data point. We can pass these embedding vectors into any downstream machine learning algorithm to include them in our prediction task. Graph neural networks (GNNs) are analogous to conventional neural networks, except that they take the graph's connections into account during the training process. It is only a slight exaggeration to say that GNNs do what other neural networks do, with the potential for better results. Part 3 of this book is dedicated to graph-enhanced machine learning.

Chapter Summary

In this chapter, we've learned that a graph is an abstract data structure consisting of vertices and connections between those vertices called edges. Graphs enable us to connect data together, to discover patterns and communities better than relational databases. Edges perform better than table joins because edges directly connect the vertices to their endpoint, making it unnecessary to read through a table and build an extra indexing structure.

Graph analytics is powerful because it efficiently explores and identifies patterns in the data. Graph analytics can improve analytics performance and uncover things not discovered by other methods.

Lastly, we have seen that graph-structured data helps us to make better predictions with machine learning models. Graph allows us to leverage relationships between data points explicitly, making our model closer to the natural phenomenon we are investigating. Modeling the relationships in such a way will enable us to learn graph representations that automatically generate features from the graph instead of hand-picking features during the feature engineering phase.

In the next chapter, we will expand your understanding of graph concepts and terminology and get you started on your way to see the world through graph-shaped lenses.

PART I

Connect

CHAPTER 2

Connect and Explore Data

In Chapter 1, we showed the potential of graph analytics and machine learning applied to human and business endeavors, and we proposed to present the details in three stages: the power of connected data, the power of graph analytics, and the power of graph machine learning. In this chapter, we will take a deep dive into the first stage: the power of connected data.

Before we delve into the power of connected data, we need to lay some groundwork. We start by introducing the concepts and nomenclature of the graph data model. If you are already familiar with graphs, you may want to skim this section to check that we're on the same page with regard to terminology. Besides graphs themselves, we'll cover the important concepts of a graph schema and traversing a graph. Traversal is how we search for data and connections in a graph.

And along the way, we talk about the differences between graph and relational databases and how we can ask questions and solve problems with graph analytics that would not be feasible in a relational database.

From that foundational understanding of what a graph is, we move on to present examples of the *power* of a graph by illustrating six ways that graph data provides you with more insight and more analytical capability than tabular data.

After completing this chapter, you should be able to:

- Use the standard terminology for describing graphs
- Know the difference between a graph schema and a graph instance
- Create a basic graph model or schema from scratch or from a relational database model
- Apply the "traversal" metaphor for searching and exploring graph data

- Understand six ways that graph data empowers your knowledge and analytics
- State the entity resolution problem and show how graphs resolve this problem

Graph Structure

In Chapter 1, we introduced you to the basic idea of a graph. In this section, we are going to go deeper. First we will establish the terminology that we will be using for the rest of this book. Then we will talk more about the idea of a graph schema, which is the key to having a plan and awareness of your data's structure.

Graph Terminology

Suppose you're organizing data about movies, actors, and directors. Maybe you work for Netflix or one of the other streaming services, or maybe you're just a fan.

Let's start with one movie, *Star Wars: A New Hope*, its three main actors, and its director. If you were building this in a relational database, you could record this information in a single table, but the table would grow quickly and rapidly become unwieldy. How would we even record details about a movie, the fact that 50 actors appeared in it, and the details of each of those actor's careers, all in one table?

Best practice for the design of relational databases would suggest putting actors, movies, and directors each into a separate table, but that would mean also adding in cross-reference tables to handle the many-to-many relationships between actors and movies and between movies and directors.

So in total, you'd need five tables just to represent this example in a relational database, as in Figure 2-1.

Separating different types of things into different tables is the right answer for organizing the data, but to see how one record relates to another, we have to rejoin the data. A query asking which actors worked with which directors would involve building a temporary table in memory called a join table that includes all possible combinations of rows across all the tables you've called, which satisfy the conditions of the query. Join tables are expensive in terms of memory and processor time.

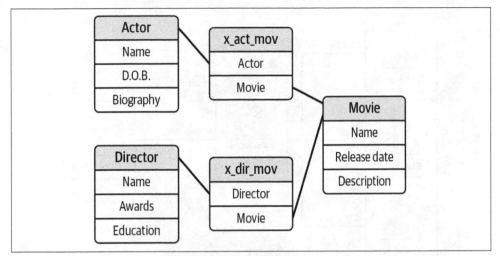

Figure 2-1. Diagram of relational tables for a simple movie database

As we can see from Figure 2-2, there is a lot of redundant data in this table join. For very large or complex databases, you would want to think of ways to structure the data and your queries to optimize the join tables.

Actor	Movie	Director
Mark Hamill	Star Wars	George Lucas
Carrie Fisher	Star Wars	George Lucas
Harrison Ford	Star Wars	George Lucas

Figure 2-2. Temporary table created from relational database query showing how three actors are linked to George Lucas via the movie Star Wars

However, if we compare that to the graph approach, as shown in Figure 2-3, one thing becomes immediately clear: the difference between a table and graph is that a graph can directly show how one data element is related to another. That is, the relationships between the data points are built into the database and don't have to be constructed at runtime. So one of the key differences between a graph and relational database is that in a graph database, the relationships between data points are *explicit*.

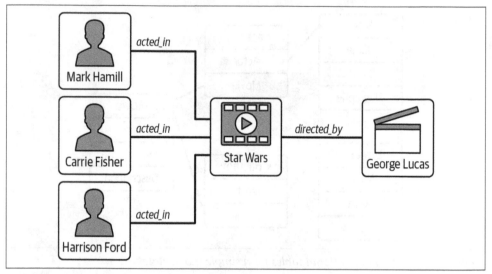

Figure 2-3. Graph showing our basic information about Star Wars

Each actor, movie, and director is called a *node* or a *vertex* (plural: *vertices*). Vertices represent things, physical or abstract. In our example, the graph has five vertices. The connections between vertices are called *edges*, which describe the relationships between the vertices. Edges are also considered data elements. This graph has four edges: three for actors showing how they are related to a movie (`acted_in`), and one for a director showing their relationship to a movie (`directed_by`). In its simplest form, a *graph* is a collection of vertices and edges. We will use the general term *object* to refer to either a vertex or an edge.

With this graph, we can answer a basic question: what actors have worked with the director George Lucas? Starting from George Lucas, we look at the movies he directed, which include *Star Wars*, and then we look at the actors in that movie, which include Mark Hamill, Carrie Fisher, and Harrison Ford.

It can be useful or even necessary to distinguish the direction of an edge. In a graph database, an edge can be *directed* or *undirected*. A *directed edge* has a specific directionality, going from a source vertex to a target vertex. We draw directed edges as arrows.

By adding a directed edge, we can also show hierarchy, that is, *The Empire Strikes Back* was the sequel to *Star Wars* (Figure 2-4).

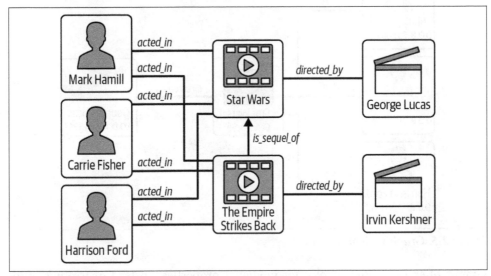

Figure 2-4. Multimovie graph with a directed edge. This shows how we begin to build up the database with additional movies and production personnel. Note the directed edge, is_sequel_of, *which provides the context to show that Empire was the sequel to Star Wars and not vice versa.*

To do more useful work with a graph, however, we will want to add more details about each vertex or edge, such as an actor's birth date or a movie's genre.

This book describes property graphs. A *property graph* is a graph where each vertex and each edge can have properties that provide the details about individual elements. If we look again at relational databases, properties are like the columns in a table. Properties are what make graphs truly useful. They add richness and context to data, which enables us to develop more nuanced queries to extract just the data that we need. Figure 2-5 shows the *Star Wars* graph with some added features.

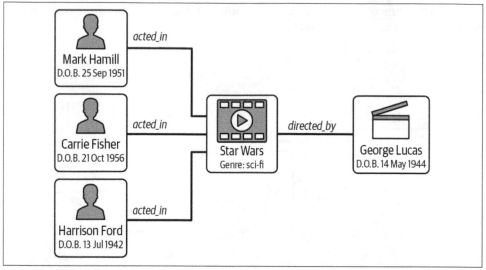

Figure 2-5. Graph with properties

Graphs offer us another choice for modeling properties. Instead of treating genre as a property of movies, we could make each genre a separate vertex. Why do this? When the property is categorical, then we expect lots of other vertices to have the same property value (e.g., there are lots of sci-fi movies). All the sci-fi movies will link to the Sci-fi vertex, making it incredibly easy to search them or to collect statistics about them, such as "what was the top-grossing sci-fi movie?" All the non-sci-fi movies have already been filtered out for you. Graph structure can not only model your core data but can also act as a search index.

Other reasons why we might want to model a property as a vertex is to improve the normalization or the data richness. *Normalization* is an approach to decomposing tables to eliminate redundancy and update complexities. Additionally, decomposing into more vertex types means we have more things that can have properties.

In our movie database example, we might want to create a new type of vertex called **Character** so we can show who played what role. Figure 2-6 shows our *Star Wars* graph with the addition of **Character** vertices. The interesting thing about Darth Vader, of course, is that he was played by two people: David Prowse (in costume) and James Earl Jones (voice). Fortunately, our database can represent this reality with a minimum of modification.

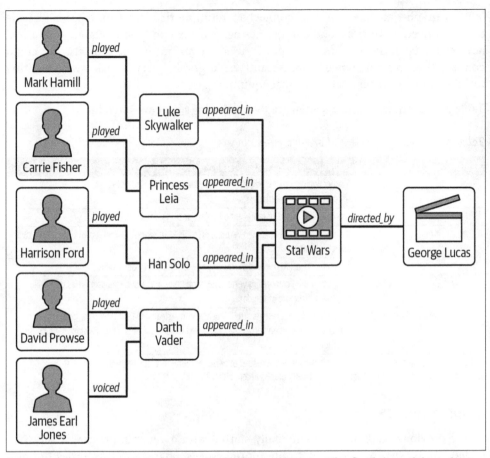

Figure 2-6. Movie graph with **Actor** *and* **Character** *types. The flexibility of this schema enables us to easily show two actors portraying one character.*

What else can we do with this graph? Well, it's flexible enough to allow us to add just about every person who was involved in the production of this movie—from the director and actors to make-up artists, special effects artists, key grip, and even best boy. Everyone who contributed to a movie could be linked using an edge called worked_on and an edge property called role, which could include director, actor, voice actor, camera operator, key grip, and so on.

If we then built up our database to include thousands of movies and everyone who had worked on them, we could use graph algorithms to answer questions like "Which actors do certain directors like to work with most?" With a graph database, you can answer less obvious questions like "Who are the specialists in science fiction special effects?" or "Which lighting technicians do certain directors like to work with most?" Interesting questions for companies that sell graphics software or lighting equipment.

With a graph database, you can connect to multiple data sources, extract just the data you need as vertices, and run queries against the combined dataset. If you had access to a database of lighting equipment used on various movie projects, you could connect that to your movie database and use a graph query to ask which lighting technicians have experience with what equipment.

Table 2-1 summarizes the essential graph terminology we have introduced.

Table 2-1. Glossary of essential graph terminology

Term	Definition
Graph	A collection of vertices, edges, and properties used to represent connected data and support semantic queries.
Vertex[a]	A graph object used to represent an object or thing. Plural: vertices.
Edge	A graph object that links two vertices, often used to represent a relationship between two objects or things.
Property	A variable associated with a vertex or edge, often used to describe it.
Schema	A database plan comprising vertex and edge types and associated properties that will define the structure of the data.
Directed edge / Undirected edge	A directed edge represents a relationship with a clear semantic direction, from a source vertex to a destination vertex. An undirected edge represents a relationship in which no direction is implied.

[a] Another commonly used alternative name is *node*. It is a matter of personal preference. It's been proposed that the upcoming ISO standard query language for property graphs accept either VERTEX or NODE.

Graph Schemas

In the previous section, we intentionally started with a very simple graph and then added complexity, by adding not only more vertices, edges, and properties but also new *types* of vertices and edges. To model and manage a graph well, especially in a business setting, it's essential to plan out your data types and properties.

We call this plan a graph *schema*, or graph *data model*, analogous to the schema or entity-relationship model for a relational database. It defines the types of vertices and edges that our graph will contain as well as the properties associated with these objects.

You could make a graph without a schema by just adding arbitrary vertices and edges, but you'd quickly find it difficult to work with and difficult to make sense of. Also, if you wanted to search the data for all the movies, for example, it would be extremely helpful to know that they are all in fact referred to as "movie" and not "film" or "motion picture"!

It's also helpful to settle on a standard set of properties for each object type. If we know all movie vertices have the same core set of properties, such as title, genre, and release date, then we can easily and confidently perform analysis on those properties.

Figure 2-7 shows a possible schema for a movie graph database. It systematically handles several of the data complexities that arose as we talked about adding more and more movies to the database.

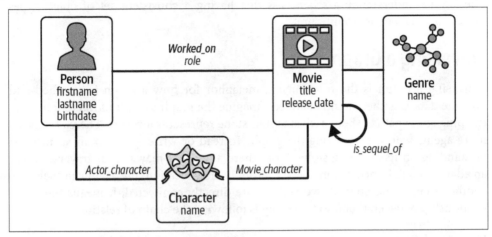

Figure 2-7. Graph schema for movie database

Let's run through the features of the schema:

- A **Person** vertex type represents a real-world person, such as George Lucas.

- The **Worked_on** edge type connects a **Person** to a **Movie**. It has a property to describe the person's role: director, producer, actor, gaffer, etc. By having the role as a property, we can support as many roles as we want with only one vertex type for persons and one edge type for working on a film. If a person had multiple roles, then the graph can have multiple edges.[1] Schemas only show one of each type of object.

- The **Character** vertex type is separate from the **Person** vertex type. One **Person** could portray more than one **Character** (Tyler Perry in the *Madea* films), or more than one **Person** could portray one **Character** (David Prowse, James Earl Jones, and Sebastian Shaw as Darth Vader in *The Return of the Jedi*).

- The **Movie** vertex type is straightforward.

- **Is_sequel_of** is a directed edge type, telling us that the source **Movie** is the sequel of the destination **Movie**.

---

1 Some graph databases would handle multiple roles by having a single Worked_on edge whose role property accepts a list of roles.

- As noted before, we chose to model the **Genre** of a movie as a vertex type instead of as a property, to make it easier to filter and analyze movies by genre.

The key to understanding schemas is that having a consistent set of object types makes your data easier to interpret.

Traversing a Graph

Traversing a graph is the fundamental metaphor for how a graph is searched and how the data is gathered and analyzed. Imagine the graph as a set of interconnecting stepping stone paths, where each stepping-stone represents a vertex. There are one or more agents who are accessing the graph. To read or write a vertex, an agent must be standing on its stepping stone. From there, the agent may step or traverse across an edge to a neighboring stone/vertex. From its new location, the agent can then take another step. Remember: if two vertices are directly connected, it means there is a relationship between them, so traversing is following the chain of relationships.

Hops and Distance

Traversing one edge is also called making a *hop*. An analogy to traversing a graph is moving on a game board, like the one shown in Figure 2-8. A graph is an exotic game board, and you traverse the graph as you would move across the game board.

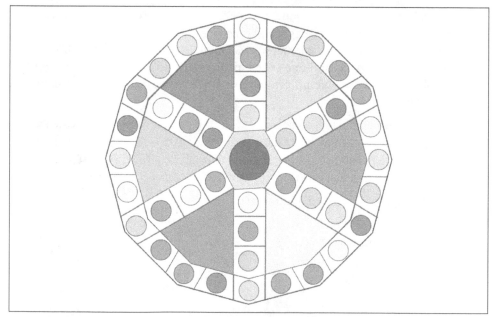

Figure 2-8. Traversing a graph is like moving on a game board

In many board games, when it is your turn, you roll a die to determine how many steps or hops to take. In other games, you may traverse the board until you reach a space of a certain type. This is exactly like traversing a graph in search of a particular vertex type.

Graph hops and distance come up in other real-world situations. You may have heard of "six degrees of separation." This refers to the belief that everyone in the United States is connected to everyone else through at most six hops of relationship. Or, if you use the LinkedIn business network app, you have probably seen that when you look at a person's profile, LinkedIn will tell you if they are connected to you directly (one hop), through two hops, or through three hops.

Traversing a graph is also how searches are conducted in graph databases. There are two basic approaches: either visit every neighbor vertex before continuing to the next level (breadth-first search) or follow a single chain of connections to the end before trying alternate paths (depth-first search). We'll go further into detail about these search types in Chapter 6.

Breadth and Depth

There are two basic approaches to systematically traversing a graph to conduct a search. Breadth-first search (BFS) means visit each of your direct neighbors before continuing the search to the next level of neighbors, the next level, and so on. Graph databases with parallel processing can accelerate BFS by having multiple traversals take place at the same time.

Depth-first search (DFS) means follow a single chain of connections as far as you can before backtracking to try other paths. Both BFS and DFS will result in eventually visiting every vertex, unless you stop because you have found what you sought.

Graph Modeling

Now you know what graphs and graph schemas are. But how do you come up with a good graph model?

Start by asking yourself these questions:

- What are the key objects or entities that I care about?
- What are the key relationships that I care about?
- What are the key properties of entities that I want to filter out?

Schema Options and Trade-Offs

As we have seen, good graph schema design represents data and relationships in a natural way that allows us to traverse vertices and edges as if they were real-world objects. As with any collection of real-world things, there are many ways we could organize our collection to optimize searching and extracting what we need.

In designing a graph database, two considerations that will influence the design are the format of our input data and our query use cases. And as we will see in this section, a key trade-off is whether we want to optimize our schema to use less memory or make queries run faster.

Vertex, edge, or property?

If you are converting tabular data into a graph, the natural thing seems to be to convert each table to a vertex type and each table column to a vertex property. In fact, a column could map to a vertex, an edge, a property of a vertex, or a property of an edge.

Entities and abstract concepts generally map to vertices, and you could think of them as nound, such as *movie* or *actor* from our earlier example. Relationships generally map to edges, and you can think of them as verbs, such as *directs* or *acts*. Descriptors are analogous to adjectives and adverbs and can map to vertex or edge properties, depending on the context and your query use case.

At first glance, it would appear that storing object attributes as close to the object as possible—that is, as properties—would deliver the most optimal solution. However, consider a use case in which you need to optimize your search for product color. Color is a quality that would usually be expected to be found as a property of a vertex, but then searching for blue objects would necessitate looking at every vertex.

In a graph, you can create a search index by defining a vertex type called `color` and linking the `color` vertex and the `product` vertex via an undirected edge. Then to find all blue objects, you simply start from the `color` vertex blue and find all linked `product` vertices. This speeds up query performance, with the trade-off being greater complexity and higher memory usage.

Edge direction

Earlier we introduced the concept of directionality in edges and noted that you can, in your design schema, define an edge type as directed or undirected. In this section, we'll discuss the benefits and trade-offs of each type. We'll also discuss a hybrid option available in the TigerGraph database.

This is so useful you might think you could use it all the time, but with all things computational, there are benefits and trade-offs in your choice of edge type.

Undirected edge

Links any two vertices of defined type with no directionality implied. The benefit is they are easy to work with when creating links and easy to traverse in either direction. For example, if users and email addresses are both vertex types, you can use an undirected edge to find someone's email but also find all the users who use that same email address—something you can't do with a directed edge.

The trade-off with an undirected edge is it does not give you contextual information such as hierarchy. If you have an enterprise graph and want to find the parent company, for example, you can't do this with undirected edges because there is no hierarchy. In this case, you would need to use a directed edge.

Directed edge

Represents a relationship with a clear semantic direction, from a source vertex to a destination vertex. The benefit to a directed edge is it gives you more contextual information. It is likely to be more efficient for the database to store and handle than an undirected edge. The trade-off, however, is you can't trace backward should you need to.

Directed edge paired with a reverse directed edge

You can have the benefits of directional semantics *and* traversing in either direction if you define two directed edge types, one for each direction. For example, to implement a family tree, you could define a **child_of** edge type to traverse down the tree and a **parent_of** edge type to traverse up the tree. The trade-off, though, is you have to maintain two edge types: every time you insert or modify one edge, you need to insert or modify its partner. The TigerGraph database makes this easier by allowing you to define the two types together and to write data ingestion jobs that handle the two together.

As you can see, your choice of edge type will be influenced by the types of queries you need to run balanced against operational overheads such as memory, speed, and coding.

 If the source vertex and destination vertex types are different, such as **Person** and **Product**, you can usually settle for an undirected edge and let the vertex types provide the directional context. It's when the two vertex types are the same and you care about direction that you must use a directed edge.

Granularity of edge type

How many different edge types do you need, and how can you optimize your use of edge types? In theory, you could have one edge type—undirected—that linked every type of vertex in your schema. The benefit would be simplicity—only one edge type to remember!—but the trade-offs would be the number of edge properties you would need for context and slower query performance.

At the other extreme, you could have a different edge type for each type of relationship. For instance, in a social network, you could have separate edge types for **coworker**, **friend**, **parent_of**, **child_of**, and so on. This would be very efficient to traverse if you were looking for just one type of relationship, such as professional networks. The trade-off is the need to define new edge types to represent new types of relationships and a loss of abstraction—that is, an increase in complexity—in your code.

Modeling interaction events

In many applications, we want to track interactions between entities, such as a financial transaction where one financial account transfers funds to another account. You might think of representing the transaction (transferring funds) as an edge between two **Account** vertices. If you have multiple occurrences, will you have multiple edges? While it seems easy to conceive of this (Figure 2-9), in the realms of both mathematical theory and real-world databases, this is not so straightforward.

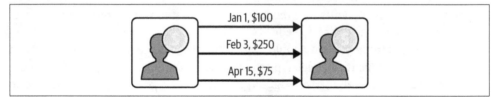

Figure 2-9. Multiple events represented as multiple edges

In mathematics, having multiple edges between a given pair of vertices goes beyond the definition of ordinary graphs into multi-edges and multigraphs. Due to this complexity, not all graph databases support this, or if they do, they don't have a convenient way to refer to a specific edge in the group. Another way to handle this is to model each interaction event as a vertex and use edges to connect the event to the participants (Figure 2-10a). Modeling an event as a vertex provides the greatest flexibility for linking it to other vertices and for designing analytics. A third way is to create a single edge between the two entities and aggregate all the transactions into an edge property (Figure 2-10b).

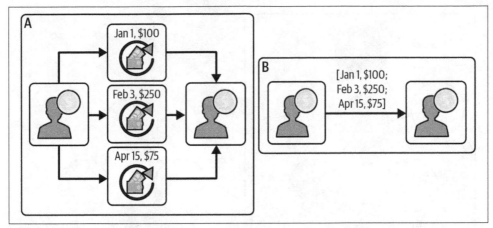

Figure 2-10. Two alternate ways to model multiple events: (a) events as vertices, and (b) a single event edge with a property that contains a list of occurrences

Table 2-2 summarizes the pros and cons of each approach. The simplest model is not always your best choice, because application requirements and database performance issues may be more important.

Table 2-2. Comparing options for modeling multiple occurrences of an interaction

Model	Benefit	Trade-off
Multiple edges	Simple model	Database support is not universal
Vertex linked to related vertices	Filtering on vertex properties Ease of analytics including community and similarity of events Advanced search tree integration	Uses more memory Takes more steps to traverse
Single edge with property recording details of occurrences	Less memory usage Fewer steps to traverse between users	Searching on transactions is less efficient Slower update/insert of the property

Adjusting your design schema based on use case

Suppose you are creating a graph database to track events in an IT network. We'll assume you would need these vertex types: **event**, **server**, **IP**, **event type**, **user**, and **device**. But what relationships would you want to analyze, and what edges would you need? The design would depend on what you wanted to focus on, and your schema could be event centered or user centered.

For the event-centered schema (Figure 2-11a), the key benefit is that all related data is just one hop away from the **event** vertex. This makes it straightforward to find communities of events, find servers that processed the most events of a given type, and find the servers that were visited by any given IP. The trade-off is that from a user perspective, the user is two hops away from a **device** or **IP** vertex.

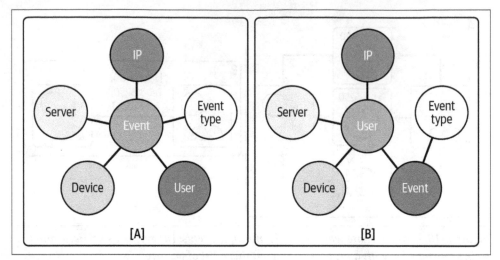

Figure 2-11. Two options for arranging the same vertex types: (a) event centered and (b) user centered

We can fix this by making our schema user centered at the expense of separating events from IPs and servers by two hops, and separating event types from devices, servers, and IPs by three hops (Figure 2-11b). However, these disadvantages might be worth the trade-off of being able to do useful user-centered analysis such as finding all users who share the same device/IP/server as a given user or profiling blocked users to try to predict who else should be blocked.

Transforming Tables in a Graph

You won't always create graph databases from scratch. Often, you'll be taking data that is already stored in tables and then moving or copying the data into a graph. But how should you reorganize the data into a graph?

Migrating data from a relational database into a graph database is a matter of mapping the tables and columns onto a graph database schema. To map data from a relational database to a graph database, we create a one-to-one correspondence between columns and graph objects. Table 2-3 outlines a simple example of mapping data from a relational database to a graph database for bank transaction data.

Table 2-3. Example of mapping tables in a relational database to vertices, edges, and properties in a graph database

Source: Relational database	Destination: Graph database
Table: Customers—multiple columns including customer_id, first_name, last_name, DOB	Vertex type: **Customer**—with corresponding properties of customer_id, first_name, last_name, DOB
Table: Banks—columns bank_id, bank_name, routing_code, address	Vertex type: **Bank**—properties bank_name, routing_code, address
Table: Accounts—columns bank_id, customer_id	Vertex type: **Account**—properties bank_id, customer_id
Table: Transactions—columns source_account, destination_account, amount	Vertex type: **Transaction**—properties source_account, destination_account, amount OR Directed edge: **Transaction**—properties source_account, destination_account, amount

The graph schema would be as shown in Figure 2-12.

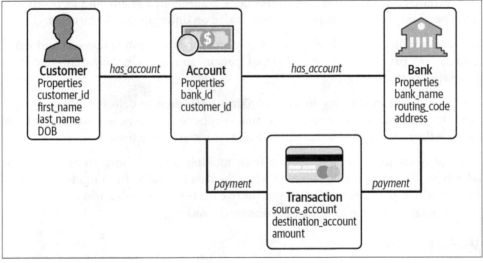

Figure 2-12. Graph schema for a simple banking database with transactions as separate vertices

One of the key decisions in creating your data schema is deciding which columns need to be mapped to their own vertices. For instance, people are generally key to understanding any real-life situation—whether they be customers, employees, or others—so they would generally map to their own vertices.

In theory, every column in a relational database could become a vertex in your schema, but this is unnecessary and would quickly become unwieldy. In the same way that you have to think about structuring a relational database, optimizing a graph database is about understanding the real-world structure of your data and how you intend to use it.

In a graph database, the key columns from your relational database become vertices and the contextual or supporting data becomes properties of those vertices. Edges generally map to foreign keys and cross-reference tables.

Some graph databases have tools that facilitate the importing of tables and mapping of foreign keys to vertex and edge IDs.

As with a relational database, a well-structured graph database eliminates redundant or repetitive data. This not only ensures efficient use of computing resources but, perhaps more importantly, ensures the consistency of your data by ensuring that it doesn't exist in different forms in different locations.

Optimizing mapping choices

Simple mapping of columns to vertices and vertex properties works, but it may not take advantage of the richness of connections available in a graph, and in reality it is often necessary to adjust mapping choices based on differing search use cases.

For instance, in a graph database for a contacts database, mobile number and email address are properties of an individual person and are generally represented as properties of that vertex.

However, if you were trying to use a banking application to detect fraud, you might want to distinguish email addresses and telephone numbers as separate vertices because they are useful in linking people and financial transactions.

It is not uncommon for information from multiple tables to map to one vertex or edge type. This is especially common when the data is coming from multiple sources, each of which provides a different perspective on the same real-world entities. Likewise, one table can map to more than one vertex and edge type.

Model Evolution

Most likely, your data is going to evolve over time, and you will need to adjust the schema to take account of new business structures and external factors. That's why schemas are designed to be flexible: to allow the system to be adapted over time without having to start from scratch.

If we look at the banking sector, for instance, financial institutions are constantly moving into new markets, either through geographical expansion or by introducing new types of products.

As a simple example, let's assume we have a bank that's always operated in a single country. The country of residence for all its customers is therefore implicit. However, moving into a second country would require updating the database to include country data. One could either add a country property to every vertex type for which it was relevant or create a new vertex type called **country** and create vertices for each country in which the bank operates.

With a flexible schema, the schema can be updated by adding the new vertex type and then linking customer vertices to the new country vertex.

Although this is a simple example, it shows how modeling data can be an evolutionary process. You can start with an initial model, perhaps one that closely resembles a prior relational database model. After you use your graph database for a while, you may learn that some model changes would serve your needs better. Two common changes are converting a vertex property into an independent vertex type and adding additional edge types.

Adapting a graph to evolving data can be simple. Adding a property, a vertex type, or an edge type is easy. Connecting two different datasets is easy, as long as we know how they relate. We can add edges to connect related entities, and we can even merge entities from two sources that represent the same real-world entity.

Graph Power

We've now seen how to build a graph, but the most important question that needs to be answered is *why* build a graph? What are the advantages? What can a graph do for you that other data structures don't do as well? We call graph technology's collected capabilities and advantages *graph power*.

What follows are the key facets of graph power. We humbly admit that this is neither the complete nor the best possible list. We suspect that others have presented lists that are more complete and more precise in a mathematical sense. Our goal, however, is not to present theory but to make a very human connection: to take the ideas that resonate with us and to share them with you, so that you will understand and experience graph power on your own.

Connecting the Dots

A graph forms an actionable body of knowledge.

As we've seen, connecting the dots is graph power at its most fundamental level. Whether it's linking actors and directors to movies or financial transactions to suspected fraudsters, a graph lets you describe the relationship between one entity and another across multiple hops.

The power of graph comes from being able to describe a network of connections, detect patterns, and extract intelligence from those patterns. While individual vertices may not contain the intelligence we are looking for, taken together, they may enable us to discover patterns in the relationships between multiple vertices that reveal new information.

With this knowledge we can begin to infer and predict from the data, like a detective joining the dots in a murder investigation.

In every detective story, the investigator gathers a set of facts, possibilities, hints, and suspicions. But these isolated bits and pieces are not the answer. The detective's magic is to stitch these pieces together into a hidden truth. They might use the pattern of known or suspected connections to predict relationships they had not been given.

When the detective has solved the mystery, they can show a sequence or network of connections that connect the suspect to the crime, along with the means, opportunity, and motive. They can likewise show that a sufficiently robust sequence of connections does not exist for any other suspect.

Did those detectives know they were doing graph analytics? Probably not, but we all do it every day in different aspects of our lives, whether that's work, family, or our network of friends. We are constantly connecting the dots to understand connections between people and people, people and things, people and ideas, and so on.

The power of graph as a data paradigm is that it closely parallels this process, making the use of graph more intuitive.

The 360 View

A 360 graph view eliminates blind spots.

Organizations of all sizes bemoan their data silos. Each department expects the other to yield up its data on demand while at the same time failing to appreciate its own inability to be open on the same basis. The problem is that business processes and the systems that we have to support them actively work against this open sharing of data.

For instance, two departments may use two different data management systems. Although both may store their data in a relational database, the data schema for each is so alien to the other that there is little hope of linking the two to enable sharing.

The problem may not be obvious if you look at it at the micro scale. If, for instance, you are compiling a record for customer X, an analyst with knowledge of the two systems in which customer data is stored will be able to easily extract the data from both, manually merge or reconcile the two records, and present a customer report. The problem comes when you want to replicate this a hundred thousand or a million times over.

And it's only by sharing the data in a holistic, integrated way that a business would be able to remove the blinders that prevent it from seeing the whole picture.

The term *Customer 360* describes a data architecture in which customer data from multiple sources and domains is brought together into a single dataset so that you have a comprehensive and holistic view of each customer.

Working with a relational database, the most obvious solution would be to merge these two departmental databases into one. Many businesses have tried grand data integration projects, but they usually end in tears because while merging data yields considerable benefits, there are also considerable trade-offs to be made that result in the loss of contextual nuance and functionality. Let's face it: there's usually a reason why the creators of a certain software package chose to construct their data schema in that particular way, and attempting to force it to conform to the schema of another system, or a new hybrid schema, will break at least one of the systems.

Graph allows you to connect databases in a natural, intuitive way without disturbing the original tables. Start by granting the graph application access to each database and then create a graph schema that links the data points from each database in a logical way. The graph database maps the relationships between the data points and does the analytical heavy lifting, leaving the source databases to carry on with what they were doing before.

If you want to see your full surroundings, you need a view that looks out across every angle—all 360 degrees. If you want to understand your full business or operational circumstances, you need data relationships across all the data you know is out there.

This is something we will look at in more depth in Chapter 3, where we will demonstrate a use case involving Customer Journey.

We have seen in the previous two points how to set up the data, and now in the next four points, we will look at how to extract meaningful intelligence from it.

Looking Deep for More Insight

Searching deep in a graph reveals vast amounts of connected information.

The "six degrees of separation" experiment conducted in the 1960s by Stanley Milgram demonstrated that just by following personal connections (and knowing that the target person is in Boston), randomly selected persons in Omaha, Nebraska, could reach the mystery person through no more than six person-to-person connections.

Since then, more rigorous experiments have shown that many graphs are so-called small-world graphs, meaning that a source vertex can reach millions and even billions of other vertices in a very small number of hops.

This vast reach in only a few hops occurs not only in social graphs but also in knowledge graphs. The ability to access this much information, and to understand how those facts relate to one another, is surely a superpower.

Suppose you have a graph that has two types of vertices: persons and areas of expertise, like the one in Figure 2-13. The graph shows *who* you know well and *what* you know well. Each person's direct connections represent what is in their own head.

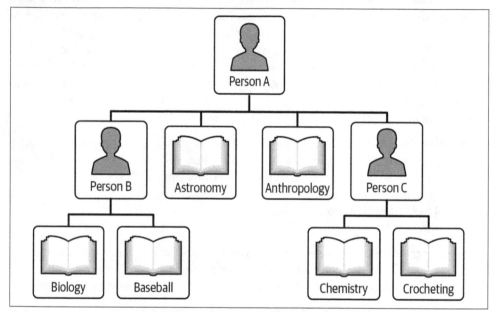

Figure 2-13. A graph showing who knows whom and their areas of expertise

From this we can readily see that A is an expert in two topics, astronomy and anthropology, but by traversing one additional hop to ask B and C what they know, A has access to four more specialties.

Now, suppose each person has 10 areas of expertise and 100 personal connections. Consider how many people and how many areas of expertise are reached by your friends' friends. There are $100 \times 100 = 10,000$ personal connections, each with 10 areas of expertise. Chances are the number of unique persons is not 10,000—you and your friends know some of the same people. Nevertheless, with each hop in a graph, you are exposed to an exponentially larger quantity of information. Looking for the answer to a question? Want to do analytics? Want to understand the big picture? Ask around, and you'll find someone who knows someone who knows.

We talk about "looking deeper" all the time, but in graph it means something particular. It is a structured way of searching for information and understanding how those facts are related. Looking deeper includes breadth-based search to consider what is accessible to you from your current position. It then traverses to some of those neighboring vertices to gain depth and see what is accessible from those new positions. Whether it's for a fraud investigation or to optimize decision making, looking deeper within a graph uncovers facts and connections that would otherwise be unknown.

As we saw in "Connecting the Dots" on page 33, one relationship on its own may be unremarkable, and there may be little if any information in a given vertex to reveal bad intentions, but thousands or even millions of vertices and edges considered in aggregate can begin to reveal new insights, which in turn leads to actionable intelligence.

Seeing and Finding Patterns

Graphs present a new perspective, revealing hidden data patterns that are easy to interpret.

As we have seen, a graph is a set of vertices and edges, but within the set of vertices and relationships, we can begin to detect patterns.

A *graph pattern* is a small, connected set of vertices and edges that can be used as a template for searching for groups of vertices and edges that have a similar configuration.

The most basic graph pattern is the data triplet: vertex → edge → vertex. The data triplet is sometimes thought of as a semantic relationship because it is related to the grammar of language and can be read as "subject → verb → object." An example is Bob → owns → boat.

We can also use graph patterns to describe higher-level objects or relationships that we have in mind. For instance, depending on the schema, a person could be linked to a number of vertices containing personal data such as address, telephone, and email. Although they are separate vertices, they are all related to that one person. Another example is a wash sale, which is the combination of two securities trades: selling a security at a loss, and then purchasing the same or a substantially similar security within 30 days.

Patterns come in different shapes. The simplest pattern, which we have looked at already, is the linear relationship between two vertices across a series of hops. The other common pattern is the star shape: many edges and vertices radiating from a central vertex.

A pattern can be Y-shaped, a pattern you would see when two vertices come together on a third vertex, which is then related to a fourth vertex. We can also have circular or recursive patterns and many more.

In contrast to relational databases, graph data is easy to visualize, and graph data patterns are easy to interpret.

A well-designed graph gives names to the vertex and edge types that reflect their meaning. When done right, you can almost look at a connected sequence of vertices and edges and read the names like a sentence. For example, consider Figure 2-14, which shows Items purchased by Persons.

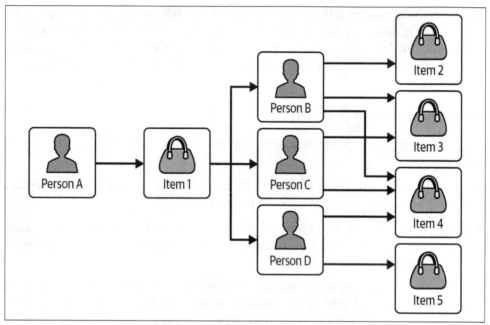

Figure 2-14. Persons who bought Item 1 and other products they bought

Starting from the left, we see that Person A (you) bought Item 1. Moving to the right, we then see another group of persons, B, C, and D, who also bought Item 1. Finally, we see some more items that were purchased by these persons. So we can say, "You bought Item 1. Other persons who bought Item 1 also bought Items 2, 3, 4, and 5." Sound familiar?

A closer analysis reveals that Item 4 was the most popular item, purchased by all three shoppers in your co-purchaser group. Item 3 was next most popular (purchased by two), and Items 2 and 5 were the least popular. With this information, we can refine our recommendations.

Many retailers use graph analytics for their recommendation analytics, and they often go deeper yet, classifying purchases by other customer properties such as gender, age, location, and time of year. We could even make recommendations based on time of day if we saw that customers were, for instance, more likely to purchase luxury items in the evening and make more pragmatic purchases in the morning.

If we also analyze the sequence of purchases, we can work out some highly personal information about customers. One large retailer was famously able to tell which

customers were pregnant and when they were due simply by focusing on the purchases of 25 products. The retailer was then able to send the customer targeted
promotional offers to coincide with the birth of their child.

Matching and Merging

*Graph is the most intuitive and efficient data structure for matching and merging
records.*

As we discussed earlier, organizations want to have a 360-degree view of their data,
but a big obstacle to this is data ambiguity. An example of data ambiguity is having
multiple versions of customer data, and the challenges of deduplicating data are well
known to many organizations.

Duplication is sometimes caused by the proliferation of enterprise systems, which
split your customer view across many databases. For instance, if you have customer
records in a number of databases—such as Salesforce, which is a customer service
database, an order-processing system, and an accounting package—the view of that
customer is divided across those systems.

To create a joined-up view of your customers, you need to query each database and
join together the records for each customer.

However, it's not always that easy because customers can end up being registered
in your databases under different reference IDs. Names can be spelled differently.
Personal information (name, phone number, email address, etc.) can change. How do
you match together the correct records?

Entity resolution matches records based on properties that are assumed to be unique
to the entities that are being represented. In the case of person records, these might
be email addresses and telephone numbers, but they could also be aggregates of
properties. For instance, we can take name, date of birth, and place of birth together
as a unique identifier because what are the chances of those three things being the
same for any two people in the world?

Entity resolution is challenging across relational databases because in order to compare entities, you need to be comparing like with like. If you are working with a
single table, you can say that similar values in similar columns indicate a match,
allowing you to resolve two entities into one, but across multiple tables, the columns
may not match. You may also have to construct elaborate table joins to include
cross-referenced data in the analysis.

By comparison, entity resolution in a graph is easy. Similar entities share similar
neighborhoods, which allows us to resolve them using similarity algorithms such as
cosine similarity and Jaccard similarity.

In entity resolution, we actually do two things:

1. Compute match likelihood scores for pairs of entities by measuring the degree of similarity of their properties and neighborhoods.
2. Merge the entities that have high enough match likelihood scores.

When it comes to merging records, we have a few options:

1. Copy the data from record B to record A, redirect the edges that pointed to B so they point to A, and delete B.
2. Create a special link called `same_as` between records A and B.
3. Create a new record called C, copy the data from A and B, redirect the links from A and B so they link to C, and finally create `same_as` edges pointing from vertex C to vertices A and B.

Which is better? The second is quicker to execute because there is only one step involved—adding an edge—but a graph query can execute the first and third options just as well. In terms of outcomes, which option is better depends on your search use case. For instance, do you prioritize richness of data or search efficiency? It might also depend on the degree of matching and merging you expect to do in your database.

We will demonstrate and discuss entity resolution with a walkthrough example in Chapter 11.

Weighing and Predicting

Graphs with weighted relationships let us easily model and analyze complex cost structures.

As we've shown, graphs are a powerful tool for analyzing relationships, but one thing to consider is that relationships don't have to be binary, on or off, black or white. Edges, representing the relationships between vertices, can be weighted to indicate the strength of the relationship, such as distance, cost, or probability.

If we weight the edges, path analysis then becomes a matter of not just tracing the links between nodes but also doing computational work such as aggregating their values.

However, weighted edges make graph analysis more complex in other ways, too. In addition to the computational work, finding shortest paths in a graph with weighted edges is algorithmically harder than in an unweighted graph. Even after you've found one weighted path to a vertex, you cannot be certain that it is the shortest path. There might be a longer path you haven't tried yet that has lower total weight.

Then again, edge weighting does not always make for a significant increase in work. In the PageRank algorithm, which computes the influence of each vertex on all other vertices, edge weighting makes little difference except that the influence that a vertex receives from a referring neighbor is multiplied by the edge weight, which adds a minimal computational overhead to the algorithm.

There are many problems that can be solved with edge weighting. Anything to do with maps, for instance, lends itself to edge weighting. You can have multiple weights per edge. Considering the map example, these could include constant weights such as distance and speed limits and variable weights such as current travel times to take account of traffic conditions.

We could use a graph of airline routes and prices to work out the optimal journey for a passenger based not only on their itinerary but also their budget constraints. Are they looking for the fastest journey regardless of price, or are they willing to accept a longer journey, perhaps with more stops, in exchange for a lower price? In both cases, you might use the same algorithm—shortest path—but prioritize different edge weights.

With access to the right data, we could even work out the probability of having a successful journey. For instance, what is the probability of our flight departing and arriving on time? For a single hop, we might accept an 80% chance that the flight wouldn't be more than an hour late, but for a two-hop trip, where the chance for the second hop not being late was 85%, the combined risk of being delayed would be 68%.

Likewise, we could look at a supply chain model and ask, what are the chances of a severe delay in the production of our finished product? If we assume that there are six steps and the reliability of each step is 99%, then the combined reliability is about 94%. In other words, there is a 6% chance that something will go wrong. We can model that across hundreds of interconnecting processes and use a shortest path algorithm to find the "safest" route that satisfies a range of conditions.

Chapter Summary

In this chapter, we have looked at graph structure and how we can use a graph database to represent data as a series of data nodes and links. In graphs, we call these vertices and edges, and they enable us to not only represent data in an intuitive way—and query it more efficiently—but also use powerful graph functions and algorithms to traverse the data and extract meaningful intelligence.

Property graphs are graphs in which every vertex and edge—which we collectively refer to as objects—can hold properties that describe that object. One property of an edge is direction, and we discussed the benefits and trade-offs of different directed edge types in indicating hierarchy and sequence.

We looked at what is meant by traversing a graph as well as "hops" and "distance." There are two approaches to traversing a graph: breadth-first search and depth-first search, each with its own benefits and trade-offs.

We looked at the importance of using a graph schema to define the structure of the database, how a consistent set of object types makes your data easier to interpret, and how it can closely relate to the real world.

Careful consideration was given to different approaches to the design, in particular the search use case and how mapping the columns of a relational database to a graph database can impact query time and the complexity of your coding.

A key step in implementing a graph database is mapping columns in a relational database to a graph, because a common use case for graph is building relationships between disparate databases. One of the decisions you have to make is which columns to map to their own objects and which to include as properties of other objects.

We looked at the evolution of databases over time and why a flexible schema is essential to ensuring your database remains up to date.

In the design of a database schema, whether that be for a relational or graph database, there are benefits and trade-offs to be made, and we looked at a few of those, including the choice of whether to map a column to an object or make it the property of an object. We also considered the choice of edge directionality and the granularity of edge types.

There are also trade-offs to be made in recording multiple events between the same two entities and tracking events in an IT network.

Finally, we looked at what we mean by graph power, including the essential question, why use graph in the first place? We looked at some general use cases, including:

- Connecting the Dots: how a graph forms an actionable body of knowledge
- The 360 View: how a 360 graph view eliminates blind spots
- Looking Deep for More Insight: how deep graph search reveals vast amounts of connected information
- Seeing and Finding Patterns: how graphs present a new perspective, revealing hidden data patterns that are easy to interpret
- Matching and Merging: why graph is the most intuitive and efficient data structure for matching and merging records
- Weighing and Predicting: how graphs with weighted relationships let us easily model and analyze complex cost structures

CHAPTER 3

See Your Customers and Business Better: 360 Graphs

This chapter will employ some real-world use cases to illustrate two of the six graph powers that we discussed in the previous chapter: "Connecting the Dots" on page 33 and the "The 360 View" on page 34. The 360 view offered by graphs helps enterprises and agencies see their data more comprehensively, which in turn enables better analytics. In the first use case, we build a Customer 360 (C360) graph to enable a company to track and understand presales customer journeys. In the second case, we build a Drug Interaction 360 graph so researchers can develop safer drug therapies.

After completing this chapter, you should be able to:

- Define the term *C360* and explain its value proposition
- Know how to model and analyze customer journeys in a graph
- Know how to use graph analytics to count and filter properties and relationships
- Set up and run a TigerGraph Cloud Starter Kit using GraphStudio
- Read and understand basic GSQL queries

Case 1: Tracing and Analyzing Customer Journeys

A business is nothing without sales. Selling, whether to consumers (B2C) or to other businesses (B2B), has become not only an art but also a science. Businesses analyze every stage of their interactions with a prospect (a potential customer) from beginning to end, hopefully resulting in a sale. According to Gartner, worldwide spending on customer relationship management (CRM) software increased by 15.6%

in 2018 to reach \$48.2 billion in 2020.[1] Salesforce has established itself as the market leader in CRM software, with approximately a 20% market share.[2]

A key way to think about the process of selling is to consider the prospective customer's experience as a series of events over time. How and when did someone engage with the business and its wares? Mapping out the interactions with a sales prospect is known as *tracing the customer's journey*.

The customer journey model is an essential tool for sales and marketing. First, it takes the customer's point of view, as they are the ultimate decision makers. Second, by realizing that the customer may need to move through stages, the business can map out what it believes will be attractive journeys that will secure many successful business deals. Third, when looking at individual journeys, we can see how far they have progressed, whether a journey has stalled, become slow, or changed course. Fourth, by analyzing the collected set of journeys, businesses can see patterns and trends and compare them to their targeted behavior. Are users in fact following the journey that was designed? Do particular engagements succeed in moving prospects forward?

There is a need for an effective and scalable data system that can collect the mixed types of data in a customer journey and support the analysis of both individual and aggregated journeys.

Solution: Customer 360 + Journey Graph

CRMs would seem to offer the solution, but they have not fully met business's needs for customer journey analysis. Designed for data to be either entered manually or ingested digitally, CRMs record and present data primarily in tabular form. The challenge comes from the fact that different types of engagements (watching a video, attending a demonstration, downloading trial software) have different characteristics. Storing mixed data like this in one table doesn't work well, so data must be spread across multiple tables. The real challenge comes from modeling the journey's sequence. The only way to follow the sequence is either through a series of costly table joins or to filter for all engagements associated with a certain person and then sort those engagements by time.

With a graph, on the other hand, we can easily model the sequence directly with edges, as shown in Figure 3-1. The journeys of all prospective customers can be

1 "CRM Market Share—Salesforce Bright Future in 2020," Nix United, February 19, 2020, *https://nix-united.com/blog/crm-market-share-salesforce-bright-future-in-2020*.

2 "Market Share of CRM Leading Vendors Worldwide 2016–2020," Statista, June 13, 2022, *https://www.statista.com/statistics/972598/crm-applications-vendors-market-share-worldwide*.

stored in one graph. Individual journeys will have similarities and intersections with one another, as persons attend the same events or engage in similar activities.

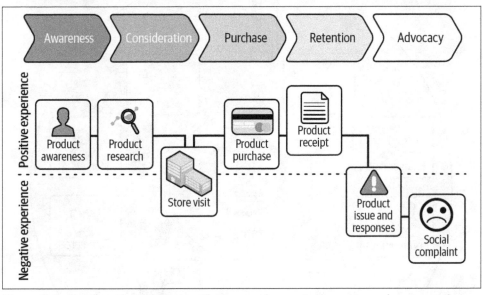

Figure 3-1. Customer journey: general stages and a particular customer's journey shown as a graph

Businesses not only want to map out customer journeys, but they also want to make them more successful: to increase customer satisfaction, to increase the percentage of journeys that end in a sale, to increase the value of sales, and to shorten the journeys. To do this, businesses need to understand the context of each customer and their decisions. This is where a 360 view helps. The 360 view is one of the unique powers of graphs we discussed in the previous chapter.

Customer 360 (C360) is a comprehensive view of a customer (or any entity of interest) created by integrating data from multiple sources, as suggested in Figure 3-2. Like customer journeys, Customer 360 is a great fit for graphs and graph analytics. A graph can support an unlimited number of relationships between one vertex (a customer) and other entities. These entities can describe not just the journey (a cold call, webinar, brochure, product demonstration, or website interaction) but also the context of the customer (current and past job titles, tenures, employers, locations, skills, interests, and education). A good 360 database will also include information about employers and industries (size, initiatives, news, etc.).

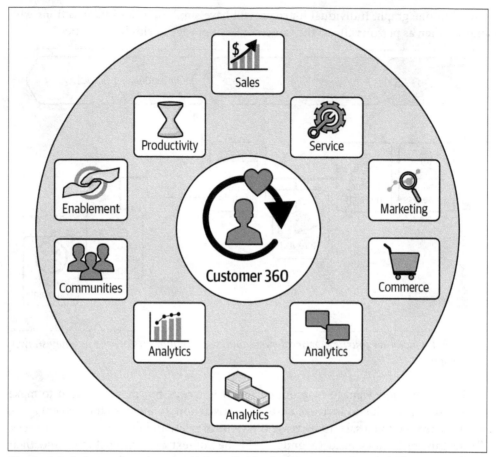

Figure 3-2. Information about a single individual connected to form a holistic view for a Customer 360 Graph

With the combination of 360° data and journey analysis, businesses are able to clearly see what is happening in the sales process, at the individual and aggregate levels, to see the context of these actions, to see where improvement is desired, and to assess the impact of efforts at sales improvement.

Our proposed solution is to develop a data model that makes it easy to examine and analyze customer journeys. The data model should also incorporate data described and related to customers to produce a Customer 360 view. The model should support queries about what events a customer journey does or doesn't contain, as well as the timing of such events.

Implementing the C360 + Journey Graph: A GraphStudio Tutorial

The implementation of a C360 and customer journey graph we present below is available as a TigerGraph Cloud Starter Kit. Starter kits are hands-on demos to teach you how graph analytics can help you with different use cases. Each kit comes with a graph schema, sample data, and queries. Don't worry if this is your first time using TigerGraph Cloud. We'll show you how to sign up for a free account and to deploy a free starter kit. Alternatively, if you have TigerGraph installed on your own machine, we'll tell you how to import the starter kit into your system. Then we'll simultaneously walk you through the design of the C360 graph and GraphStudio in general.

Figure 3-3 maps out the two paths toward setting up a starter kit. In the following sections, we'll first tell you how to create a TigerGraph Cloud account. Then we'll walk you through the steps for getting and loading a starter kit, first for TigerGraph Cloud users and then for TigerGraph on-premises users.

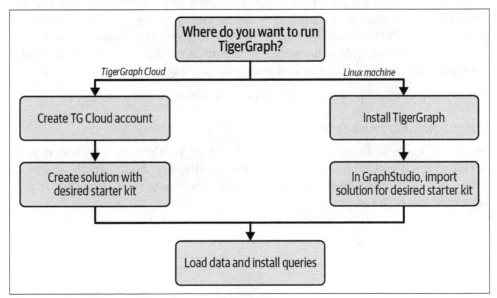

Figure 3-3. Setting up a TigerGraph Starter Kit

Create a TigerGraph Cloud Account

If this is your first time using TigerGraph Cloud, you need to set up an account. It's simple and free:

1. In a web browser, go to *tgcloud.io*.

2. Click the "Sign up" button and fill out the form. The sign-up form may ask you to create an organization. An organization can contain and manage multiple users and multiple databases under one account.

3. When you submit the form, TigerGraph Cloud will then ask you to go to your email to verify your account. You now have a TigerGraph Cloud account!

In the next section, we'll tell you how to create a TigerGraph Cloud database, with your choice of starter kit.

Get and Install the Customer 360 Starter Kit

We are going to use the starter kit called "Customer 360 – Attribution and Engagement Graph." If you are a TigerGraph Cloud user, you can get the starter kit as part of a new database deployment. If you are running TigerGraph on your own computer, you can download the starter kit files from the TigerGraph website (*http://www.tigergraph.com*) and then upload them into your TigerGraph instance.

The next two sections go over the details for these two options.

Deploy a cloud instance with a starter kit

When you log in to TigerGraph Cloud, the first page visible is the My Clusters page. A cluster is a TigerGraph database deployment, with or without a graph schema or data. Click the Create Cluster button, which will take you to the Create Cluster page (shown in Figure 3-4).

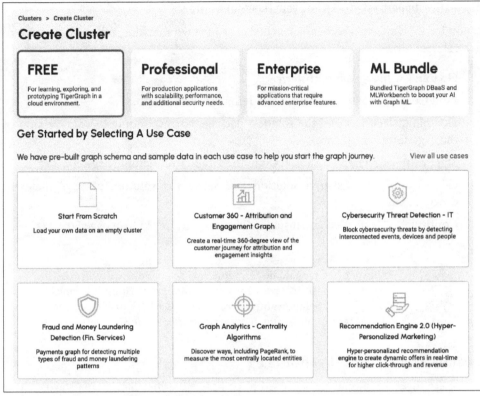

Figure 3-4. TigerGraph Cloud Create Cluster menu

Then follow these steps:

1. Confirm the service tier for your cluster. On the Create Cluster page, you'll see it defaults to the free tier. Larger and more powerful clusters incur hourly charges. For the exercises in this book, the free size should be fine. You can upgrade a cluster after deploying it, if you wish.

2. Select a starter kit by use case. If the kit you want isn't displayed, click on "View all use cases" to see more choices. In this case, it's "Customer 360 – Attribution and Engagement Graph." For the free tier, that's it. In a few minutes, your database instance will be ready.

3. If you decide to create a paid tier instance, then you have more choices to make: cloud platform provider, instance size, region, disk size, and cluster configuration. You can follow this tutorial with the default values for all of these.

4. Once your cluster instance is ready, it will be listed on the My Clusters page. Click its Tools button. From the menu that appears, select GraphStudio.

5. Continue to "Load data and install queries for a starter kit" on page 50.

Alternative: Import a starter kit into your TigerGraph instance

If you have TigerGraph software installed on your own machine, follow these steps to get a starter kit:

1. Go to *www.tigergraph.com/starterkits*.

2. Find Customer 360—Attribution and Engagement Graph.

3. Download Data Set and the solution package corresponding to your version of the TigerGraph platform.

4. Start your TigerGraph instance. Go to the GraphStudio home page.

5. Click Import An Existing Solution and select the solution package that you downloaded.

6. Continue to "Load data and install queries for a starter kit" on page 50.

 Importing a GraphStudio Solution will delete your existing database. If you wish to save your current design, perform a Graph-Studio Export Solution and also run a database backup as described on the TigerGraph documentation site (*https://oreil.ly/LoDnj*).

Load data and install queries for a starter kit

There are three additional steps needed to complete the installation of a starter kit. If you know GraphStudio and just want to know how to install a starter kit, then follow these steps:

1. Go to the Design Schema page. On the menu on the left, switch from the Global view to the starter kit's local graph view. It might be called MyGraph, or it might have a customized name like AntiFraud.

2. Go to the Load Data page. Wait about five seconds until the Load Data button on the left end of the top menu becomes active. Click the button and wait for the data to finish loading. You can track the loading progress in the timeline display at the lower right.

3. Go to the Write Queries page. Above the list of queries, click the Install All Queries button and wait for the installation to complete.

An Overview of GraphStudio

TigerGraph's GraphStudio is a complete graph solution development kit, covering every stage in the process from developing a graph model to running queries. It is organized as a series of views or pages, each one for a different task in the development process.

Because this is our first time through GraphStudio together, we are going to walk through all five stages: Design Schema, Map Data to Graph, Load Data, Explore Graph, and Write Queries. At each stage, we will both explain the general purpose of the page and guide you through details of the specific starter kit we are working with. In future chapters, we will skip over most of the generalities and only talk about the starter kit details.

If we were beginning with an empty database, we would need to do additional design work, such as creating a graph model. Having a starter kit lets you skip most of this and get right to exploring and querying an example dataset.

 How to create a graph model in GraphStudio is just one of the many topics covered in TigerGraph's online documentation at *docs.tigergraph.com*. The official TigerGraph YouTube channel is also a valuable resource for tutorials.

Design a Graph Schema

The starter kit is preloaded with a graph model based on commonly used data objects in Salesforce and similar CRM software. The name of the graph in this starter kit is *MyGraph*. When you start GraphStudio, you are initially at the global graph level. You are not yet working on a particular graph. In a TigerGraph database, the global level is used to define data types that are potentially available to all users and all graphs. See the section labeled "Global types" in Figure 3-5. A database can then host one or more graphs. A graph can contain local types, and it can include some or all of the global types. See graphs G1 and G2 in the figure.

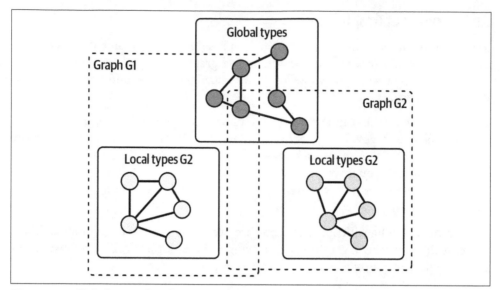

Figure 3-5. Global types, local types, and graphs in a TigerGraph database

To work on a graph, you need to select the graph, which moves you from the global level to the local graph level. To switch to a local graph, click on the circular icon in the upper left corner. A drop-down menu will appear, showing you the available graphs and letting you create a new graph. Click on MyGraph (step 2). Just below that, click on Design Schema to be sure we're starting at the right place.

You should now see a graph model or schema like the one in Figure 3-6 in the main display panel.

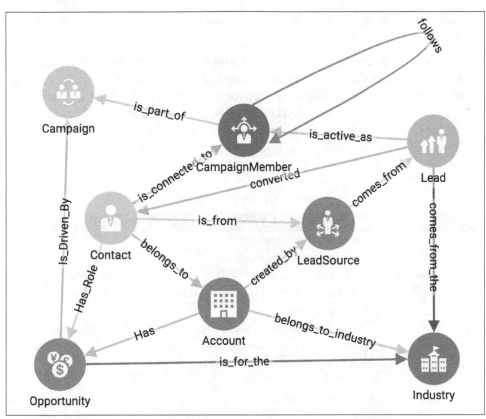

Figure 3-6. Graph schema for CRM data (see a larger version of this figure at https://oreil.ly/gpam0306)

A graph schema defines the *types* of data objects to be stored in the database. If the schema is depicted visually, then each data type is shown once. This schema has 8 vertex types and 14 edge types.

The central vertex type is **Contact**, which is a prospective buyer of the product. However, a **Contact** is not just any prospective buyer, which reflects the fact that a person buying a B2B product on behalf of a company is not making a spur-of-the-moment decision. Instead, the person transitions through stages of the buying process. We call the person's flow through the buying process the *customer journey*.

One real-world person might show up more than once in the database. If the vendor conducts a marketing **Campaign**, then persons who respond to the campaign show up as **CampaignMember** vertices. Also, if a third party, a **LeadSource**, provides contact information about a potential buyer, then the potential buyer shows up as a **Lead**. A **Salesperson** engages a **Lead** to see if there is a realistic possibility of a sale. If there is, then the **Lead**'s information is copied to a new vertex type called a **Contact**. This

Contact and their source **Lead** represent the same physical person but at different stages of the customer journey.

Table 3-1 contains descriptions of all eight vertex types. In some cases, the description of one vertex type talks about how it is related to another vertex type. For example, an **Account** is "an organization that a **Contact** belongs to." Looking at Figure 3-6, you can see an edge type called **belongs_to** between **Account** and **Contact**. There are 13 other edge types in the figure. The edge types have descriptive names, so if you understand the vertex types, you should be able to figure out the meaning of the edges.

Table 3-1. Vertex types in the Salesforce Customer 360 graph model

Vertex type	Description
Account	An organization that a **Contact** belongs to
Campaign	A marketing initiative intended to generate **Leads**
CampaignMember	A persona who responds to a **Campaign**
Contact	A **Lead** who is now associated with a sales **Opportunity**
Industry	A business sector of an **Account**
Lead	A person who is a potential buyer of the product but is not yet associated with an **Opportunity**
LeadSource	A channel through which a **Lead** finds out about the product
Opportunity	A potential sales transaction, characterized by a monetary amount

Data Loading

In TigerGraph starter kits, the data is included, but it is not yet loaded into the database. To load the data, switch to the Load Data page (step 1 of Figure 3-7), wait a few seconds until the Load button in the upper left of the main panel becomes active, and then click it (step 2). You can watch the progress of the loading in the real-time chart at the right (not shown). Loading the 34K vertices and 105K edges should take two minutes on the TGCloud free instances; it's faster on the paid instances.

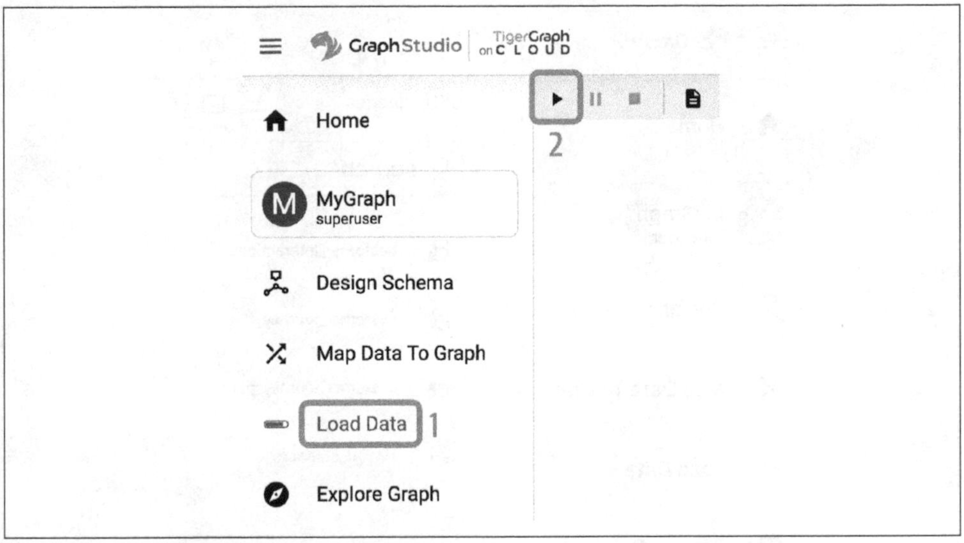

Figure 3-7. Loading data in a starter kit

Queries and Analytics

We will analyze the graph and run graph algorithms by composing and executing queries in GSQL, TigerGraph's graph query language. When you first deploy a new starter kit, you need to install the queries. Switch to the Write Queries page (step 1 of Figure 3-8). Then click the Install All icon at the top right of the list of queries (step 2).

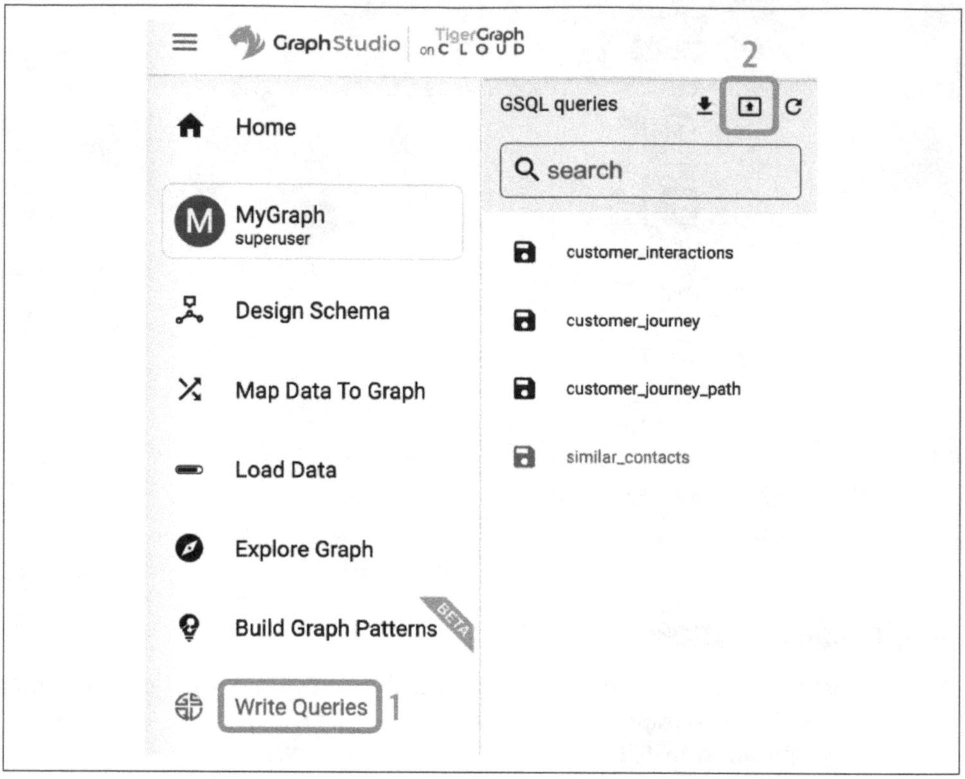

![GraphStudio TigerGraph on CLOUD interface screenshot. Left sidebar navigation: Home, MyGraph (superuser, marked M), Design Schema, Map Data To Graph, Load Data, Explore Graph, Build Graph Patterns (BETA), Write Queries (labeled 1). Right panel: GSQL queries with download/install/refresh icons (install icon labeled 2), search box, and query list: customer_interactions, customer_journey, customer_journey_path, similar_contacts.]

Figure 3-8. Installing queries

Learning and Using GSQL

The GSQL examples in this book are intended to show you some of the techniques to express informational and analytical queries of a graph database. While the examples are written in GSQL, it is not necessary for you to become fluent, nor do we even try to teach it in a rigorous way. If you know basic SQL and are familiar with a general-purpose language like Python, we believe you will be able to follow our explanations of the queries with a little effort. When we want to make a particular point about the GSQL language, we will use a note box like this.

For our Customer 360 use case, we will discuss three queries:

Customer interaction subgraph

This query generates a subgraph that gives us a holistic view of the customer journey. The subgraph embodies the interactions that the customer has with the company's campaigns. The query starts with a given customer of type **Contact** vertex. From there, it collects **Account**, **Opportunity**, and **CampaignMember** vertices that the customer had interacted with. Furthermore, for each of the **Campaign Member** elements, a **Campaign** is selected as well. Finally, the query returns the resulting customer interaction subgraph.

Customer journey

This query finds all the **CampaignMember** elements that the customer has interacted with during a time period. The query starts with a given **Contact** and filters for all the **CampaignMember** elements that have been in touch with the **Contact** between a start time and end time. Unlike the first query, we don't return a subgraph with the connections between the **Contact** and **CampaignMember**. Here we return a sorted list of **CampaignMember** vertices.

Similar contacts

This query returns contacts similar to a given **Contact**. If the given **Contact** was successfully converted to a paying customer, this query can find additional good candidates for conversion. This query implements the Jaccard similarity measure in GSQL to calculate the similarity between a given **Contact** and other **Contact** vertices who share a similar **Campaign**. Then the contacts with the highest similarity score will be returned.

For each of the three queries, we'll give a high-level explanation, directions for running them in TigerGraph's GraphStudio, what to expect as a result, and a closer look at some of the GSQL code in the queries.

Customer interaction subgraph

The customer_interactions query takes one argument: a customer who is a natural person of type **Contact**. First, we select all the **Account** identities that **belongs_to** the given **Contact**. Then we find all the **Opportunity** vertices connected to the **Contact**. In addition, the **Contact** vertex has a connection to one or more **CampaignMember**, who is a natural person that is part of a **Campaign**. Figure 3-9 illustrates the relationships uncovered by this query.

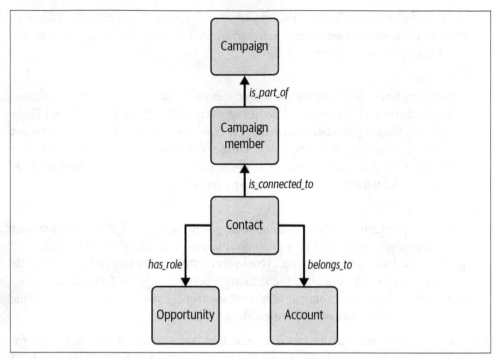

*Figure 3-9. **Contact** vertex and edges*

Do: Run the GSQL query `customer_interaction` by selecting the query name from the list (step 1 in Figure 3-10) and then clicking the Run icon above the code panel (step 2). This query has one input parameter: the "Contact" field lets us fill in a name of the customer. If you look at the query code pane (Figure 3-10), you will see a comment that suggests an example value for Contact: `Sam-Eisenberg`.

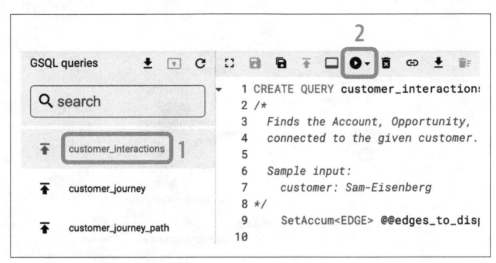

Figure 3-10. Running the `customer_interaction` query

Use your mouse to copy and paste values from the code window into the query parameter input boxes.

The output will appear in the result panel below the query-editing panel. The graph may look scrambled initially. To clean up the appearance, click the Change Layout (force) button in the lower right corner of the output and select force. Then the output should look something like Figure 3-11.

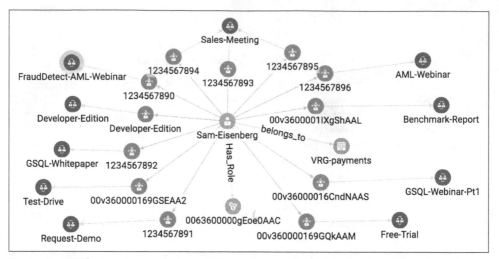

Figure 3-11. The `customer_interaction` *query result with input* `Sam-Eisenberg` *(see a larger version of this figure at https://oreil.ly/gpam0311)*

Now we will look at how the GSQL query `cust_journey_subgraph` works. Refer to the code block that follows:

```
CREATE QUERY customer_interactions(VERTEX<Contact> customer) {
/*
    Finds the Account, Opportunity, CampaignMembers, and Campaigns
    connected to the given customer.

    Sample input:
      customer: Sam-Eisenberg
*/
    SetAccum<EDGE> @@edges_to_display; // accumulator declaration(s) ❶

    cust = { customer }; // make into a vertex set  ❷

    // Get the customer's connected Accounts  ❸
    accts = SELECT t FROM cust:s -(belongs_to>:e)- Account:t
        ACCUM @@edges_to_display += e;

    // Get the customer's connected Opportunities  ❹
    opps = SELECT t FROM cust:s -(Has_Role>:e)- Opportunity:t
        ACCUM @@edges_to_display += e;

    // Get the customer's connected CampaignMembers  ❺
    campMems = SELECT t FROM cust:s -(is_connected_to>:e)- CampaignMember:t
        ACCUM @@edges_to_display += e;

    // Get the Campaigns connects to those CampaignMembers  ❻
    campaigns = SELECT t FROM campMems:s -(is_part_of>:e)- Campaign:t
        ACCUM @@edges_to_display += e;
```

```
    // Print (display) the collected vertices and connecting edges. ❼
    interactions = accts UNION opps UNION campMems UNION campaigns;
    PRINT cust, interactions;
    PRINT @@edges_to_display;
}
```

In the first line, we define the name of the query and its input parameters. To find a customer subgraph, we need one parameter for the customer, a vertex of type **Contact**. Next we declare some variables. At ❶ we define a variable, a set of edges called @@edges_to_display.

GSQL Query Structure

A GSQL query is a named parameterizable procedure. The main body is a sequence of SELECT statements that traverse and analyze the graph one or more hops at a time. The inputs and outputs of a SELECT statement are vertex set variables. The output of the query as a whole is explicitly stated with PRINT statements.

To begin traversing the graph, we need to define a vertex set that contains our starting point or points. At ❷ we create a vertex set called cust consisting of the **Contact** from the input parameters. Then at ❸ we use a SELECT statement to start to gather the customer's interactions. The clause FROM cust:s -(belongs_to:e)- Account:t means traverse from cust across **belongs_to** edges to **Account** vertices. The notations :e and :t define alias variables for the edges and target vertices, respectively. The ACCUM clause acts like a FOREACH for the alias variables. In effect, each e edge that fits the FROM pattern is added to the @@edges_to_display accumulator. Lastly, the initial clause accts = SELECT t means that this statement returns a vertex set called accts consisting of the t alias vertices.

GSQL Accumulators

Accumulators, a unique feature of the GSQL language, are data objects that have a special operation called *accumulate*, indicated by the += operator. The exact meaning of += varies depending on the accumulator type, but it always is used to accept additional input data to update the accumulator's external value. Accumulators can accept multiple asynchronous accumulate operations, and thus they are ideal for concurrent/parallel processing. The @@ prefix indicates a global accumulator. A @ prefix indicates a set of local (also known as vertex-attached) accumulators. Local means each vertex in the query has its own independent instance of this accumulator. For example, @interact_size is a local accumulator of type SumAccum<INT>. SumAccum<INT> is typically used to count.

At ❹ we do something similar, but here we select the vertices and edges where the customer has a role in creating an **Opportunity**. The selected vertices are in the variable Opps; the selected edges are added to @@edges_to_display. Next, at ❺ we find the `CampaignMember` vertices that are connected to the customer and update @@edges_to_display again with the results. We then start from the campaign_members we selected in the previous step (FROM campMems) and find the vertices and edges of each **CampaignMember** that is part of a **Campaign**, then update @@edges_to_display again with the results at ❻. In ❼ we combine the vertices selected in steps ❸, ❹, ❺, and ❻ into one variable called interactions. Finally, we print (output) the input customer, its interactions, and their connecting edges (@@_edges_to_display). When the output contains vertices or edges, GraphStudio will display them graphically in the pane below the code pane. The output pane's menu has options to format the output as JSON or tables as well.

Customer journey

The customer_journey query shows all **CampaignMember** and **Account** vertices that have a relationship with the customer during a given time period. Here we want to see more than just what marketing interactions a customer had; we want to see the sequence of activities. Let's take a look at the GSQL implementation.

This GSQL query takes four parameters:

```
CREATE QUERY customer_journey(VERTEX<Contact> customer,
    SET<STRING> campaign_type_set, DATETIME start_time, DATETIME end_time) {
```

The first parameter is a vertex of type **Contact** and represents the customer that we are interested in. The second parameter is a list of campaign types to include. Leaving it empty will include all campaign types. The third and fourth parameters are of DATETIME types, and we use these parameters to determine the time window in which our query should be executed.

Next we take advantage of local accumulators to act like instance variables of a vertex class. We will add three string properties to each selected **CampaignMember**:

```
SumAccum<STRING> @cam_type, @cam_name, @cam_desc;
```

First we select the **Account** to which our target customer belongs:

```
start = { customer };
account = SELECT t FROM start -(belongs_to>)- Account:t;
```

Then we select all **CampaignMember** vertices that are connected to the customer within the given time window:

```
campaign_members =
        SELECT c
        FROM start-(is_connected_to>)- CampaignMember:c
```

```
    WHERE c.CreatedDate >= start_time
        AND c.CreatedDate <= end_time;
```

Next we check that each of these **CampaignMembers** belongs to one of the campaign types designated in the input parameters. To do this, we need to traverse from each **CampaignMember** to its **Campaign**. While we are at it, we copy some information from the **Campaigns**:

```
CM =
    SELECT c FROM campaign_members:c -(is_part_of>)- Campaign:t
    WHERE campaign_type_set.size() == 0
    OR t.Campaign_Type IN campaign_type_set
    ACCUM c.@cam_type = t.Campaign_Type,
        c.@cam_name = t.Name,
        c.@cam_desc = t.Description
    ORDER BY c.FirstRespondedDate;
```

The ORDER BY clause at the end sorts the selected **CampaignMember** vertices by their effective date.

The comments at the beginning of the query suggest some inputs to try. Click the Run Query button, then copy and paste the suggested inputs into the parameter text boxes on the left. For campaign_type_set, click the + symbol to add a value to the set. For the datetime parameters start_time and end_time, notice that Graph-Studio accepts values in YYYY-MM-DD format. Scroll down if needed to get to the Run Query button. The output should include **Contact** Sam-Eisenberg, **Account** VRG-Payments, and seven **CampaignMember** elements. These are the components of Sam's customer journey during the given time period.

To see the time sequence of the journey, switch to the JSON or table view output modes. Or you can run the customer_journey_path query, whose output is shown in Figure 3-12. It is identical to the customer_journey query, except for several extra lines of GSQL code, which insert directed edges from one **CampaignMember** vertex to the next. The code is a bit complex for this early in the book, so we won't describe how it works. Also note that you need to run customer_journey_path twice: once to create the path edges, and again in order to see them.

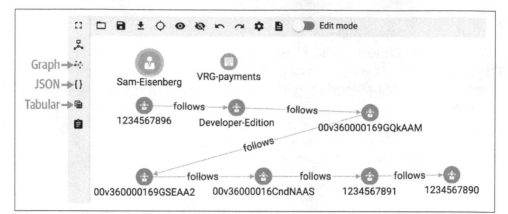

Figure 3-12. Output of `customer_journey_path` *query for* `Sam-Eisenberg` *(see a larger version of this figure at https://oreil.ly/gpam0312)*

Similar customers

Before we implement similarity measures, we need to determine first for which attribute we want to compute the similarity. In our case, we want to compute the similarity for customers based on participation in similar sets of marketing campaigns. To measure this, we use Jaccard similarity. Jaccard similarity is not exclusively applicable for graph-structured data. It is a way to measure the similarity between two sets, based on how many items that belong to one set also belong to the other set, divided by the total number of distinct items appearing in either set. In the case of a graph, every vertex has a set of neighboring vertices. So graph-based Jaccard similarity measures the overlap of the neighbor set of one vertex with the neighbor set of another vertex. In other words, how many common neighbors are there, relative to the total number of neighbors?

Our situation is a little more complicated, because we want to assess the similarity of associations to campaigns; however, `Campaigns` are two hops away from `Contacts` rather than being directly connected. Furthermore, we allow the user to filter by types of campaigns to count.

Let's walk through the GSQL code for the `similar_contacts` query. This query accepts three parameters. The first parameter `source_customer` is a vertex of type **Contact** and represents the customer for whom we want to find similar customers. The second parameter is the set of campaign types (strings) that the user wants to consider. The third parameter is an integer value to determine how many similar customers we want to return:

```
CREATE QUERY similar_contacts(VERTEX<Contact> source_customer,
                    SET<STRING> campaign_types, INT top_k = 5) {
```

We start with declaring four accumulators. The first three are integer counts: the number of campaigns for our input customer (`@@size_A`), the number of campaigns for each candidate contact (`@size_B`), and the number of campaigns that they have in common (`@size_intersection`). There's only one input, so `@@size_A` is a global accumulator. The others are vertex-attached local accumulators. We also have a FLOAT type local accumulator to store the computed similarity value:

```
    SumAccum<INT> @@size_A, @size_B, @intersection_size;
    SumAccum<FLOAT> @similarity;
```

Then we get the value of `@@size_A` using the `outdegree()` function, specifying edge type **is_connected_to**:

```
A = SELECT s
        FROM A:s
        ACCUM @@set_size_A += s.outdegree("is_connected_to");
```

Now we traverse from `source_customer` across two hops to go first to **CampaignMember** and then the **Campaign** vertices. This corresponds to steps 1 and 2 in Figure 3-13. Note the WHERE clause for checking the campaign types:

```
    campaign_mem_set =
      SELECT t
      FROM A:s -(is_connected_to>:e)- CampaignMember:t;

    campaign_set =
      SELECT t
      FROM campaign_mem_set:s -(is_part_of>:e)- Campaign:t
      WHERE campaign_types.size() == 0 OR (t.Campaign_Type IN campaign_types);
```

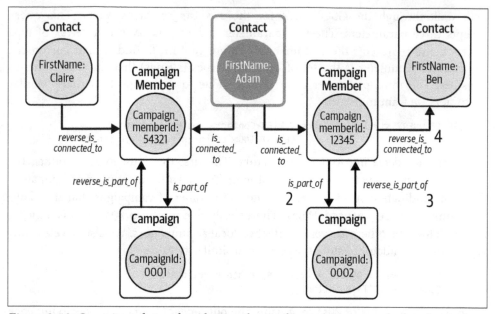

Figure 3-13. Overview of steps for selecting the similar customers to calculate Jaccard similarity score

The next phase is a great example of the graph-based approach to analytics. This query's task is "find all the Contacts B that have relationships similar to those of Contact A." Rather than searching all possible **Contacts** and then comparing their relationships, we go to A's related entities, then walk backward from there to candidate **Contacts**. These are steps 3 and 4 in Figure 3-13. The reasoning is that this forward-then-backward walk across the relationships automatically filters out candidates that have nothing in common. And if we are clever, we can measure the degree of similarity while we are traversing.

Compare the GSQL code for step 3 with the code for step 2. Notice how the directionality indicator for the directed edge changed from a > suffix to a < prefix:

```
rev_campaign_mem_set =
    SELECT t
    FROM campaign_set:s -(<is_part_of:e)- CampaignMember:t;
```

The last hop is more complicated because it incorporates the Jaccard computation. The hop itself is as expected, with a `WHERE` clause to exclude going back to our `source_customer`:

```
B = SELECT t
    FROM rev_campaign_mem_set:s -(<is_connected_to:e)- Contact:t
    WHERE t != source_customer
```

Recall that an `ACCUM` clause acts like a `FOREACH` block iterated across every path that satisfies the preceding `FROM-WHERE` clauses. The following code incrementally counts the size of the intersection between A's and B's campaign sets, and also sets `@size_B` for this particular **Contact**:

```
ACCUM t.@intersection_size += 1,
      t.@size_B = t.outdegree("is_connected_to")
```

Now we can calculate the Jaccard similarity. As its name implies, a `POST-ACCUM` clause usually takes place after an `ACCUM` clause. The two most important rules about `POST-ACCUM` are 1) it can use the accumulator results of the preceding `ACCUM` clause, and 2) it can only work with vertex variables, not edge variables. We use one of the standard formulations for Jaccard similarity. The denominator is equivalent to the number of unique items in sets A and B. The 1.0 in the numerator is to perform floating point arithmetic instead of integer arithmetic:

```
POST-ACCUM t.@similarity = t.@intersection_size*1.0/
                          (@@size_A + t.@size_B - t.@intersection_size)
```

Finally, we order the resulting similarity score from highest to lowest, and we only take the top_k results to print:

```
ORDER BY t.@similarity DESC
LIMIT top_k;

PRINT @@size_A;
PRINT B[B.FirstName, B.LastName, B.@similarity, B.@size_B];
```

We went through the implementation of Jaccard similarity both to show you how easily some graph algorithms can be implemented in GSQL and to help you understand the approach if you want to write your own queries and analytics. TigerGraph provides an extensive library of prewritten graph data science algorithms, which we will present later in the book.

Case 2: Analyzing Drug Adverse Reactions

In our second use case, we seek to analyze the adverse reactions to drug treatments.

Today's healthcare system covers 30% of the world's data volume, and its compound annual growth is projected to be 36% by 2025.[3] This data collection ranges from external sources such as the US Food and Drug Administration (FDA) and National Databases Medical Associations to privately owned datasets from health insurance companies. Organizations mine this data for valuable insights to create targeted

---

3 "The Healthcare Data Explosion," RBC Capital Markets, accessed May 21, 2023, *https://www.rbccm.com/en/gib/healthcare/episode/the_healthcare_data_explosion*.

content and engagement campaigns, improve health insurance plans, and develop medicines. Developing better medical therapies is our focus for this use case.

When developing medicines, it is vital to have clear insight into the composition of drugs, how they interact with one another, and what side effects they might cause. Therefore, the FDA requires every drug manufacturer to monitor how its drugs are being used with other drugs and report on any adverse reaction.

Analysts and researchers want to find relationships among various drugs, patients who use them, and the possible side effects. Do doctors prescribe the same drug to people in a particular postal district, or are their assessments mainly built upon patients who went to the same college? When a patient reports an adverse reaction to a given drug, other patients might also be in danger, given their drug interaction history. Without a view of how these drug interactions occur and to whom the drugs prescriptions are given, research in this field becomes challenging, and it could threaten public health when vital links between drugs and side effects are overlooked.

Solution: Drug Interaction 360 Graph

The growing amount of healthcare data brings challenges in combining external and internal data sources at a large scale and presenting this in a meaningful way. The applications in this domain require an approach that can not only handle this large amount of data but also find hidden patterns among the various data sources.

Graph databases are an ideal data platform for the discovery and analysis of drug interactions. With a graph database, we can form a 360 view of key entities and connect the dots to expose all possible correlations among patients, the drug interactions that have incurred, and the manufacturers of those drugs.

In contrast, relational and NoSQL databases store data in separate tables and rely on the analyst's domain expertise to choose which tables to join, and each join is an expensive operation. The discovery of interactions and correlations is limited to the particular cases that the analysts checked by forming particular sequences of table joins. For this case, a tabular structure is less conducive to scientific discovery than a graph structure.

Implementation

To illustrate a drug interaction 360 graph, we will use the TigerGraph Cloud Starter Kit called "Healthcare Graph (Drug Interaction/FAERS)." To follow along, see the earlier instructions for how to deploy a TigerGraph Cloud Starter Kit. Load the data and install the queries.

The data we are using for this use case is publicly available from the US FDA. It contains quarterly data from the FDA's Adverse Event Reporting System (FAERS), including demographic and administrative information on the drug, patient outcome, and reaction from case reports. The FDA releases the data as seven tables. The documentation includes an entity-relationship diagram, which is suggestive of a two-hub 360 graph. However, investigating this data using relational database techniques would require creating many join tables. With graph databases, we can traverse these relationships much easier.

Graph Schema

To improve the visibility and analysis of the data, we propose to transform the seven tables into 10 vertex types and 10 edge types. We split the Drug table into **Drug** and **DrugSequence** vertex types, and we split the Demographic table into **ReportedCase**, **Patient**, and **PharmaCompany** tables. These splits give us the agility to shift our focus as needed and to more easily see the interplay between different factors. For every **ReportedCase**, we can find information about the patient, the drug manufacturer, the patient's reaction, the source of the report, the outcome, and the various drugs the patient has been taking. For every **DrugSequence**, we can find the related drug, the indication, and the patient's therapy.

Table 3-2 describes the 10 vertex types, and Figure 3-14 shows how they are connected. The starter kit contains data from one calendar quarter. In total, there are 1.87M vertices and 3.35M edges.

Table 3-2. Vertex types in the Drug Information model

Vertex type	Description	Instances
DrugSequence	A sequence of **Drug** elements	689,312
Drug	A drug that is part of a **DrugSequence**	40,622
Indication	An indication (medical condition) that can be treated with a **DrugSequence**	422,145
Therapy	A therapy where the **DrugSequence** is used	268,244
ReportedCase	A reported case of side effects	211,414
Patient	A person who reported a case	211,414
Outcome	A result after assessment of a **ReportedCase**	7
ReportSource	A source type for a **ReportedCase**	9
Reaction	A reaction from a **ReportedCase**	9,791
PharmaCompany	A pharmaceutical company that manufactures a **Drug**	7,740

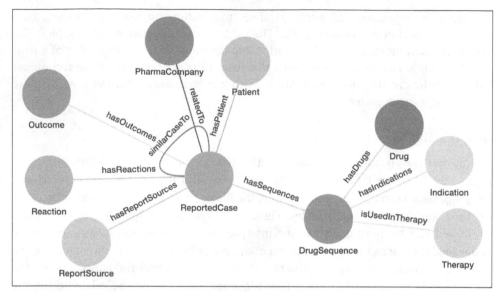

Figure 3-14. Graph schema of Drug Information data (see a larger version of this figure at https://oreil.ly/gpam0314)

Queries and Analytics

The drug interaction starter kit comes with three queries as examples of drug interaction analysis. From these examples, a studious analyst can see how to construct other queries and even more complex queries.

Find similar reported cases based on reactions
> Finding cases with similar sets of reactions can lead to understanding root causes. This query starts from a given reported case and calculates its similarity to other cases, based on the similarity of reactions of the patients. Then it returns the top-scoring similar cases.

Most reported drugs for a company
> Pharmaceutical companies want to know which of their drugs are receiving the most reports of adverse reactions. Government regulatory agencies might also want to know this. This query performs that calculation for them.

Top side effects for top drugs
> Pharmaceuticals and regulators want to know not only which drugs are being reported but also what the top side effects are. This query selects the topmost **Drug** type for a given **Company** and counts how many times each **Reaction** for that drug is reported.

Find similar reported cases

Things that have similar characteristics are similar, but how exactly do we measure this? You must decide what characteristics matter and how to assess the strength of similarity. In a graph, an entity's characteristics include not only its attributes but also its relationships. Looking at Figure 3-14, you can see that **ReportedCase** is surrounded by relationships to six other vertex types, which are all potential similarity factors. It also has an edge type **similarCaseTo**, where the results of similarity calculations can be stored.

The query implements relationship-based similarity scoring: `jaccard_nbor_reaction`. The query's first argument, `source`, is the **ReportedCase** of interest. The `etype` argument specifies what type of relationships to consider. The `top_k` argument determines how many reported cases the query returns, and `sampSize` invokes sampling if each instance of a **Reaction** (or other characteristic) has more than this threshold number of related cases.

Once we specify which characteristics to consider, we still need to apply a formula for measuring similarity. This query uses Jaccard similarity, the most commonly used measure when the property is categorical rather than numeric. We only know if a reaction occurs, not its strength, so the data is categorical.

```
CREATE QUERY jaccard_nbor_reaction(VERTEX source, STRING etype
  ="hasReactions", INT top_k=100, INT sampSize=100) FOR GRAPH faers {
  //example: ReportedCase=100640876
/*
Calculates the Jaccard Similarity between a given vertex and every other
vertex. A simplified version of the generic purpose algorithm
jacccard_nbor_ss in the GSQL Graph Data Science Library
https://github.com/tigergraph/gsql-graph-algorithms
*/
    SumAccum<INT> @intersection_size, @@set_size_A, @set_size_B;
    SumAccum<FLOAT> @similarity;
    SumAccum<INT> @@t_Size;

    Start (ANY) = {source}; ❶
    Start = SELECT s
        FROM Start:s
        ACCUM @@set_size_A += s.outdegree(etype); ❷

    Neighbors = SELECT t ❸
        FROM Start:s-(etype:e)-:t;❹
```

Similar to the first query in our first case example, we need to define the vertices where we start our traversal. We do this at ❶. Then to compute the Jaccard calculation, we need the size of the source vertex's neighbor set, which we obtain by applying the `out_degree` function and specifying `etype` at ❷. At ❸, we collect **Neighbors** by traversing from **Start** over every `etype` edge.

The expression `Start:s-(etype:e)-:t`, at ❹, represents a traversal pattern in the graph. This particular pattern means:

1. Begin with a member of the set `Start`.
2. Connect to an edge of type `etype`.
3. Through that edge, arrive at any target vertex.

The expression also defines three aliases for the three parts of the pattern: `s`, `e`, and `t`. The result of the FROM clause is a set of tuples (`s`, `e`, `t`) that satisfy the pattern. The alias `t` represents a member of the set of target vertices. These aliases are local; they can only be used within this SELECT block. They are unrelated to the aliases in other SELECT blocks.

At ❺ we select other vertices. We do this by checking if `etype` is `reactionTo`; then `Neighbors` will comprise all the **Reactions** of the given source **ReportedCase**. Then we build a set of **ReportedCases** by traversing from the `Neighbors` across `etype` edges again. If the out degree of a neighbor is greater than `sampSize`, we traverse only a sample of the connecting edges. We exclude the source vertex from the selection at ❻.

```
Others = SELECT t ❺
     FROM Neighbors:s -(:e)- :t
     SAMPLE sampSize EDGE when s.outdegree(etype) > sampSize
     WHERE t != source ❻
     ACCUM t.@intersection_size += 1,
         t.@set_size_B = t.outdegree(etype)
     POST-ACCUM t.@similarity = t.@intersection_size*1.0/ ❼
             (@@set_size_A + t.@set_size_B - t.@intersection_size),
         @@tSize += 1
     ORDER BY t.@similarity DESC ❼
     LIMIT top_k;

PRINT Others;
PRINT @@t_Size, Others.size();
```

 This pattern (traverse to neighbors, traverse back along the same edge type, exclude the starting vertex) is a common technique to find entities that have something in common with the starting entity. It is the graph-based technique for collaborative filtering recommendation.

At ❼ we compute the Jaccard similarity score between the source vertex and each member of `Others`. Given two sets A and B, *Jaccard*(A, B) is defined as:

(intersection of A and B) / (size of A + size of B – intersection of A and B)

The efficient GSQL implementation is a little subtle. We will not go into line-by-line detail, but we will point out two paradigms:

- In our case, the sets are composed of neighbors of A and B. We do not start from sets A and B and then compute their intersection. We start from A, go to its neighbors, then go to their neighbors. This finds all B sets such that intersection(A,B) is not empty.

- We use distributed processing to perform operations on multiple members of a set concurrently. The ACCUM and POST-ACCUM clauses in GSQL are implicit FOREACH loops, specifying what to do for each member of the iteration sets. The order of iteration is unspecified. The TigerGraph compute engine may operate on multiple iterations concurrently.

An ACCUM clause acts like a FOREACH loop on each set of connected vertices and edges that satisfy the preceding FROM/SAMPLE/WHERE clauses, that is, on each pattern tuple. In this SELECT block, s refers to a member of Neighbors, which is a **Reaction**, and t refers to a **ReportedCase** having that **Reaction**. A POST-ACCUM clause is another FOREACH loop, but it can only operate on one vertex alias (e.g., either s or t).

At ❼ we order the Others vertices by descending similarity score and then prune the set to include only the top_k vertices. Finally, we print all the vertices in Others and the @@t_Size value.

Running the query with suggested source case 100640876 and then viewing the results in tabular form, we discover three **ReportedCase** instances with a perfect similarity score of 1: 103126041, 101749293, and 102852841. Then there are several others with similarity scores of 0.5.

Most reported drug for a company

The most_reported_drugs_for_company query takes three parameters. The first parameter, company_name, selects the company for which we want to find the topmost reported drugs. The second parameter k determines how many drug types we wish to return. Lastly, the third parameter filters DrugSequence elements with the given role value:

```
CREATE QUERY most_reported_drugs_for_company(
    STRING company_name="PFIZER",INT k=5, STRING role="PS") {
    // Possible values for role: PS, SS, I, C
    // PS = primary suspect drug, SS = secondary suspect drug
    // C = concomitant, I = interacting

    // Keep count of how many times each drug is mentioned.
    SumAccum<INT> @num_Cases;
```

Reflect on the words "most *reported drug* for a *company*." We can logically conclude that the query must traverse **ReportedCase**, **Drug**, and **PharmaCompany** vertices. Take a look back at Figure 3-14 to see how these vertex types are connected:

```
Drug - DrugSequence - ReportedCase - PharmaCompany
```

There are three hops from **Drug** to **PharmaCompany**; our query will perform its work in three stages. Composing GSQL as multistage procedures instead of multiple separate queries enables the use of accumulators as temporary storage values for both performance and functionality.

First, we find all the **ReportedCase** vertices that relate to the company given as an input parameter. Drilling down: we build a vertex set that contains all the **Company** vertices, because GSQL requires that a graph traversal begin with a vertex set. Then we select all the **ReportedCase** vertices that link to a **Company** vertex, as long as that company's name matches the company_name argument:

```
// 1. Find all cases where the given pharma company is the 'mfr_sndr'
    Company = {PharmaCompany.*};
    Cases = SELECT c
        FROM Company:s -(relatedTo:e)- ReportedCase:c
        WHERE s.mfr_sndr == company_name;
```

We then traverse from the selected **ReportedCase** vertices from the set that we collected above to their associated **DrugSequence** vertices. After that, we filter the **DrugSequence** set to only include those whose role matches the query's role argument:

```
// 2. Find all drug sequences for the selected cases.
    DrugSeqs = SELECT ds
        FROM Cases:c -(hasSequences:e)- DrugSequence:ds
        WHERE (role == "" OR ds.role_cod == role);
```

In the final part of the code, we connect the **DrugSequence** vertices that we selected in the second part with their associated **Drug** vertices. Of course, we need to do more than just find the drugs. We count how many cases feature a particular drug, then sort the drugs by decreasing count, and select the k most frequently mentioned drugs:

```
// 3. Count occurrences of each drug mentioned in each drug sequence.
    TopDrugs = SELECT d
        FROM DrugSeqs:ds -(hasDrugs:e)-> Drug:d
        ACCUM d.@num_Cases += 1
        ORDER BY d.@num_Cases DESC
        LIMIT k;

    PRINT TopDrugs;
}
```

Running this query with default input values (company_name="PFIZER", k=5, role="PS"), we get the drugs Lyrica, Lipitor, Chantix, Celebrex, and Viagra. Looking at the JSON or tabular output, we see the number of cases are 2682, 1259, 1189 ,1022, and 847, respectively.

Top side effects for top drugs

The query `top_side_effects_for_top_drugs` returns the top side effect for the most reported **Drug** of a given **Company**. Like the previous query, it also wants to find the most reported drug of a company, but it does additional work to count the side effects. Its parameter list looks the same as that of `most_reported_drugs_for_com pany`; however, here k refers to not only the topmost reported drugs but also the topmost frequent side effects:

```
CREATE QUERY top_side_effects_for_top_drugs(STRING company_name="PFIZER",
    INT k=5, STRING role="PS") FOR GRAPH faers SYNTAX v2 {
    // Possible values for role: PS, SS, I, C
    // PS = primary suspect drug, SS = secondary suspect drug
    // C = concomitant, I = interacting

    // Define a heap which sorts the reaction map (below) by count.
    TYPEDEF TUPLE<STRING name, INT cnt> tally;
    HeapAccum<tally>(k, cnt DESC) @top_Reactions;

    // Keep count of how many times each reaction or drug is mentioned.
    ListAccum<STRING> @reaction_List;
    SumAccum<INT> @num_Cases;
    MapAccum<STRING, INT> @reaction_Tally;
```

As we did for the previous query, let's look at the name and description of the query to understand what vertex and edge types we must traverse. We can see that we need to include **ReportedCase**, **Drug**, and **PharmaCompany**, as well as **Reaction** (side effect). This sets up a Y-shaped graph traversal pattern:

```
Drug - DrugSequence - ReportedCase - PharmaCompany
                             \- Reaction
```

This query has five stages. Stages 1, 3, and 4 of this query are the same or are slightly enhanced versions of Stages 1, 2, and 3 in the `most_reported_drugs_for_company` query.

Stage 1 is the same as Stage 1 of `most_reported_drugs_for_company`—find all the **ReportedCase** vertices that relate to the company given as an input parameter:

```
// 1. Find all cases where the given pharma company is the 'mfr_sndr'
    Company = {PharmaCompany.*};
    Cases = SELECT c
        FROM Company:s -(relatedTo:e)- ReportedCase:c
        WHERE s.mfr_sndr == company_name;
```

Stage 2 is new: now that we have a set of **ReportedCase** vertices, we can count their associated **Reactions**. We traverse all the **ReportedCase – Reaction** edges and then add each reaction type r.pt of a case c to a string list attached to that case c:

```
// 2. For each case, attach a list of its reactions.
   Tally = SELECT r
       FROM Cases:c -(hasReactions:e)- Reaction:r
       ACCUM c.@reaction_List += r.pt;
```

In Stage 3, we then traverse from the selected **ReportedCase** vertices from Stage 1 to their associated **DrugSequence** vertices. We perform the traversal first, and then filter the **DrugSequence** set to include only those whose role matches the query's role argument. After that, we copy the list of reactions attached to **ReportedCase** vertices to their associated **DrugSequences**. This last step is a GSQL technique to move data to where we need it:

```
// 3. Find all drug sequences for the selected cases, and transfer
//     the reaction list to the drug sequence.
   DrugSeqs = SELECT ds
       FROM Cases:c -(hasSequences:e)- DrugSequence:ds
       WHERE (role == "" OR ds.role_cod == role)
       ACCUM ds.@reaction_List = c.@reaction_List;
```

In Stage 4, we connect the **DrugSequence** vertices selected in Stage 2 with their associated **Drug** vertices. Besides counting the number of cases for a drug, we also count the occurrences of each **Reaction**:

```
// 4. Count occurrences of each drug mentioned in each drug sequence.
//     Also count the occurrences of each reaction.
   TopDrugs = SELECT d
       FROM DrugSeqs:ds -(hasDrugs:e)- Drug:d
       ACCUM d.@num_Cases += 1,
           FOREACH reaction in ds.@reaction_List DO
               d.@reaction_Tally += (reaction -> 1)
           END
       ORDER BY d.@num_Cases DESC
       LIMIT k;
```

Finally, in Stage 5, we take only the top k side effects. We do this by counting each reaction in tally, sorting them in descending order, and returning the top ones:

```
// 5. Find only the Top K side effects for each selected Drug.
   TopDrugs = SELECT d
       FROM TopDrugs:d
       ACCUM
           FOREACH (reaction, cnt) IN d.@reaction_Tally DO
               d.@top_Reactions += tally(reaction,cnt)
           END
       ORDER BY d.@num_Cases DESC;

   PRINT TopDrugs[TopDrugs.prod_ai, TopDrugs.@num_Cases,
```

```
                TopDrugs.@top_Reactions];
   }
```

If you run this query with the default inputs (which are the same as those of the previous query), the visual output looks the same. The difference is the `Top Drugs.@top_Reactions` accumulator. The best way to see this is to look at the JSON output. For Lyrica, the most reported drug from Pfizer, we have the following values:

```
"TopDrugs.@top_Reactions": [
  { "cnt": 459,"name": "Pain"},
  { "cnt": 373, "name": "Drug ineffective" },
  { "cnt": 167, "name": "Malaise" },
  { "cnt": 145, "name": "Feeling abnormal" },
  { "cnt": 145, "name": "Pain in extremity" }
],
```

Chapter Summary

In this chapter, we delved into two use cases to demonstrate the power of graphs to help users see the relationships in their data more clearly and completely. We introduced TigerGraph Starter Kits—demonstration databases and queries, preinstalled on TigerGraph Cloud instances—that show the basics of a variety of different use cases. We walked through the process of obtaining and installing a Customer 360 starter kit. At the same time, we walked through the first several steps of using GraphStudio, TigerGraph's graphical user interface.

We also introduced you to GSQL, the procedural SQL-like graph query language used by the TigerGraph graph database. Readers who know SQL and a conventional programming language should be able to learn GSQL without much trouble. To demonstrate how GSQL can help our analysis with graphs, we delved into two use cases. In the first use case, we defined a customer journey and described how sales groups benefit from recording and analyzing them. We then showed how a Customer 360 graph provides a powerful and flexible way to integrate customer data, which can then be represented as customer journeys. We walked through the three GSQL queries, which explore and analyze the customer journeys. In the second use case, we showed how a 360 graph can be used to show all the possible interactions and correlations among drugs used for medical treatment. Such analysis is vital for detecting and then taking action on adverse side effects.

CHAPTER 4

Studying Startup Investments

In this chapter, we will dive into the world of startup investments. This real-world use case shows us how three of the six graph powers help us to reveal high-potential investment opportunities. The first graph power, connecting the dots, allows us to view how various actors in the investment landscape are connected. The second graph power, looking deep, offers investors a method to include connected information about those actors in our analysis. The third graph power, weighing and predicting, enables us to utilize past funding events and investment portfolios to predict the success rate of future investments.

After completing this chapter, you should be able to:

- Explain how connecting the dots, looking deep, and weighing and predicting address search and analysis needs
- Model and analyze startup investment opportunities
- Traverse multihop relationships to filter deeper connected information
- Read and understand more advanced GSQL queries

Goal: Find Promising Startups

Investing in a startup is an exciting and lucrative way of building wealth. Investors poured over $156 billion into US startups in 2020. Those startups generated over

$290 billion of liquidity.[1] However, 9 out of 10 startups will fail, and with only 40% becoming profitable, it becomes a challenge to bet on the right horse.[2]

Startups start with a founding team consisting of only a few members. Over time, as a startup goes through different development stages, its product improves, and the team grows. To fund these developments, the startup needs money from investors. From the perspective of investment, one way to identify which startup is a proper candidate to finance is by looking at the composition of the startup team and its organization. Startups that have the right people at the right places in their organizations tend to have higher chances of success. Therefore, startups led by founders with a positive track record of building up companies are more likely to succeed in other companies. Another way to assess the investment opportunity is by looking at the startup's existing investors. Investors with a high return on their investment portfolio show that they can see the potential of startups in the early stages and help them grow into more profitable businesses.

Investing in startups is a risky and complex assessment that requires understanding the product and market it tries to take on and the people and organizations that drive it. Investors need to have an overview of the relationships between these aspects that help support the analysis of a startup's potential.

Solution: A Startup Investment Graph

Data to support the assessment of investments is mainly unstructured because it is collected from different sources. One example of such a source is the Crunchbase dataset. This dataset contains information on investment rounds, founders, companies, investors, and investment portfolios. However, the dataset is in raw format, meaning that the data is not structured to answer the questions we have on the entities related to startups for investment purposes. Data about startups and the entities contributing to the current state is hidden from us unless we query for the data explicitly. With graphs, we can form a schema centered around a target startup that we want to investigate and view the impact of other entities on the startup.

Investing in startups occurs in a series of funding events, as shown in Figure 4-1. Startups typically want to raise more money from a more extensive mixture of investors in every later funding stage. Knowing the timing and sequence of events throughout these funding stages is essential to validate successful investment interactions. Graphs can provide a complete overview of an investment network by searching for multihop chains of events. By doing this, we can connect angel investors and venture

---

1 Alex Wilhelm, "In 2020, VCs Invested $428M into US-Based Startups Every Day," TechCrunch, January 19, 2021, *https://techcrunch.com/2021/01/19/in-2020-vcs-invested-428m-into-us-based-startups-every-day.*

2 Sandeep Babu, "STARTUP STATISTICS—The Numbers You Need to Know," Small Business Trends, March 28, 2023, *https://smallbiztrends.com/2022/12/startup-statistics.html.*

capitalists through different funding stages and expose their investment portfolios' success rates over time.

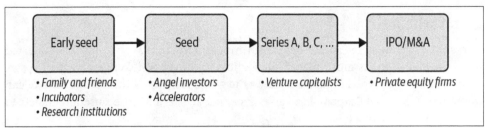

Figure 4-1. Startup funding stages and types of investors per stage

Traditional relational database queries provide us with a snapshot of an event and the state of each entity at a single point in time. However, when assessing investment portfolios, we need to understand the relationships between investors and the companies they have invested in and how these relationships have evolved. Graphs solve this by showing the investment portfolio as a series of events using multihop queries. We can also use multiple hops to perform complex searches and filtering, such as "find companies that have board members who are from a top-ranked VC firm and who previously served on the board of startups that had successful exits."

For example, we want to know what startups colleagues of a successful investor are investing in now. This insight allows us to utilize successful investors' expertise and network based on their past investments. A multihop query can realize this by first selecting one or more successful investors. We might already have some in mind, or we could find them by counting the number of successful investors per investor; that would be one hop. The second hop selects all financial organizations where the investors work. The third hop query selects colleagues at those financial organizations, and the fourth hop selects other funding events where those colleagues participate.

Implementing a Startup Investment Graph and Queries

TigerGraph Cloud offers a starter kit for the startup investment analysis use case. In the remainder of this chapter, we will describe how we model startups and their funding with a graph schema. Then we'll look at four different graph analyses that could help an investor select promising startups.

The Crunchbase Starter Kit

Use the TigerGraph Cloud account that you created in Chapter 3 to deploy a new use case and select "Enterprise Knowledge Graph (Crunchbase)." Once this starter kit is installed, follow the steps in the section "Load data and install queries for a starter kit" on page 50 in Chapter 3.

Graph Schema

The starter kit includes actual data from investments in startups in 2013 collected by Crunchbase. It has more than 575K vertices and over 664K edges, with 10 vertex types and 24 edge types. Figure 4-2 shows the graph schema of this starter kit. We can immediately see that **Company** is a vertex type that acts as a hub because it connects to many other vertex types.

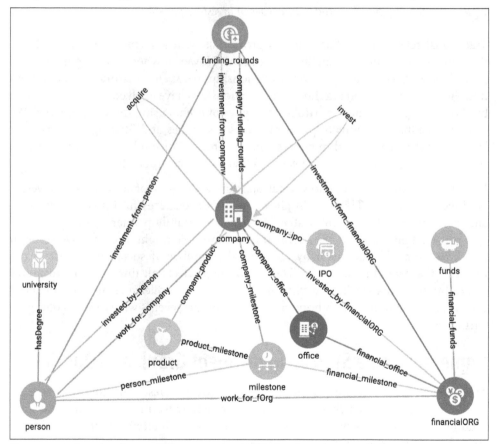

Figure 4-2. Graph schema for Enterprise Knowledge Graph (Crunchbase) (see a larger version of this figure at https://oreil.ly/gpam0402)

Furthermore, there are two types of self edges. A **Company** can **acquire** another **Company**, and a **Company** can also **invest** in another **Company**. A **Person** type vertex, on the other hand, does not have self edges, which means that a social connection always goes through another vertex type such as **University**, **Financial_Org**, **Funding_Rounds**, or **Company**. For example, if a **Person** works for a company, this type of relationship is indicated with the edge type **work_for_company**.

In Table 4-1, we describe the 10 vertex types in the starter kit. From the description, we can see that **Company** vertices have potential relationships with many other vertex types. Some of them even have multiple relationship types that connect to **Company**. For example, a **Person** can invest in a **Company**, but it can also work for a **Company**.

Table 4-1. Vertex types in the Crunchbase Starter Kit

Vertex type	Description
Company	A company
Funding_Rounds	An investment event where a **Company** invests or receives funds
Person	A natural person who works for a **Company** or invests in a **Company**
University	A university institution
Financial_Org	A financial institution that invests in a **Company**
Funds	A financial investment
Office	A physical office of a **Company**
IPO	An initial public offering of a **Company**
Product	A product or service of a **Company**
Milestone	A milestone that a **Company** has accomplished

Queries and Analytics

Let's look at the queries in the Enterprise Knowledge Graph (Crunchbase) Starter Kit. There are four queries in this starter kit. Each query is designed to answer questions that a potential investor or employer might ask.

Key role discovery

This query finds all the persons with a key role at a given **Company** and its parent companies. A key role for a **Person** is defined as serving as a founder, CEO, CTO, director, or executive for the **Company** where they work.

Investor successful exits

Given a certain investor, this query finds the startups that had a successful exit within a certain number of years after the investor invested. A successful exit is when a company has an IPO or is acquired by another company. The visual output of the query is the subgraph of the given investor with all its relationships with **IPO** and acquiring **Company** elements. An investor could be any element of type **Person**, **Financial_Org**, or **Company**.

Top startups based on board

> This query ranks startups based on the number of times that a current board member working for a top investment firm (**Financial_Org**) was also a board member of a previous startup that had a successful exit. Investment firms are ranked by the amount of funds they invested in the past *N* years. Board members are scored according to their number of successful exits. In addition, the query filters output startups that are beyond a certain funding-round stage.

Top startups based on leader

> This query ranks startups based on the number of times one of its founders previously worked at another **Company**, during an early stage of that company, which then went on to have a successful exit. The search is filtered to look only at a given industry sector.

Key role discovery

The key_role_discovery query has two arguments. The first argument, company_name, is our target **Company** for which we want to find the persons who played key roles either there or at a parent company. The second argument, k, determines how many hops from our starting company_name we will search for parent companies. This query fits very naturally with a graph model because of the k hops parameter. Figure 4-3 shows part of the graph traversal for two hops. Starting from company Com A, we could find connections to a parent company Com B and two key persons, Ben and Adam. We then look to see if Com B has key persons or has another parent company.

We'll now walk you through the GSQL implementation. In your starter kit, look for the query called key_role_discovery. Select it so you can see the code.

First, we declare some accumulators[3] in which to gather our output objects, @@output_vertices and @@output_edges. We also declare visited to mark vertices that the query has encountered already, to avoid double-counting or searching in circles. In this dataset, if a time variable does not have a genuine value, it is set to code 0, which translates to January 1, 1970. We declare TNULL as a more descriptive name for this situation:

```
OrAccum @visited;
SetAccum<VERTEX> @@output_vertices;
SetAccum<EDGE> @@output_edges;
DATETIME TNULL = to_datetime("1970-01-01 00:00:00");
```

---

3 Accumulators were described in Chapter 3.

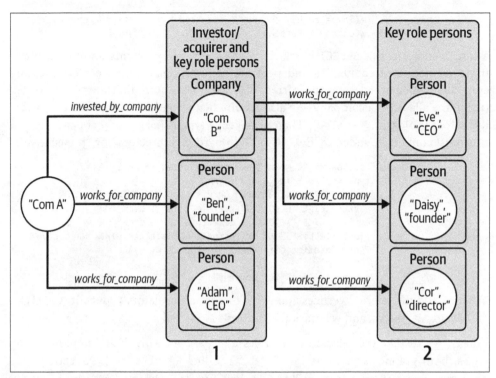

Figure 4-3. Graph traversal pattern to find employees who have a key role at a company and its parent companies

Next, we select all the company elements whose name attribute matches the input parameter company_name. The functions lower(trim()) remove any leading or trailing blank spaces and convert all the letters to lowercase so that differences in capitalization won't matter. Each vertex whose name matches is added to the @@out put_vertices set and is also marked as @visited:

```
Linked_companies (ANY) = SELECT tgt
    FROM Company:tgt
    WHERE lower(trim(tgt.name)) == lower(trim(company_name))
    ACCUM @@output_vertices += tgt
    POST-ACCUM tgt.@visited = TRUE;
```

Now, we start a WHILE loop to look for key persons and parent companies up to k levels deep. At each iteration, we select all **Company** elements that have an **inves ted_by_company**, **acquired_by**, or **work_for_company** edge to a **Company** or **Person**. This is a good example of the importance of selecting descriptive names for your vertices and edges:

```
WHILE TRUE LIMIT k DO
    Linked_companies = SELECT tgt
        FROM Linked_companies:s
```

```
- ((invested_by_company> | acquired_by> | work_for_company):e)
- (Company | Person):tgt
```

There is more to this SELECT block. Its **WHERE** clause performs additional filtering of the selected companies and persons. First, to make sure we are traversing company-to-person edges in the correct direction, we require that the source vertex (using the alias s) is a company. We also require that we haven't visited the target vertex before (NOT tgt.@visited). Then, if the edge type is **work_for_company**, the job title must contain "founder," "CEO," "CTO," "[b]oard [of] directors," or "[e]xecutive":

```
WHERE s.type == "Company" AND tgt.@visited == FALSE AND
    (e.type == "work_for_company" AND
      (e.title LIKE "%founder%" OR e.title LIKE "%Founder%" OR
       e.title LIKE "%CEO%" OR e.title LIKE "% ceo%" OR
       e.title LIKE "%CTO%" OR e.title LIKE "% cto%" OR
       ((e.title LIKE "%oard%irectors%" OR e.title LIKE "%xecutive%")
         AND datetime_diff(e.end_at, TNULL) == 0))
    ) OR
    e.type != "work_for_company"
```

We then add the selected vertices and edges to our accumulators @@output_vertices and @@output_edges, and we mark the vertices as visited.

Finally, we display the selected companies and persons with their interconnecting edges, both graphically and as JSON data. The line Results = {@@output_verti ces} creates a vertex set from a SetAccum<VERTEX>. If we printed @@output_vertex directly, we would see only the vertices' IDs. Printing a vertex set like Results will display all of the vertices' properties:

```
IF @@output_vertices.size() != 0 THEN
    Results = {@@output_vertices}; // conversion to output more that just id
    PRINT Results;
    PRINT @@output_edges;
ELSE
    PRINT "No parties with key relations to the company found within ", k,
        " steps" AS msg;
```

GSQL: Printing Vertices

For efficiency, accumulators containing vertices store only their IDs. To print vertex properties, copy the accumulator into a regular vertex set and print the vertex set.

In Figure 4-4, we show the output when company_name = LuckyCal and k = 3. While the name of the company in the center is missing, we can see that it is Facebook, based on the list of founders, including Mark Zuckerberg.

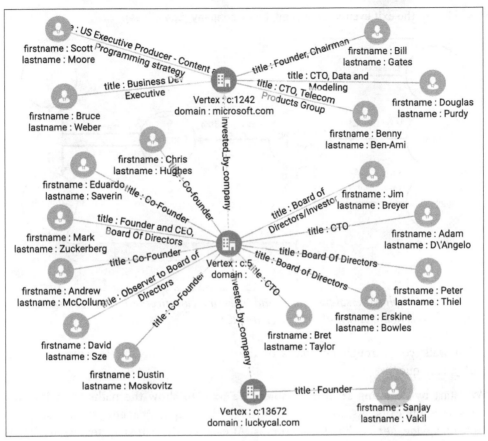

Figure 4-4. Key role discovery when company_name = LuckyCal *and k = 3 (see a larger version of this figure at https://oreil.ly/gpam0404)*

Investor successful exits

The `investor_successful_exits` query finds the achievement of a given investor, where achievement is measured by the number of investments that lead to IPOs and acquisitions. It takes three arguments. `investor_name` is the name of our target investor of whom we want to know the achievements, and `investor_type` is the type of investor, which could be **Company**, **Person**, or **Financial_Org**. We use year to test if an exit occurred soon enough after the funding. We can answer this query by using the following graph traversal pattern as illustrated in Figure 4-5. Start from the selected investor vertex (`investor_name`):

1. Hop to the funding rounds the investor participated in.
2. Hop to the companies funded by these rounds.

3. Hop to the exit events (**acquired_by** or **company_ipo** edges).

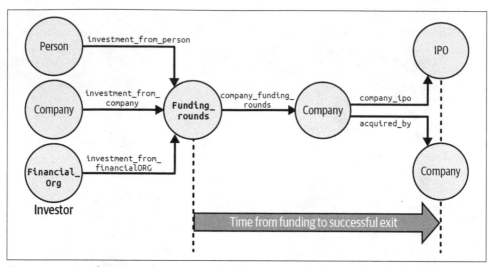

Figure 4-5. Graph traversal pattern to find investors with successful exits (see a larger version of this figure at https://oreil.ly/gpam0405)

We'll walk you through key parts of the GSQL code for the investor_success ful_exits query.

We start by declaring several variables. We want to show the paths from investor to successful exits. As we traverse through the graph, @parent_vertex_set and @parent_edge_set act like breadcrumbs. At each newly visited vertex, we use them to record how we got there. After we reach the end, we use these accumulators to find our way back. During the backtrack, we gather all the vertices and edges on these paths into the global accumulators @@result_vertex_set and @@result_edge_set:

```
SetAccum<VERTEX> @parent_vertex_set;
SetAccum<EDGE> @parent_edge_set;
SetAccum<VERTEX> @@result_vertex_set;
SetAccum<EDGE> @@result_edge_set;
```

Next we create the Start set of vertices, using a CASE statement and the investor_type parameter to select the type of investors indicated by the user:

```
Start (ANY) = {};
CASE lower(trim(investor_type))
    WHEN "person"      THEN Start = {Person.*};
    WHEN "company"     THEN Start = {Company.*};
    WHEN "financialorg"  THEN Start = {Financial_Org.*};
END;
```

We complete the preliminaries by finding the individual investor who has investor_name. If the investor is a **Person**, we check the attribute called fullname; otherwise, we check the attribute called name:

```
Investor (ANY) = SELECT inv
    FROM Start:inv
    WHERE ( inv.type == "Person"
            AND lower(trim(inv.fullname)) == lower(trim(investor_name))
          ) OR lower(trim(inv.name)) == lower(trim(investor_name));
```

Now we begin our graph hops. First we select all the **Funding_Rounds** linked to the investor. At each selected **Funding_Rounds** vertex, we store the identity of the vertex and edge traversed to arrive there. The target vertices of this hop are stored in a variable called Funding_rounds:

```
Funding_rounds = SELECT tgt
    FROM Investor:s - ((investment_from_company | investment_from_person |
        investment_from_financialORG):e) - Funding_Rounds:tgt
    ACCUM
        tgt.@parent_vertex_set += s,
        tgt.@parent_edge_set += e;
```

Now we take another hop from the selected funding rounds to the companies they funded. An investor can invest in a company at more than one funding round. For example, in Figure 4-6, we see that Ted Leonsis invested in Revolution Money in both rounds B and C. An investor's success should be judged from the time of their first investment. Each **Funding_Rounds** vertex sends its funded_at parameter value to a MinAccum @min_invested_time, which remembers the minimum value that it is given:

```
Invested_companies = SELECT tgt
    FROM Funding_rounds:s - ((company_funding_rounds):e) - Company:tgt
    ACCUM
        tgt.@parent_vertex_set += s,
        tgt.@parent_edge_set += e,
        tgt.@min_invested_time += s.funded_at;
```

Finally, for each company that received investment funding, we look to see if it had a successful exit within the required time window. A **company_ipo** or **acquired_by** edge indicates an exit. If it was an IPO, we check that the IPO date (the public_at attribute) is later than the investment date but not more than the value of years later. An analogous check is performed on the acquired_at attribute if it was an acquisition event:

```
IPO_acquired_companies = SELECT tgt
    FROM Invested_companies:s - ((company_ipo | acquired_by>):e) -:tgt
    ACCUM
        tgt.@parent_vertex_set += s,
        tgt.@parent_edge_set += e,
        // See if IPO occurred within `years` after Investor's investment
```

```
IF (e.type == "company_ipo"
    AND datetime_diff(tgt.public_at, s.@min_invested_time) > 0
    AND datetime_diff(
    tgt.public_at, s.@min_invested_time) <= years * SECS_PER_YR)
// See if Acquisition occurred within `years` of investment
OR (e.type == "acquired_by"
    AND datetime_diff(e.acquired_at, s.@min_invested_time) > 0
    AND datetime_diff(
    e.acquired_at, s.@min_invested_time) <= years * SECS_PER_YR)
THEN @@result_vertex_set += tgt
END;
```

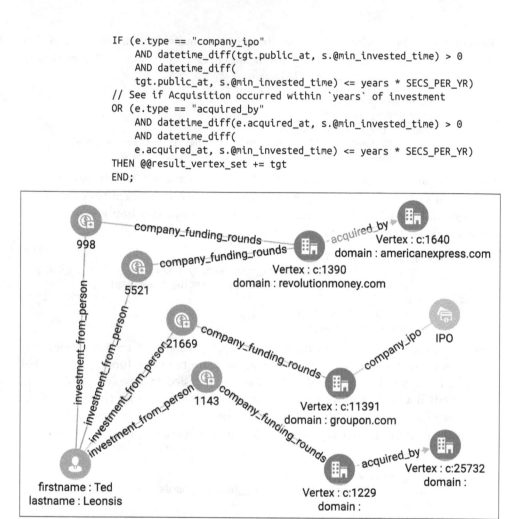

Figure 4-6. Investor successful exits when `investor_name` = *Ted Leonsis and* `years` = *3 (see a larger version of this figure at https://oreil.ly/gpam0406)*

If we only wanted to know how many successful exits our investor had, or the company details of those exits, we would be done. However, it's interesting to graphically show the paths from investor → funding → company → exit, as in Figure 4-6. To gather that information, we traverse from the exit vertices backward to the investor, using the breadcrumbs (@parent_vertex_set and @parent_edge_set) that we set previously:

```
Children = {@@result_vertex_set};
PRINT Children.size() as Num_Successful_Exits;
WHILE(Children.size() > 0) DO
    Start = SELECT s
        FROM Children:s
```

```
        ACCUM
            @@parents += s.@parent_vertex_set,
            @@result_edge_set += s.@parent_edge_set;

    @@result_vertex_set += @@parents;
    Children = {@@parents};
    @@parents.clear();
```

Top startups based on board

The `top_startups_based_on_board` query adds some complexity by adding in two forms of ranking: top-performing investment companies and top-performing leaders at those investment companies. It starts by identifying the **Financial_Org** entities that have invested the most money in recent years. Then, we rank **Persons** at those organizations according to the number of times they were on the board of a startup **Company** and guided it to a successful exit. Then, we display any pre-exit **Companies** that currently have one of these successful executives as a board member.

The `top_startups_based_on_board` query has four input parameters:

k_orgs
> The number of top financial institutions we want to include in our selection scope

num_persons
> The number of top board members to select

max_funding_round
> Filters the final list of promising startups to exclude those that have received investment funding at a later stage than max_funding_round

past_n_years
> Sets the time window for money invested by **Financial_Org**

We can implement this query according to the following steps, most of which correspond to a graph hop; these steps are illustrated in Figure 4-7:

1. Compute how much **Funding_Rounds** investment each **Financial_Org** made in the past N years [Hop 1].

2. Rank the **Financial_Org** by the investment amount and take the top k_orgs.

3. Find **Persons** who work for a top k **Financial_Org** (from step 2) [Hop 2].

4. Find companies at which those **Persons** (from step 3) served as board members [Hop 3].

5. Rank those **Persons** (from step 3) by the number of times they were on the board of a **Company** (from step 4) before its successful exit [Hop 4].

6. Find pre-exit **Company** vertices that have a top board member **Person** (from step 5). Filter these companies by the funding round cutoff [Hop 5].

This query declares several accumulators and other variables to assist with this computation. There are also two interesting data preparation steps. One stores some currency exchange rates in a lookup table. Another makes a list of all the funding round codes @@allowed_funding_rounds up to our max_cutoff_round.

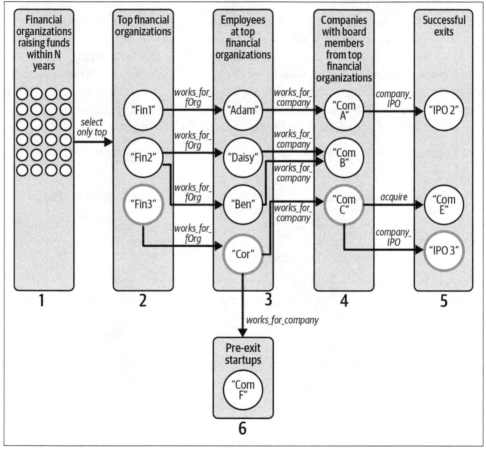

Figure 4-7. Graph traversal pattern to find promising startups based on successful board members from top financial organizations

Our first graph hop is also a data preparation step. Our Crunchbase graph schema stores the IPO or acquisition date of a company on an edge. Copy that data so that it is also available with the companies themselves:

```
Comp = SELECT c
    FROM (Company):c - ((company_ipo|acquired_by>):e) - (IPO|Company):x
    ACCUM
```

```
CASE WHEN
  e.type == "company_ipo" AND datetime_diff(x.public_at, T0) != 0
THEN
  c.@t_exit += x.public_at
END,
CASE WHEN
  e.type == "acquired_by" AND datetime_diff(e.acquired_at,T0) != 0
THEN
  c.@t_exit += e.acquired_at
END;
```

In the next hop, we connect **Financial_Org** vertices with their investment **Funds** in order to tally the investments of the past_n_years and then take the top k organizations. The WHERE clause filters for the desired time range. To take the top k, GSQL offers ORDER BY and LIMIT clauses, just as in SQL:

```
Top_orgs = SELECT org
    FROM (Financial_Org):org - (financial_funds:e) - Funds:f
    WHERE datetime_diff(END_2013, f.funded_at) <= past_n_years*SECS_PER_YR
    ACCUM org.@amount +=
        (f.raised_amount / @@currency2USD.get(f.raised_currency_code)),
        f.@visited = TRUE
    ORDER BY org.@amount DESC
    LIMIT k_orgs;
```

Advanced GSQL users may sometimes choose to use HeapAccum instead of ORDER BY/LIMIT because sorting a small heap takes less computer memory than the global sort that ORDER BY performs.

Next, we select all employees (**Person** who **work_for_fOrg**) at these top financial organizations (the Top_org vertex set from the previous step):

```
Persons_at_top_orgs = SELECT p
    FROM Top_orgs:o - (work_for_fOrg:e) - Person:p;
```

From these Persons_at_top_orgs, we want to select the ones that satisfied the following criteria for helping to lead a successful exit:

- Their job title included "Board."
- The company has had an exit (c.@t_exit.size() != 0).
- The person has a valid work start date (datetime_diff(w.start_at, T0) != 0).
- The company's exit occurred after the board member joined.

The following code performs that selection:

```
Top_board_members = SELECT p
    FROM Persons_at_top_orgs:p - (work_for_company:w) - Company:c
    WHERE (w.title LIKE "%Board%" OR w.title LIKE "%board%")
        AND c.@t_exit.size() != 0 AND datetime_diff(w.start_at, T0) != 0
        AND datetime_diff(c.@t_exit.get(0), w.start_at) > 0
```

After finding these successful startup board members, we build a list of these successful startup companies (@@comp_set). We also have each such **Company** record its key board member (c@board_set), and we tally the successful exits of each key person (p.@amount += 1). Finally, we take the most prolific board members (ORDER BY and LIMIT):

```
ACCUM
    @@comp_set += c,
    c.@board_set += p,
    p.@amount += 1
ORDER BY p.@amount DESC
LIMIT num_persons;
```

Then we find all pre-exit **Company** entities that have a top_board_member:

```
Top_startups = SELECT c
    FROM Top_board_members:s - (work_for_company:w) - Company:c
    WHERE (w.title LIKE "%Board%" OR w.title LIKE "%board%")
        AND w.start_at != T0
        AND c.status == "operating" AND c.@t_exit.size() == 0;
```

Finally, we include only those pre-exit companies whose **Funding_Rounds** have been early enough to satisfy the max_cutoff_round limit:

```
Top_early_startups = SELECT r
    FROM Top_startups:s - (company_funding_rounds:e) - Funding_Rounds:r
    ACCUM
        s.@visited += TRUE,
        IF @allowed_funding_rounds.contains(r.funding_round_code) THEN
            r.@visited = TRUE
        ELSE
            s.@early += FALSE
        END;
```

The remainder of the query is used to trace back from the top board members to display the companies they worked for and their successful exits.

Figure 4-8 shows the results when we set k_orgs = 10, num_persons = 2, max_funding_round = b, and past_n_years = 10. The two key board members are Jim Goetz and Jim Breyer, who both work for Accel Partners. Goetz has had four successful exits, while Breyer has had three. The recommended startups are companies linked to Goetz or Breyer that don't yet have an exit: Nimble Storage, Ruckus Wireless, HubSpot, Booyah, and Etsy.[4]

---

4 We are analyzing Crunchbase's 2013 data. A few of these startups did succeed; others did not.

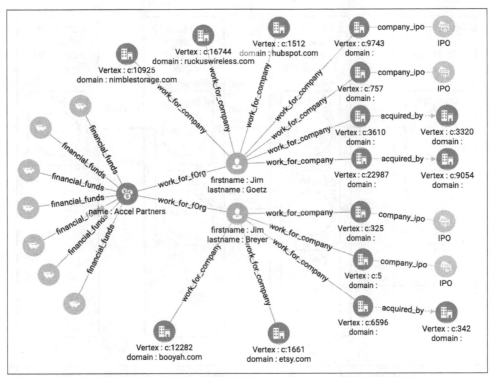

Figure 4-8. Graph output for top startups based on board members (see a larger version of this figure at https://oreil.ly/gpam0408)

Top startups based on leader

Our last query in this starter kit is similar to the previous one, except that rather than looking for top board members, we are looking for founders. This query takes three arguments. `max_funding_round` is the funding round cutoff, meaning that we only select startups whose investment rounds have been no later than `max_funding_round`. Argument `return_size` is the number of top startups we want to retrieve from our query, and `sector` is the industry sector we want to filter out the result.

Figure 4-9 illustrates how we construct this query as a series of graph hops:

1. Find all companies that have IPOed or been acquired [Hop 1].

2. Find employees who contributed to the companies in step 1 [Hop 2].

3. Find startups whose founder also was a key employee from step 2 [Hop 3]. Filter the startups based on the cutoff round and sector.

4. Find companies whose founders have the most successful connections.

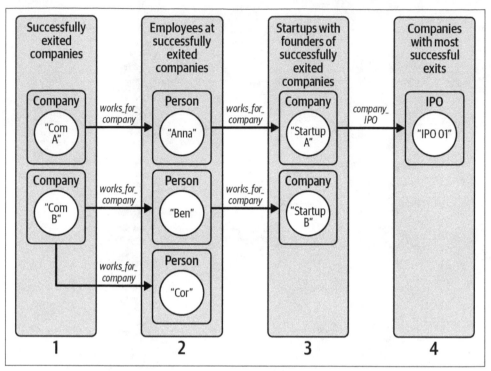

Figure 4-9. Graph traversal pattern to find promising startups based on successful founders

This query introduces some data structures that we haven't seen before: a TUPIL and a HeapAccum. A GSQL tuple is a user-defined data type composed of a set of basic existing types. A Company_Score tuple consists of a **Company** vertex followed by an integer. A HeapAccum manages a sorted list of tuples up to a user-specified maximum number of items. Our HeapAccum @@top_companies_heap holds Company_Score tuples sorted by their score values. The heap can contain up to return_size companies:

```
TYPEDEF TUPLE<VERTEX<Company> company, INT score> Company_Score;
HeapAccum<Score_Results>(return_size, score DESC) @@top_companies_heap;
```

We also define two nested MapAccums. A map is like a lookup table. Looking at the structural definition of @@person_company_leave_date_map, this means that for a given person, we record when that person left a given company. For @@person_com pany_employment_map, we record the employment relationship between a **Person** and a **Company**:

```
// Declare map to store when an employee left which company
MapAccum<VERTEX<Person>,
    MapAccum<VERTEX<Company>, DATETIME>> @@person_company_leave_date_map;
```

```
            MapAccum<VERTEX<person>,
                MapAccum<VERTEX<Company>, EDGE>> @@person_company_employment_map;
```

Now we find all the companies with an IPO or that have been acquired by another company. For clearer code, one code block finds IPO companies, another focuses on acquisitions, and then we merge the two sets of companies. For the IPOs, we traverse from **IPO** vertices to **Company** vertices. We check that the IPO has a valid `public_at` attribute. Once selected, we tag each **Company** with the path back to the **IPO** vertex and with the `public_at` date. We tag the company as no longer in the startup phase:

```
IPO_companies = SELECT c
    FROM IPO:i - (company_ipo:e) - Company:c
    //Filter out companies with null acquisition time (not yet acquired)
    WHERE datetime_diff(i.public_at, TNULL) != 0
    ACCUM
        c.@parent_vertex_set += i,
        c.@parent_edge_set += e,
        c.@min_public_date = i.public_at,
        c.@is_still_startup += FALSE;
```

A similar code block finds the `acquired_companies`. The edge type is different (**acquire** instead of **company_ipo**), and the effective data attribute is different (`acquired_at` instead of `public_at`).

We then join the output sets from these two blocks:

```
IPO_acquired_companies = IPO_companies UNION Acquired_companies;
```

Next we select all the persons who have worked for a successfully exited company before the exit event. For each such person, we store their relevant information into the nested maps that we described earlier. Notice the `->` operator used to specify a map's key `->` value pair:

```
Startup_employees = SELECT p
    FROM IPO_acquired_companies:c - (work_for_company:e) - Person:p
      WHERE datetime_diff(e.start_at, TNULL) != 0
        AND datetime_diff(e.end_at, TNULL) != 0
        AND datetime_diff(e.start_at, c.@min_public_date) < 0
      ACCUM
            @@person_company_employment_map += (p -> (c -> e)),
            @@person_company_leave_date_map += (p -> (c -> e.end_at));
```

Now we find the startups where these successful-exit employees are currently a founder, filtered by industry. The checks for the startup status and founder status are performed in the WHERE clause:

```
New_startups = SELECT c
    FROM startup_employees :p - (work_for_company :e) - Company :c
    WHERE c.@is_still_startup
        AND c.@early_startup
        AND c.status != "acquired"
        AND c.status != "ipo"
```

```
                AND e.title LIKE "%ounder%"
                AND lower(trim(c.category_code)) == lower(trim(sector))
                AND datetime_diff(e.start_at, TNULL) != 0
                AND datetime_diff(e.end_at, TNULL) != 0
```

After selecting these startups, we tally the founders' past successes:

```
ACCUM
// Tally the founder:past-success relationships per new company
    FOREACH (past_company, leave_date)
    IN @@person_company_leave_date_map.get(p) DO
        IF datetime_diff(e.start_at, leave_date) > 0 THEN
            p.@parent_edge_set +=
                @@person_company_employment_map.get(p).get(past_company),
            p.@company_list += past_company,
            c.@parent_vertex_set += p,
            c.@parent_edge_set += e,
            c.@sum_ipo_acquire += 1
        END
    END
HAVING c.@sum_ipo_acquire > 0;
```

Select companies where the founders have the most relationships with successfully exited companies. We use the `HeapAccum` we described previously to rank the companies based on the tally of successful exits of its founder(s):

```
Top_companies = SELECT c
    FROM Startups_from_employees:c
    ACCUM @@top_score_results_heap += Score_Results(c, c.@sum_ipo_acquire);
PRINT @@top_score_results_heap;

FOREACH item IN @@top_score_results_heap DO
    @@output_vertex_set += item.company;
END;
```

Figure 4-10 shows the results when the input arguments are `max_funding_round` = c, `return_size` = 5, and `sector` = software. The five selected startups are listed on the right. Looking at the second company from the top, we read from right to left: Packet Trap Networks is selected because founder Steve Goodman was a Founder/CEO of Lasso Logic, which was acquired by SonicWALL.

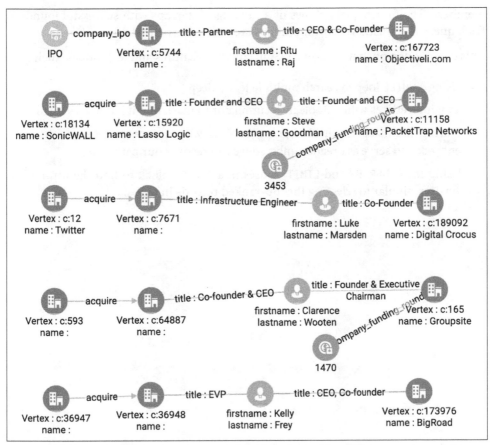

Figure 4-10. Graph output of top startups based on leader (see a larger version of this figure at https://oreil.ly/gpam0410)

Chapter Summary

In this chapter, we have seen how we can use graph analytics to answer important questions and gain valuable insight about startup investments. Looking at the graph schema for Crunchbase data, we've seen that such data is highly interconnected. In the case of investment advice, we often look to past performance as an indicator of possible future results. So we look for one pattern (success in the past) and see if there is potential for a repeat of that pattern. This type of pattern search or similarity search is typical of graph analytics.

We have discussed four queries in this chapter to identify those patterns that can help us investigate investment opportunities. The first query identifies all persons with key roles within a company. The second query identifies successful startup exits from an investor. The third query shows us a ranking of startups with successful board members. The fourth query shows us a ranking of startups with successful founders. Each query demonstrated how multihops are utilized to benefit our analyses.

This chapter demonstrated several GSQL language features and techniques, such as:

- Using a `WHILE` loop to search multiple levels deep
- Tagging vertices with a Boolean accumulator to mark that it has been visited
- During multistep traversal, tagging vertices with a `parent_vertex` and a `parent_edge` to serve as breadcrumbs, so we can recover our paths later
- Using the `ORDER BY` and `LIMIT` clauses in a `SELECT` block to find the top-ranked vertices, similar to selecting the top-ranked records in SQL

CHAPTER 5

Detecting Fraud and Money Laundering Patterns

In this chapter, we take on the serious problem of fraud and money laundering. Fraud is typically conducted by one or more parties as a multistep process. Sometimes, the only way to distinguish fraud or money laundering from legitimate activity is to detect a characteristic or unusual pattern of activity. Modeling the activity and relationships with a graph enables us to detect suspicious activity by searching for those patterns along with checking for their frequency.

After completing this chapter, you should be able to:

- Describe coordinated activity among multiple parties in terms of a graph pattern
- Use a multihop or iterated single-hop graph traversal to perform a deep search
- Describe bidirectional search and its advantages
- Understand the use of timestamps to find a time sequence

Goal: Detect Financial Crimes

Financial institutions are responsible for averting criminal money flows through the economic infrastructure. According to The Financial Action Task Force (FATF), illicit funds amount to 3.6% of global GDP.[1] A well-known criminal activity is money laundering, or disguising the origin of money earned through illicit means. According to

---

1 "What Is Money Laundering?" fatf-gafi, accessed May 22, 2023, *https://www.fatf-gafi.org/en/pages/frequently-asked-questions.html#tabs-36503a8663-item-6ff811783c-tab*.

the FATF, 2.7% of global GDP is laundered per year. Banks are legally obligated to investigate their clients' payment behavior and report any suspicious activities.

Other types of financial fraud include identity theft, where someone uses another person's accounts without permission, and Ponzi schemes, which are characterized by money flowing from newer investors to earlier investors without actually going to an external venture.

Banks have built a wide range of applications and procedures into their daily operations to identify and detect financial crimes. Broadly speaking, these techniques can fall into two areas.

The first area of investigation, Know Your Customer (KYC), looks into the client profile. Similar to what we've seen in Chapter 3 with the Customer 360 use case, analysts need to conduct client due diligence. This client risk assessment can happen at multiple stages of the client lifecycle, such as during new client takeover (NCTO) or during a periodic review.

The second area of investigation, transaction monitoring, mainly focuses on identifying criminal behavior through bank transactions. Here, analysts try to identify unusual payment patterns between senders and beneficiaries. Although these two investigation areas often overlap from a bank operational perspective and on a risk management level, we will mainly focus on transaction monitoring in this chapter.

Transaction monitoring involves thorough investigations into entities that show suspicious payment behavior. Analysts start these investigations from entities flagged as suspicious and move from there to explore high-risk interactions. Thus, analysts do not know the complete picture of how the money flows and lack visibility on where the flagged entity is in the entire money trail. To gain this visibility, they have to query step-by-step the next payment interaction to build up a complete picture of the payment network. Therefore, analysts need an approach that helps them retrieve a set of consecutive payments and the parties involved in those payments.

Solution: Modeling Financial Crimes as Network Patterns

Traditional transaction monitoring relies on rule-based systems where client behavior is checked against fixed risk indicators. Such a risk indicator could be when, for example, clients received $15,000 cash in their account and immediately sent that money to several third-party accounts. This could be normal income and expense activity, or it could be part of a money laundering technique called layering. It indicates a suspicious activity because it revolves around a large amount of cash, and that money moves to several third parties, making it harder to trace its origin.

There are two major problems with relying on rule-based risk indicators. First, the analyst is still required to do an in-depth follow-up investigation on flagged clients, which involves querying consecutive payments between different clients. Second, rule-based risk indicators have been limited in their sophistication due to the challenge of extracting deep patterns from tabular data.

When modeling this problem as a network, it becomes easier to identify high-risk patterns because we can visualize the money flow directly from the graph data model. Doing so shows us how the money moves in a network and which parties are involved in those payment interactions. This graph approach solves the first problem because the graph pattern search will discover the consecutive payments for the analyst. It also solves the second problem because the network will expose all the relationships between involved parties, including those that the analysts do not explicitly query.

Later in this book, we will see how graph machine learning can do an even better job of detecting financial crime patterns.

Implementing Financial Crime Pattern Searches

TigerGraph provides a starter kit for fraud and money laundering detection. Follow the installation steps from Chapter 3 to install the starter kit. After the installation, we will use the starter kit to design our money laundering network and explore how we can detect suspicious payment interactions on this network.

The Fraud and Money Laundering Detection Starter Kit

Using TigerGraph Cloud, deploy a new cloud cluster and select "Fraud and Money Laundering Detection" as the use case. Once this starter kit is installed, follow the steps in the section "Load data and install queries for a starter kit" on page 50 in Chapter 3.

Graph Schema

The Fraud and Money Laundering Detection Starter Kit contains over 4.3M vertices and 7M edges, with a schema that has four vertex types and five edge types. Figure 5-1 shows the graph schema of this starter kit.

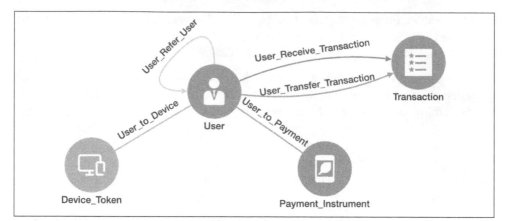

Figure 5-1. Graph schema for the Fraud and Money Laundering Detection Starter Kit (see a larger version of this figure at https://oreil.ly/gpam0501)

In Table 5-1 we describe the four vertex types. A **User** has a central role in a payment interaction, where it can receive and send payments. **Transaction** is the payment itself. **Device_Token** is a unique ID number that refers to the device used for the payment, and **Payment_Instrument** refers to the type of instrument used for the payment.

Table 5-1. Vertex types in the Fraud and Money Laundering Detection Starter Kit

Vertex type	Description
User	A person who is involved in a payment
Transaction	A payment
Device_Token	A unique ID number used to carry out the **Transaction**
Payment_Instrument	An instrument to execute the payment

There are two types of relationships between **User** and **Transaction**. A **User** can receive a transaction, denoted with **User_Receive_Transaction**, or a **User** can send a transaction, marked with **User_Transfer_Transaction**. A **User** can refer another **User**, which is indicated by **User_Refer_User**. The edge type **User_to_Payment** links a **User** to a **Payment_Instrument** (check, cash, warrant, etc.) used to carry out a transaction. Finally, the **User_to_Device** edge type connects a **User** to the **Device_Token** used when making an electronic payment.

Queries and Analytics

The queries included in this starter kit showcase how graphs can help analysts detect high-risk payment behavior to combat fraud and money laundering. We'll first give a high-level description of the pattern that each query looks for and how this pertains

---

to transaction fraud or money laundering. We then go into depth for three of them to give you a better idea of how they are implemented.

Circle detection

This query detects when money moves in a circular flow. It selects the `Transaction` elements that form a time sequence from an input `User` and then return to that `User`. If the amount of money that comes back is close to the amount that went out, then this may indicate money laundering.

Invited user behavior

This query looks for suspicious patterns of `User_Refer_User` behavior, which may indicate that a `User` is collaborating with other parties to collect referral bonuses. It looks at the number of referrals within two hops of a source `User` and at the number of transactions these users have conducted.

Multitransaction

This query showcases the payments between two networks of `User` elements. Starting with an input `Transaction`, the first group is a network of `User` elements related to the sending party. The second group is a network of `User` elements from the receiving party. The query visualizes the two networks and any money flows between them.

Repeated user

This query discovers if there is a connection among `User` elements that send money to the same receiver. It starts with the input `User`, who receives money, and selects all other `User` elements that send the money to that input `User`. Then it checks if there is a path between those senders using `Device_Token`, `Payment_Instrument`, and `User`.

Same receiver sender

This query detects if a `User` uses a fake account to send money to itself. Given an input `Transaction`, this query returns true if the receiver and sender can be linked to each other by `Device_Token` and `Payment_Instrument`.

Transferred amount

This query looks within a given time window for the total amount of funds transferred out from the `Users` who are connected within a few hops of a source `User`. While not directly suspicious, a high volume of funds could help to build the case for anti-money-laundering layering.

We now take a closer look at the invited user behavior, multitransaction, and circle detection queries.

Invited user behavior

This pattern assumes that a **User** can earn tiered referral bonuses for referring many new **User** to an electronic payment service. This query contains a two-hop traversal implementation, as illustrated in Figure 5-2. We start our traversal from a given `input_user`. The first hop selects all the **User** elements that are invited by this `input_user`. Then, with the second hop, we collect all the **User** elements that the first-order invitees invite. We then aggregate the transaction amount of those invitees. The `input_user` is a fraudulent **User** if the amount of money directly being transferred is high while the aggregated money from the second-order invitees is low or zero. The intuition behind this is that `input_user` has many fake referrals that fuel itself with referral bonuses so that it can send a large number of transactions.

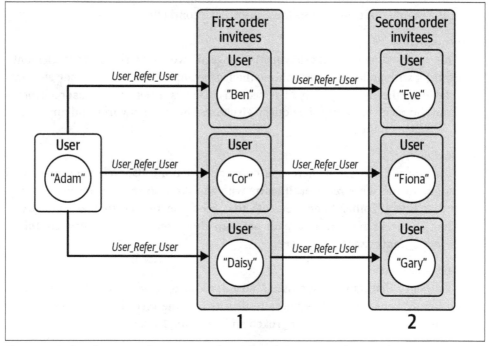

Figure 5-2. Graph traversal pattern to detect fraudulent users that conduct activities to earn referral bonuses

First we declare some accumulator variables to store our aggregated data:

```
SumAccum<INT> @@num_invited_persons;
SumAccum<FLOAT> @@total_amount_sent;
SetAccum<EDGE> @@edges_to_display;
```

The SumAccum `@@num_invited_persons` counts the number of second-hop invitees. The SumAccum `@@total_amount_sent` aggregates the amount of all transactions from the one-hop invitees. The `SumAccum @@edges_to_display` gathers all the edges (`User_Ref_User`) between the input **User** and a referred **User**, so that the visualization system knows to display them.

Then we find the one-hop invitees referred by the source **User**. We save each edge between the `Start` **User** and an invitee in `@@display_edge_set`:

```
Start = {input_user};

First_invitees = SELECT t
    FROM Start:s -(User_Refer_User>:e)- :t
    ACCUM @@edges_to_display += e;
```

> In the `FROM` clause, we don't need to specify what type of vertices we are targeting because the edge type (**User_Refer_User**) only permits one type of target vertex (**User**).

Next, we add up the amount of money that these first-order invitees have sent out. Each **Transaction** has an attribute called `amount`:

```
Trans = SELECT t
    FROM First_invitees:s -(User_Transfer_Transaction>:e)- :t
    ACCUM
        @@total_amount_sent += t.amount,
        @@edges_to_display += e;
```

Finally, we get the additional invitees referred by first-hop invitees:

```
Second_invitees = SELECT t
    FROM First_invitees:s -(User_Refer_User>:e)- :t
    WHERE t != input_user
    ACCUM @@edges_to_display += e
    POST-ACCUM (t) @@num_invited_persons += 1;
```

This search looks very much like the first hop, with two additional steps:

1. We check that we are not hopping back to the source **User**.

2. We count the number of second-order invitees.

If you run the algorithm with the three suggested input users (115637, 25680893, 22120362), you'll see they have referred one or a few users, who in turn have referred zero or a few users. Looking at the JSON results, you'll see between $0 and $709 in total payments.

Multitransaction

Analysts believe that criminals often transfer money between two networks. The following query exposes this intuition. Given any input transaction, the first network consists of related accounts from the sender of that transaction, and the second network consists of associated accounts from the receiving party. Then we look for payment activities among all parties from those two networks. This query assembles those networks and finds any interactions between them, using the execution flow illustrated in Figure 5-3.

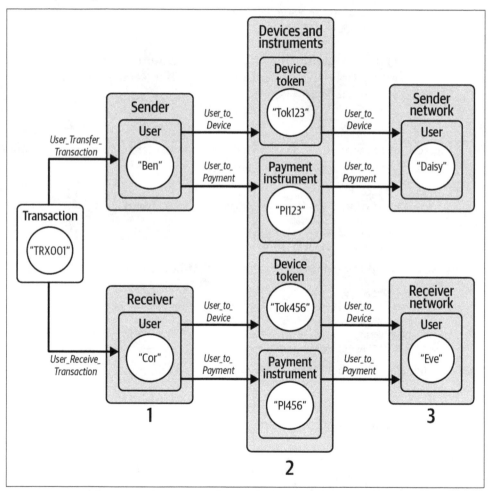

Figure 5-3. Graph traversal pattern to find transaction networks from sending and receiving parties

We start with selecting the sender and receiver **User** elements for a given **Transaction** by traversing **User_Transfer_Transaction** or **User_Receive_Transaction** edge types:

```
Sender_receiver (ANY) = SELECT t
    FROM Start:s
      -((<User_Receive_Transaction|<User_Transfer_Transaction):e)- :t
```

 In the FROM clause, we are traversing from a **Transaction** (source_transaction) to **User** elements, which is the reverse direction of the **User_Receive_Transaction** and **User_Transfer_Transaction** edges. That is why the direction arrows point to the left and are on the left side of the edge type names. Alternatively, if those edges have reverse edge types defined, we could use their reverse edges instead (and use right-facing arrows.)

We use cases to determine if the **User** is a receiving or sending party of the **Transaction**. If a **User** connects to a **Transaction** via **User_Receive_Transaction**, we set @from_receiver to true and add that **User** to the @@receiver_set. In other cases, the **User** is a sending party of the **Transaction**, so we set @from_sender to true and add this **User** to @@sender_set:

```
CASE WHEN e.type == "User_Receive_Transaction" THEN
    t.@from_receiver += TRUE,
    @@receiver_set += t
ELSE
    t.@from_sender += TRUE,
    @@sender_set += t
```

Now that we know the sender and receiver, we find **User** elements that belong to the receiving or sending party. That is, we traverse over **User_to_Device** or **User_to_Payment** edges and add **User** elements to either the @@sender_set or @@receiver_set if they exist within four hops (WHILE Start.size() > 0 LIMIT MAX_HOPS DO). Since it takes two hops to make a transaction (sender → transaction → recipient), four hops equals a chain of two transactions:

```
WHILE Sender_receiver.size() > 0 LIMIT MAX_HOPS DO
    Sender_receiver = SELECT t
    FROM Sender_receiver:s -((User_to_Device|User_to_Payment):e)- :t
    WHERE t.@from_receiver == FALSE AND t.@from_sender == FALSE
    ACCUM
        t.@from_receiver += s.@from_receiver,
        t.@from_sender += s.@from_sender,
        @@edges_to_display += e
    POST-ACCUM
        CASE WHEN t.type == "User" AND t.@from_sender == TRUE THEN
            @@sender_set += t
```

```
                    WHEN t.@from_receiver == TRUE THEN
                        @@receiver_set += t
```

If we end up at a **User** vertex type and that **User** is a sending party, we add that **User** to @@sender_set. If t.@from_receiver is true, then the **User** belongs to the receiving party, and we add that **User** to @@receiver_set.

After forming the sending and receiving groups, we now look for transactions other than the source transaction that connect the sender and receiver groups. First, we find transactions adjacent to the receiver set:

```
Receivers = {@@receiver_set};
Receivers = SELECT t
    FROM Receivers:s
        -((User_Receive_Transaction>|User_Transfer_Transaction>):e)- :t
....
```

Then, we find transactions adjacent to the sender set:

```
Senders = {@@sender_set};
Connecting_transactions = SELECT t
    FROM Senders:
        -((User_Receive_Transaction>|User_Transfer_Transaction>):e)- :t
    WHERE t != input_transaction
    ACCUM
        t.@from_sender += s.@from_sender,
        @@edges_to_display += e
    HAVING t.@from_receiver AND t.@from_sender;
```

The HAVING clause checks whether a transaction is considered part of the receiving group and the sending group.

Running the query with one of the suggested transaction IDs (32, 33, or 37), the output will look like one connected community, because there is at least one transaction in addition to the input transaction that joins the sender community to the receiver community. Try a different input ID, and the output will likely look like two separate communities, joined only by the input transaction.

Circle detection

The essence of money laundering is transfering money between enough parties that it becomes a challenge to trace its origin. Criminals have several routing schemas to mask the source of their illicit money. A popular transfer schema is one where the money is transferred via various intermediaries to return eventually to one of the senders. In this case, the money traverses in a circular pattern. A circular money flow is not itself a crime. What makes it criminal is intent and if any of the transitions are by themselves fraudulent. Characteristics of a circular flow—the size of the loop, the amount of money transferred, the percentage of money returned to the sender, the

---

time delays between transactions, and how many of the individual transactions are out of the ordinary—are also useful indicators.

With graphs, we can detect such circular patterns easier than with traditional databases because we can hop repeatedly from one transaction to the next until a transaction arrives at the originator. As we explained in Chapter 2, graph hops are computationally much cheaper than table joins in a relational database.

In Figure 5-4, we see such a circular money flow. In this example, Adam is the originator and sends $100 to Ben. Ben sends $60 to Cor, and she sends $40 to Daisy, who in turn sends $100 back to Adam. We show in this example that Ben, Cor, and Daisy do not send the same amount of money they have received to the next person in the chain. Criminals do this to add another layer of noise by making the starting amount branch out into different chunks across various intermediaries, making it harder to find out who the originator is and what amount is being laundered.

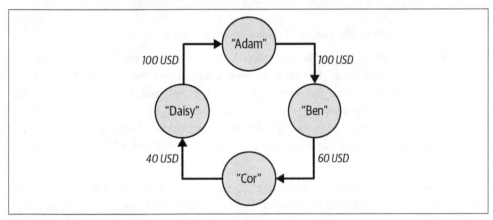

Figure 5-4. Example circular money flow

The query `circle_detection` finds all the circular transaction chains starting from a given **User** (`source_id`) that have up to a maximum number of transactions per circle (`max_transactions`). Since there are two hops per transaction (sender → transaction → recipient), the circles can have up to twice as many hops. To be a valid circle, the sequence of transactions in a circle must move forward in time. For example, for this to be a valid circle:

`source_id → txn_A → txn_B → txn_C → source_id`

then `txn_A.ts < txn_B.ts < txn_C.ts`, where `ts` is the timestamp of a transaction.

Because there are so many possible paths to check, the query's implementation employs a couple of performance and filtering techniques. The first one is bidirectional search, which searches forward from the starting point while simultaneously searching backward from the ending point. It is faster to conduct two half-length searches than one full-length search. When the two searches intersect, you have a complete path.

The second technique filters out paths that can't meet the forward time travel requirement:

```
Seed = {source_id};
Seed = SELECT src
    FROM Seed:src - ((User_Transfer_Transaction>|User_Receive_Transaction>):e)
                  - Transaction:tgt
    ACCUM
        CASE WHEN
          e.type == "User_Transfer_Transaction"
        THEN
          @@min_src_send_time += tgt.ts
        ELSE
          @@max_src_receive_time += tgt.ts
        END
    ...
    HAVING @@max_src_receive_time >= @@min_src_send_time;
```

Starting from source_id, make one step both forward (**User_Transfer_Transaction**) and backward (**User_Receive_Transaction**). Find the earliest time of any transaction sent by source_id (@@min_src_send_time) and the latest time of any transaction received by source_id (@@max_src_receive_time). Check to make sure that @@max_src_receive_time >= @@min_src_send_time. These global limits will also be used later to check the plausibility of other transactions, which are candidates for a circular path.

Then we begin Phase 1 of the search. Starting from source_id, step forward two hops (equals one transaction). Using Figure 5-4 as an example, this would step from Adam to Ben. Also traverse two hops backward (Adam to Daisy). Iterate this combination of steps, moving forward (or backward) in time until each direction has stepped halfway around a maximum size circle. Table 5-2 shows the paths that would be traversed if we consider the graph of Figure 5-4.

Table 5-2. Forward and reverse paths, using the graph of Figure 5-4

Iteration	1	2	3
Forward	Adam→Ben	Ben→Cor	Cor→Daisy
Reverse	Adam→Daisy	Daisy→Cor	Cor→Ben

The following code snippet shows a simplified version of one iteration of the forward traversal. For brevity, the checking of timing and step constraints has been omitted:

```
Fwd_set = SELECT tgt
    FROM Fwd_set:src - (User_Transfer_Transaction>:e) - Transaction:tgt
    WHERE tgt.ts >= @@min_src_send_time
        AND src.@min_fwd_dist < GSQL_INT_MAX
```

```
        AND tgt.@min_fwd_dist == GSQL_INT_MAX
    ACCUM tgt.@min_fwd_dist += src.@min_fwd_dist + 1
    … // POST-ACCUM clause to check time and step constraints
    ;

Fwd_set = SELECT tgt
    FROM Fwd_set:src - (<User_Receive_Transaction:e) - User:tgt
    WHERE src.@min_fwd_dist < GSQL_INT_MAX
        AND tgt.@min_fwd_dist == GSQL_INT_MAX
    ACCUM tgt.@min_fwd_dist += src.@min_fwd_dist + 1
… // POST-ACCUM clause to check time and step constraints
    HAVING tgt != source_id;
```

Looking at Table 5-2, we see that after the second iteration, a forward path and a reverse path have met at a common point: Cor. We have a circle! But wait. What if the Ben→Cor timestamp is later than the Cor→Daisy timestamp? If so, then it's not a *valid* circle.

In Phase 2 of the query, we discover and validate circular paths by doing the following. For the forward search, continue traversing forward but only along paths that were previously traversed in the reverse direction and that move forward in time. In our example, if max_transactions = 2 so that Phase 1 got as far as Ben→Cor, then Phase 2 could continue on to Cor→Daisy, but only because we had already traversed Daisy→Cor in Phase 1 and only if the timestamps continue to increase:

```
Fwd_set = SELECT tgt
    FROM Fwd_set:src - (User_Transfer_Transaction>:e) - Transaction:tgt
    // tgt must have been touched in the reverse search above
    WHERE tgt.@min_rev_dist < GSQL_INT_MAX
        AND tgt.ts >= @@min_src_send_time
        AND src.@min_fwd_dist < GSQL_INT_MAX
        AND tgt.@min_fwd_dist == GSQL_INT_MAX
    ACCUM tgt.@min_fwd_dist += src.@min_fwd_dist + 1
    POST-ACCUM
        CASE WHEN
          tgt.@min_fwd_dist < GSQL_INT_MAX
          AND tgt.@min_rev_dist < GSQL_INT_MAX
          AND tgt.@min_fwd_dist + tgt.@min_rev_dist
              <= 2 * STEP_HIGH_LIMIT
        THEN
          tgt.@is_valid = TRUE
        END;

Fwd_set = SELECT tgt
    FROM Fwd_set:src - (<User_Receive_Transaction:e) - User:tgt
    //tgt must have been touched in the reverse search above
    WHERE tgt.@min_rev_dist < GSQL_INT_MAX
        AND src.@min_fwd_dist < GSQL_INT_MAX
        AND tgt.@min_fwd_dist == GSQL_INT_MAX
    ACCUM tgt.@min_fwd_dist += src.@min_fwd_dist + 1
    POST-ACCUM
```

```
CASE WHEN
    tgt.@min_fwd_dist < GSQL_INT_MAX
    AND tgt.@min_rev_dist < GSQL_INT_MAX
    AND tgt.@min_fwd_dist + tgt.@min_rev_dist
        <= 2 * STEP_HIGH_LIMIT
THEN
    tgt.@is_valid = TRUE
END
HAVING tgt != source_id;
```

After Phase 2, we have found our circles. There is a Phase 3 that traverses the circles and marks the vertices and edges so that they can be displayed. Figure 5-5 and Figure 5-6 show example results from circle detection, for maximum circle sizes of four, five, and six transactions. As the circle size limit increases, more circles are found.

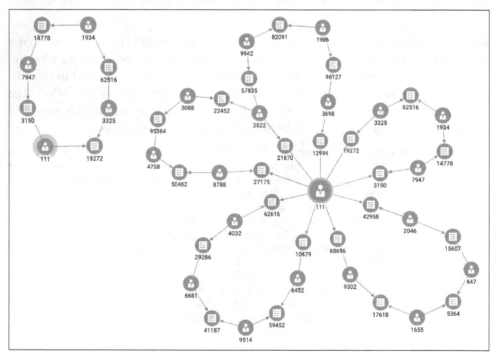

Figure 5-5. Circle detection results for source_id *= 111 and* max_transactions *of 4 and 5, respectively (see a larger version of this figure at https://oreil.ly/gpam0505)*

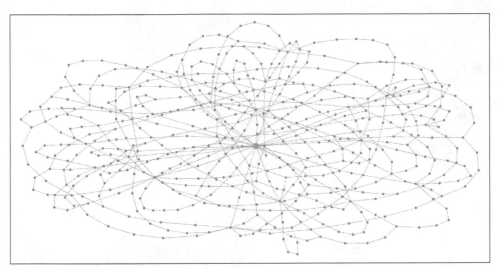

Figure 5-6. Circle detection results for source_id = 111 *and* max_transactions = 6 *(see a larger version of this figure at https://oreil.ly/gpam0506)*

Chapter Summary

Financial fraud is a serious and costly problem that most businesses and all financial institutions must face. Better and faster techniques to detect and stop fraud are needed. We showed that graph data modeling and graph queries are powerful ways to detect suspicious patterns of activity that would have otherwise gone unnoticed. Graph modeling makes it easy to address three key phases for searching for patterns: describing the search, performing the search, and examining the results. Later in the book, we'll show how graph machine learning provides more sophisticated and accurate fraud detection.

More specifically, we have discussed three queries to detect and combat fraud and money laundering. The first query demonstrated how we could detect if money flows in a circular pattern. The second query showed how graphs could find suspicious user behavior within a referral program. The third query showcased the money flow between two networks of people. The fourth query showed how we could find connections between people who send their money to the same person. The fifth query detected whether someone used a fake account to send money to themselves. The last query we discussed was about detecting a high volume of money transfers to a person.

In the next chapter, we will offer a systematic approach to analyzing graphs. In particular, we will delve into the rewarding world of graph measures and graph algorithms.

PART II

Analyze

CHAPTER 6

Analyzing Connections for Deeper Insight

In the preceding chapters, we learned that representing data as a graph gives us the power to look more deeply and broadly across our data so we can answer questions more accurately and with more insight. We've looked at several use cases to see examples of how to model data as a graph and how to query it. Now we want to take a more methodical look at graph analytics. What do we mean when we say graph analytics? What are some specific techniques we can use for graph analytics?

After completing this chapter, you should be able to:

- Define graph analytics and describe what distinguishes it from general data analytics

- Understand graph analytics' requirements and some key methods, including breadth-first search and parallel processing

- Define several categories of graph algorithms that are useful for analytics

- List a few algorithms within each category and give examples of real-world uses

Understanding Graph Analytics

Let's start by defining data analytics in general. *Data analytics* is making useful observations and drawing conclusions about a body of data to help people understand the significance of the data. Analytics transforms data into useful insights. Graph analytics does the same thing, except that the structure of the data affects which data we will examine and in what order. Connections are a form of data, and the connections drive the course of the analysis.

Another distinguishing aspect of graph analytics is that it is good for addressing questions *about* the connections. You could ask what the shortest chain of connections is between Customer A and Customer B in a tabular set of data, but you are much better equipped to perform that analysis if your data is a graph. We can summarize our thoughts as follows:

> Graph analytics is making observations and drawing conclusions *on* connected data and *about* connected data.

Requirements for Analytics

To make an observation about a body of data, it's obvious that we have to examine all of that data or the rel evant subset and that there will be some form of computation involved. If our data collection contains all sales transactions for a certain year, a simple analysis would be to compute the total sales for each month and then to see if the sales are trending upward, downward, or moving in a more complex way. If the data is organized into a table, then we imagine scanning down the table, reading each row. We also imagine that we need some place to hold our results—the monthly sales. In fact, we'll probably want to keep a running total as we read each row and add its sales to one of the monthly sums.

Graph analytics has similar requirements: reading all the relevant data, performing calculations and decisions on each data point, holding temporary results, and reporting final results. The primary difference between graph analytics and tabular analytics is that the graph's connections affect both the nature of the data items and the order in which we scan the data. There are also choices of methodology or architecture that can make the computations and memory storage more efficient.

Graph Traversal Methods

In graph analytics, we follow the connections that lead us from one data point to the next. Using the metaphor of the graph being a network of walking paths, it's common to say that we *walk* or *traverse* the graph. At first, it may seem that you want to follow a chain of connections, the way an individual would walk. However, when you look at the task you are trying to accomplish, it turns out that it may make more sense to explore all the one-hop direct connections from your present position one at a time, before following a connection of a connection. Following a chain of connections is called *depth-first search (DFS)*, and looking at all of your direct connections before moving to the next tier of connections is called *breadth-first search (BFS)*. We mentioned these briefly in Chapter 2.

The following workflow explains both BFS and DFS. The difference is in the order in which work gets processed, reflected in the order of vertices in the `Places_to_Explore` list:

1. Put the source vertex into a processing list called `Places_to_Explore`. As a list, it has an order, front to back.

2. Remove the first vertex from the front of the Places_to_Explore list. If that vertex is marked as Already_Visited, then skip steps 3 and 4.

3. Perform whatever work you want to do for each vertex, such as checking whether a value matches your search query. Now mark the vertex as Already_Visited.

4. From the current vertex, get a list of all of its connected edges. If BFS, add that list to the *end* of the Places_to_Explore list (queue). If DFS, add that list to the front of the Places_to_Explore list (stack).

5. Repeat steps 2 to 4 until the Places_to_Explore list is empty.

With BFS, we follow a "fair" system in which every newly encountered vertex goes to the back of the line. As a consequence, vertices get processed level by level, all the vertices one hop from the source, then all the vertices two hops from the sources, and so on. With DFS, we follow a "greedy" system, which processes one child of the source and then puts its neighbors at the front of the line instead of at the back.[1] That means that in the third step, one lucky vertex that is three hops from the source will get attention. In Figure 6-1, we see an example of BFS and DFS. Initially, only vertex 1 has a number. The other numbers are assigned in the order of visit.

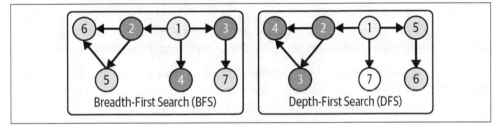

Figure 6-1. Overview of breadth-first search (BFS) versus depth-first search (DFS) methods

BFS is superior when you are looking for something as close as possible to the ground truth best answer. Shortest path algorithms use BFS. DFS can be good if you expect the answer to be multihop and there are many paths that satisfy the task.

If we intend to explore the entire graph and we have only one worker to process information, then BFS and DFS have roughly equivalent efficiency. However, if parallel processing is available, then BFS wins out almost every time.

---

1 DFS prioritization is analogous to primogeniture for inheritance of titles, where the firstborn child has priority for inheritance.

Parallel Processing

Parallel rocessing is being able to do two or more tasks at the same time to cut down on latency, that is, the total time from start to finish. To benefit from parallel processing, the overall task needs to be able to be split into multiple subtasks that can be performed independently ("parallelizable"), and you must have multiple processors. In addition, there is some management work to know how to split the task and then merge the separate results into a final result.

BFS and parallel processing go well together. Most graph analytics tasks that use BFS can be performed more efficiently with parallel processing. Imagine you want to create a detailed map of a road network. You have a troop of surveyors (multiple processors) who all start at Point A. At every fork in the road, you split up your troops to get the work done faster (BFS with parallel processing). With software, you have an advantage over the physical world. When one processor is finished with its current task, it can jump to anywhere in the data network where it is needed for the next task.

Aggregation

One of the fundamental tasks in analytics is *aggregation*: taking a set of values, performing some operation on them, and producing a single result that characterizes the set. The most common aggregation functions are count, sum, and average.

Consider this analysis of purchase behavior: given a **Customer-Purchases-Products** graph, find the three most purchased products that are bought within one week after Product X and in the same product family as Product X. Here is how we can solve it with graph analytics:

1. Start at the vertex representing Product X.

2. Traverse along **Purchases** edges to find all the **Customers** who purchased Product X. At each of those traversal paths, note the purchase date.

3. From each of those **Customers**, scan their other **Purchases** edges for the one-week time window starting from that purchase date. For every **Product** that fits in that time window, add it to a global data structure, which allows adding new items and also updating the count of such items.

4. Sort the global counts to find the three most popular follow-up purchases.

Let's analyze that workflow and what would be needed:

*   Starting from a single vertex, we used BFS for two hops, filtering the second hop by a date range determined by the first hop. BFS requires bookkeeping (the `Places_to_Explore` list mentioned previously). You've already seen in previous

---

chapters how the GSQL language has built-in support, using a SELECT-FROM-ACCUM statement and saving the result of one level of traversal as the vertex set result of that statement.

- Each path of the BFS needs to temporarily keep track of its own time window. The math is simple here: add seven days to a given timestamp. GSQL has local variables that can perform the task of temporarily holding data for later analysis.

- The main aggregation work is collecting the follow-up purchases and finding which are the three most popular. We need a global data structure that each processing agent can access to add a new item. The simplest data structure would be a list that can hold duplicate instances of the same item. After we finish looking for follow-up purchases, we would then need to read through the list to see how many times each item is mentioned and to sort the counts to get the top three. A more sophisticated way would be to use a *map* that holds data pairs: productID:count. This would require support for two operations: insert a new productID and increment a count. If we want to use parallel BFS, we need to be able to support concurrent inserts and increments. After getting the final counts, we need to sort to get the top three.

The GSQL language provides built-in support for parallel aggregation using objects called accumulators. Accumulators can be global or per vertex. Accumulators can hold scalar values, like a sum or average, or they can hold collections, like a list, set, map, or heap. For this example of finding the most popular follow-up purchases, a global MapAccum would satisfy most of the work.

Using Graph Algorithms for Analytics

Some analytics tasks require writing custom database queries: the question being asked is unique and quite specific to the dataset and use case. In other cases, the analytical question is fairly common. Having a library of standard analytical tools, with parameters so they can be adjusted to specific datasets and tasks, can be very useful. For graph analytics, we have such a toolkit; it's a *graph algorithm library*, or *graph data science library*, as they are sometimes known. Earlier in the book, we described graph algorithms as a type of graph query, used a similarity algorithm, and mentioned a few other algorithm types like shortest path. We've intentionally kept their use to a minimum until this chapter, where we can go into depth.

Graph Algorithms as Tools

First, let's define the term *algorithm*. An algorithm is an unambiguous, step-by-step, and finite set of instructions to perform a specific task. Think of an algorithm like a precise recipe. When you have an algorithm for a task, you know the task is achievable. For a subclass called *deterministic algorithms*, the same input always yields the same output, no matter who performs the algorithm or when. Algorithms aren't just for analytics. For example, there's an algorithm for storing your color and font size preferences for an ereader, and a companion algorithm for applying your preferences every time you start the reader. Those aren't really analytical tasks, but they are tasks nonetheless.

When we say *graph algorithms*, however, it suggests more than just "algorithms about graphs." First, the term usually implies algorithms that are *generic* in the sense that they are designed to work on a whole class of graphs—say, any graph with undirected edges—rather than only graphs with certain schema and semantic details, such as banking transaction graphs. Second, the term *graph algorithms* often refers to solutions for *analytical* tasks.

By focusing on generic analytical tasks, graph algorithms become excellent tools for graph analytics. Over the years, theorists and data analysts have identified a number of common and generic analytical tasks for graphs, and have developed algorithms to perform these tasks. A graph algorithm library is a thoughtful collection of graph algorithms, able to perform a variety of different tasks. The library collection is crafted to span a breadth of useful functions, and hence it is a toolkit.

Just as with skilled trades like woodworking or automobile repair, data analytics requires training and experience to use the tools well. As a graph algorithm user, you need to learn what types of tasks you can perform with each algorithm, what type of material (data) it is designed for, what is the right way to use it, and when not to use it at all. As you grow in sophistication, you will better appreciate the trade-offs between algorithms that perform similar functions. You will also see innovative ways to use an algorithm and how using algorithms in combination can perform more complex and sophisticated tasks than any single algorithm.

Because we are talking about software and data, data analysts have one advantage over craftspersons using forged steel tools on wood and metal materials: our tools and our materials are extremely malleable. As an algorithm user, it is helpful but not essential to understand how an algorithm works. By analogy, you don't need to know how to design a voltmeter in order to measure a battery's voltage. However, if you want to modify an algorithm to better fit your situation, then it is necessary to understand that algorithm at least in part.

Any user of graph algorithms needs to follow one cautionary note: apply an algorithm only to those vertices and edges that are semantically appropriate for your desired analysis. Most real-world graphs contain multiple types of vertices and edges, each with their own semantic roles. For example, we might have **Book** and **Reader** vertices and **Bought**, **Read**, and **Reviewed** edges. While you could run PageRank on the whole graph, the results would not make much sense, because it doesn't make sense to rank **Books** and **Readers** on the same scale. Due to their generic nature, most graph algorithms ignore semantic typing. Whether your analysis will be meaningful when types are ignored is something that you will have to decide.

We've covered a lot of important concepts so far, so let's summarize:

- Graph analytics leverages data connections to obtain deeper insights about the data.
- Breadth-first search, parallel processing, and aggregation are key ingredients of efficient graph analytics.
- Graph algorithms act as tools for common graph analytics tasks.
- You can perform more complex tasks by using them in combination.
- Using graph algorithms is a craft. The more you know about the tools and the materials, the better a craftsperson you will be.

Table 6-1 shows the key terminologies of data analytics and algorithms that we have introduced in this chapter.

Table 6-1. Glossary of graph analytics and algorithm terms

Term	Definition
Data analytics	The process of analyzing data using statistical methods to obtain insights
Graph analytics	A subset of data analytics that focuses on analyzing relationships between entities in a graph
Algorithm	An unambiguous, step-by-step, and finite set of instructions to perform a specific task
Deterministic algorithm	A subset of algorithms where the same inputs will always produce the same results
Graph algorithm	A subset of algorithms that are generic for a class of graphs and a solution to analyze graph structures
Walk/traverse a graph	The process of exploring the vertices and edges of the graph in a specific order from the present position

Graph Algorithm Categories

Consider a couple more examples of graph analytics tasks:

Community ranking
    In a social network, rank subcommunities based on the average number of new discussions per member per week.

Similar patient profiles
    Given a patient with certain symptoms, personal background, and treatment to date, find similar patients so that successes and setbacks can be compared, leading to better overall care.

The first task presumes we have well-defined communities. In some cases, we want communities defined not by labels but by actual social behavior. We have graph algorithms to find communities based on connections and relational behavior. The second task presumes we have a way to measure similarity. There is also a family of algorithms for graph-based similarity.

This section provides an overview of the most common graph algorithms and algorithm categories in graph analytics today. We will look at five categories:

- Paths and trees
- Centrality
- Community
- Similarity
- Classification and prediction

Path and tree algorithms

One of the classic graph-based tasks is to find the *shortest path* from one vertex to another. Knowing a shortest path is useful not only for finding the best delivery and communication routes but also for seeing if persons or processes are closely associated. Is this person or organization closely associated with parties of concern? We can also use shortest path analysis to check the lineage or provenance of a document or other product.

The task might seem easy, but consider this example: suppose you wanted to get in touch with a famous but private person, say Keanu Reeves. It is a personal matter, so you can only go through personal contacts, and the fewer intermediary contacts, the better. You don't know which of your acquaintances might know this person. Therefore, you ask all of them if they know Mr. Reeves. None of them do, so would they please ask their acquaintances? Every contact asks their acquaintances to check until finally someone knows Keanu Reeves personally.

This connection-of-a-connection process is exactly how we find shortest paths in an unweighted graph. It is in fact breadth-first search. You can see how parallel processing would be appropriate. All of your acquaintances can work simultaneously to check their acquaintances.

Figure 6-2 shows an example. In round 1, you (vertex A) check all of your direct connections (B, C, and D). Each of them gets marked with a 1. In round 2, each of these newly visited vertices checks their connections. B has two connections (A and E), but only E is new. C has three connections, but only F is new. D has no connections that have not been visited before. Therefore, E and F are our new "frontier" vertices and are marked with a 2. In round 3, G and H are our frontier vertices. H is in fact Keanu Reeves, so we are done. Note that there are two paths:

A-B-E-H and A-C-F-H. Also note that while we were looking for the path to Keanu Reeves, we also found paths to intermediate vertices like E and F.

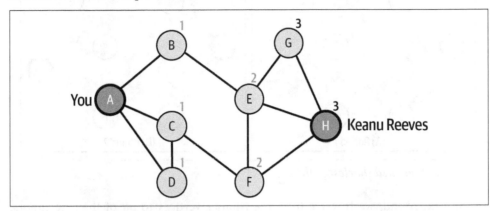

Figure 6-2. Unweighted shortest path

How much compute effort does it take to get our answer? It depends on how close our destination happens to be. Computer scientists often look at the worst case or average effort. Since our algorithm finds paths to intermediate vertices, what if we change that task: find a path starting from one source and to every destination? If we traverse every edge in the graph exactly once, we should be able to get our answer. Actually, we might need to traverse twice: initially, we attempt A→B, then later B→A and discover that we have already been to A. We'll need to mark each vertex as visited, set a distance, and later check that it's been visited. So we have some activities that scale with the number of edges (E), and some that scale with the number of vertices (V). So the total amount of effort is on the order of E + V. In standard notation, we say it is O(E + V), pronounced "big oh E plus V." In a connected graph, E is always at least as big as V, and we care about the biggest factor, so we can simplify it to O(E).

What if some connections are better than others? For example, it might be three blocks from your house to a store, but some blocks are longer than others. This is the *shortest path in a weighted graph* problem. When the edges are weighted, we have to proceed more carefully, because a path with more steps might still be the less costly one. In Figure 6-3, we have added weights to the edges and displayed the first two rounds of a modified search algorithm, attributed to computer science pioneer Edsger Dijkstra. First, we initialize every vertex with the length of the best-known path. Since we don't know any paths yet (except from A to A), every distance is set to infinity at first. Then in round 1, we traverse from A to each of its neighbors. We label each of them with the actual length of the edge traversed plus the distance from the source of that edge back to the starting point. For example, to get to B, the total distance is the weight of edge A-B, plus the distance of source A back to the starting point, distance(A,A) = 2 + 0 = 2.

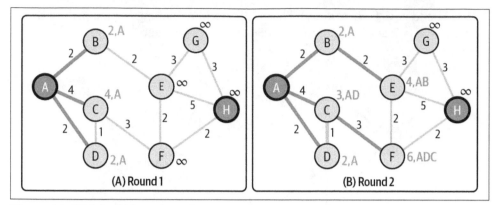

Figure 6-3. Weighted shortest path

In the next round, we traverse from the frontier vertices to *all* of their neighbors. Here we see a difference from the unweighted path algorithm. We consider the path from D to C, even though C has been visited before. We see that the path A-D-C has a total length of weight(A,D) + distance(D,C) = 2 + 1 = 3. This is less than the length of the path A-C = 4. C will be marked with the path and length of the *shortest* of the several paths found so far. In a weighted graph, even after we have found a path, we might need to keep searching to see if there is a path with more hops but less total weight. For this reason, finding the shortest path in a weighted graph takes more compute effort than in an unweighted graph.

We'll consider one more path task, the *minimal spanning tree* (MST) problem. In graph theory, a tree is a set of N vertices and exactly N−1 edges that connect the vertices. An interesting side effect is that there will be exactly one path in the tree to get from each vertex to each other vertex. A minimal spanning tree in a weighted graph is a tree that has the least total edge weight. One use of MST is to provide connectivity at the lowest total cost, such as paving the least amount of road or provisioning the least amount of network cable.

There are several algorithms of similar efficiency for solving the MST problem. Prim's algorithm is perhaps the simplest to describe. We'll use Figure 6-4 as an example:

1. Make a list of all the edges, sorted by weight.
2. Pick an edge with least weight (C-D). Every edge we pick becomes part of our tree.
3. Pick the lightest edge that has one end in the partial tree and one end not: (A-D).
4. Repeat step 3 until we have a total of N−1 edges.

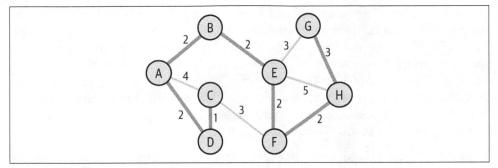

Figure 6-4. Minimal spanning tree

Following these rules, the next selected edges will be A-B, B-E, E-F, and F-H. Then we have a tie. Both E-G and H-G have a weight of 3, so either one can be used to complete our tree.

Centrality algorithms

Which is the most centrally located vertex in a graph? That depends on how we define centrality. The TigerGraph Graph Data Science (GDS) Library has more than 10 different centrality algorithms.

Closeness centrality scores each vertex based on the average distance from it to every other vertex in the graph. Typically, we invert this average distance, so that we get higher scores for shorter distances. Closeness centrality matters to organizations that want to select the best location for their retail store, government office, or distribution center. If they want to minimize the average distance that patrons or packages need to travel, they use closeness centrality. How do we measure distance? Shortest path algorithms can do this. While there are more efficient ways to measure average distance than to calculate every individual shortest path, the principle still holds: algorithms can be building blocks for solving more complex problems. There are variations of closeness centrality for directed graphs and for weighted graphs.

Let's compute some closeness centralities for the weighted graph in Figure 6-4. Vertices E and F look like they might be near the center. For E, we want the shortest path distances to A, B, C, D, F, G, and H. By visual inspection, we see that the distances are $4 + 2 + 5 + 6 + 2 + 3 + 4 = 26$. For F, we want distances to A, B, C, D, E, G, and H, which are $6 + 4 + 3 + 4 + 2 + 5 + 2 = 26$, so it's a tie.

Harmonic centrality is a minor variation of closeness centrality. Instead of being the inverse of the average distance, harmonic centrality is the average (or sum) of the inverse distances. One advantage of harmonic centrality is that it can deal with unconnected vertices by saying their distance is infinite, whose inverse value is simply zero. This brings up a key point when selecting an algorithm: do you need to handle unconnected vertices?

Betweenness centrality poses a different situation: suppose you consider all the shortest paths in a graph, from each vertex to each other vertex. If there are multiple shortest paths (as we saw in Figure 6-2), consider all of them. Which vertex sits on the most paths? A vertex with high betweenness is not necessarily the destination, but it will get a lot of pass-through traffic. Whether you are trying to find the best location for a gas station or assessing which network routers are most vital, betweenness can be a key measure. Again, we see that one algorithm (shortest path) is a building block for another (betweenness).

It might surprise you to know that PageRank can be categorized as a centrality algorithm. PageRank was designed to find the most important web pages on the internet. More precisely, PageRank measures *referential authority* in which a page's importance increases if more pages point to it or if the authority of those pages is higher. Another way of looking at it is the *random surfer* model.

Imagine someone is surfing the internet. They start on a random page. Each minute, the surfer goes to another page. Most of the time, they follow a link on that page to another page; every link has equal probability of being chosen. There is a small fixed probability of not following a link and just going directly to a random page. After a very long time, what is the probability that the random surfer will be on a particular page? The probability is that page's PageRank score. Pages that get visited more often due to the graph's pattern of connections are deemed to have higher centrality. The mathematical magic of PageRank is that the rankings aren't affected by where you start the random walk. Note that PageRank is designed for directed graphs, whereas most of the tasks we have looked at so far are sensible for either directed or undirected graphs.

Community algorithms

Another meaningful analysis of graphs is to understand the implicit groupings of vertices, based on how they connect to one another. High levels of interaction imply high levels of influence, resilience, or information passing, which is useful to understand and predict everything from market segmentation and fraudster behavior to group resilience to viral spread of ideas or biological contagions.

There are a number of possible ways to define a community, each with a corresponding algorithm or algorithms. We can sort them based on how many connections to the community are required to be considered part of the community. At the low end of the spectrum, when only a single connection is sufficient to be considered part of the community, we call the group a *connected component*, or just *component* for short. At the high end for connectivity, when every vertex has a direct connection to every other community member, this is a *complete subgraph*. The vertices of a complete subgraph constitute a *clique*. In between these extremes are k-cores. A *k-core* is a subgraph where every vertex has direct connections to k or more other members.

A connected component is a k-core where k = 1. A clique containing c vertices is a k-core where k = (c −1), the largest possible value for k.

Figure 6-5 shows these three classes of communities applied to the same graph. On the left, every vertex is a member of one of three connected components. In the center graph, we have two k-cores for k = 2, but four vertices are excluded. On the right, we have two small cliques; many vertices do not qualify.

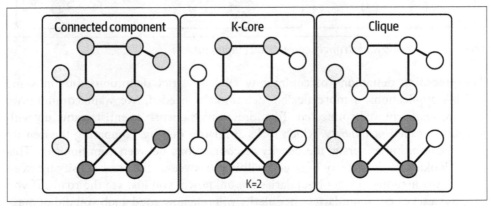

Figure 6-5. Community types classified by density of connection

Any of these definitions can enforce edge directionality; for connected components, we even have names for this. If the edges are undirected (or we ignore the directionality), then we call it a *weakly connected component* (WCC). If the edges are directed and it is possible for each vertex to reach every other vertex by following a directed path, then it is a *strongly connected component* (SCC). In Figure 6-6, we add directionality to the edges of our example graph and see how this can rule out some vertices.

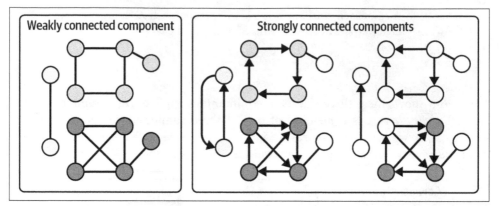

Figure 6-6. Weakly and strongly connected components

The preceding definitions of community all have strict definitions, but in some real-life applications, a more flexible definition is needed. We want communities that are *relatively* well connected. To address this, network scientists came up with a measure called *modularity*, which looks at relative density, comparing the density within communities versus the density of connections between communities. This is like looking at the density of streets within cities versus the road density between cities. Now imagine the city boundaries are unknown; you just see the roads. If you propose a set of city boundaries, modularity will rate how good a job you did of maximizing the goal of "dense inside; not dense outside." Modularity is a scoring system, not an algorithm. A modularity-based community algorithm finds the community boundaries that produce the highest modularity score.

To measure modularity (Q), we first partition the vertices into a set of communities so that every vertex belongs to one community. Then, considering each edge as one case, we calculate some totals and averages:

Q = [actual fraction of edges that fall within a community]

minus [expected fraction of edges if edges were distributed at random]

"Expected" is used in the statistical sense. If you flip a coin many times, you expect 50/50 odds of heads versus tails. Modularity can handle weighted edges by using weights instead of simple counts:

Q = [average weight of edges that fall within a community]

minus [expected weight of edges if edges were distributed at random]

Note that the average is taken over the total number of edges. Edges that run from one community to another add zero to the numerator and add their weight to the denominator. It is designed this way so that edges that run between communities hurt your average and lower your modularity score.

What do we mean by "distributed at random"? Each vertex v has a certain number of edges that connect to it: the *degree* of a vertex is $d(v)$ = total number (or total weight) of v's edges. Imagine that each of these $d(v)$ edges picks a random destination vertex. The bigger $d(v)$ is, the more likely that one or more of those random edges will make a connection to a particular destination vertex. The expected (i.e., statistical average) number of connections between a vertex $v1$ and a vertex $v2$ can be computed as:

$$E_{rand}[wt(v1, v2)] = \frac{d(v1)d(v2)}{2m}$$

where m is the total number of edges in the graph. For the mathematically inclined, the complete formula for modularity Q is:

$$Q = \frac{1}{2m} \sum_{i,j \in G} \left[wt(i,j) - \frac{d(i)d(j)}{2m}\right] \delta(comm(i), comm(j))$$

where $wt(i,j)$ is the weight of the edge between i and j, $comm(i)$ is the community ID of vertex i, and $\delta(a, b)$ is the Kronecker delta function, which equals 1 if a and b are equal and 0 otherwise.

There are a number of algorithms that try to efficiently search for the community assignment that yields the highest modularity. Figure 6-7 shows two possible community groupings, but there is an exponentially large number of possible groupings. Therefore, algorithms take some shortcuts and make some assumptions to efficiently find a very good answer, if not the best answer.

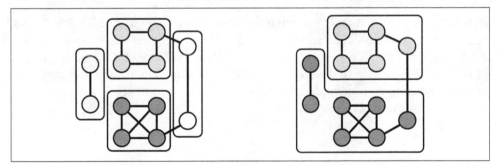

Figure 6-7. Two possible community colorings for the same graph

The most established modularity optimization algorithm is the *Louvain algorithm*, named after the University of Louvain. Louvain starts by considering each individual vertex as a community. It then tests each vertex to see if the global modularity would be improved by merging it with one of its neighboring communities and treating the merged community as a single vertex. After performing one round of mergings, it repeats with the new set of larger communities. It stops when merging no longer improves the modularity. Several improvements to the speed and clustering quality of Louvain have been proposed. The *Leiden algorithm* incorporates many of these improvements.

Similarity algorithms

What makes two things similar? We usually identify similarities by looking at observable or known properties: color, size, function, and so forth. A passenger car and a motorcycle are similar because they are both motorized land vehicles for one or a few passengers. A motorcycle and a bicycle are similar because they are both two-wheeled vehicles. But how do we decide whether a motorcycle is more similar to a car or to a bicycle? For that matter, how would we make such decisions for a set of persons, products, medical conditions, or financial transactions? We need to agree upon a system for measuring similarity. Is there some way that we can let the graph itself suggest how to measure similarity?

A graph can give us contextual information to help us decide how to determine similarity. Consider the following axiom:

> An entity is characterized by its properties, its relationships, and its neighborhood.

Therefore, if two vertices have similar properties, similar relationships, and similar neighborhoods, then they should be similar. What do we mean by similar neighborhoods? Let's start with a simpler case—the exact same neighborhood:

> Two entities are similar if they connect to the same neighbors.

In Figure 6-8, Person A and Person B have three identical types of edges (**Purchased**, **hasAccount**, and **Knows**), connecting to the three exact same vertices (Phone model Y, Bank Z, and Person C, respectively). It is not necessary, however, to include all types of relationships or to give them equal weight. If you care about social networks, for example, you can consider only friends. If you care about financial matters, you can consider only financial relationships.

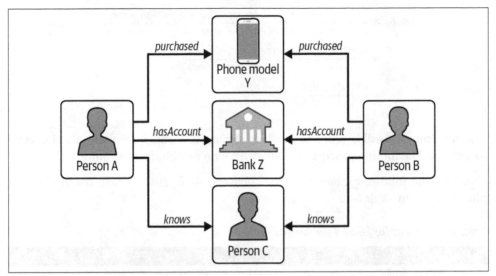

Figure 6-8. Two persons sharing the same neighborhood

To reiterate the difference between community and similarity: all five entities in Figure 6-8 are part of a connected component called *community*. However, we would not say that all five are *similar* to one another. The only case of similarity suggested by these relationships is Person A being similar to Person B.

Neighborhood similarity

It's rare to find two entities that have exactly the same neighborhoods. We'd like a way to measure and rank the degree of neighborhood similarity. The two most common measures for ranking neighborhood similarity are Jaccard similarity and cosine similarity. Some others are overlap similarity and Pearson similarity.

Jaccard similarity

Jaccard similarity measures the relative overlap between two general sets. Suppose you run Bucket List Travel Advisors, and you want to compare your travelers to one another based on which destinations they have visited. Jaccard similarity would be a good method for you to use; the two sets would be the destinations visited by each of two customers being compared. To formulate Jaccard similarity in general terms, suppose the two sets are $N(a)$, the neighborhood of vertex a, and $N(b)$, the neighborhood of vertex b. Then the Jaccard similarity of a and b is:

$$jaccard(a, b) = \frac{number\_of\_shared\_neighbors}{size(N(a)) + size(N(b)) - number\_of\_shared\_neighbors}$$

$$= \frac{number\_of\_shared\_neighbors}{number\_of\_unique\_neighbors}$$

$$= \frac{|N(a) \cap N(b)|}{|N(a) \cup N(b)|}$$

The maximum possible score is 1, which occurs if *a* and *b* have exactly the same neighbors. The minimum score is 0 if they have no neighbors in common.

Consider the following example: three travelers, A, B, and C, have traveled to the places shown in Table 6-2.

Table 6-2. Dataset for Jaccard similarity example[a]

Destinations	A	B	C
Amazon Rainforest, Brazil	✓	✓	
Grand Canyon, USA	✓	✓	✓
Great Wall, China	✓		✓
Machu Picchu, Peru	✓	✓	
Paris, France	✓		✓
Pyramids, Egypt		✓	
Safari, Kenya		✓	
Taj Mahal, India			✓
Uluru, Australia		✓	
Venice, Italy	✓		✓

[a] The use of a table for our small example may suggest that a graph structure is not needed. We assume you already decided to organize your data as a graph. The table is an easy way to explain Jaccard similarity.

We can use the table's data to compute Jaccard similarities for each pair of travelers:

- A and B have three destinations in common (Amazon, Grand Canyon, and Machu Picchu). Collectively, they have been to nine destinations: jaccard(A, B) = 3/9 = 0.33.

- B and C have only one destination in common (Grand Canyon). Collectively they have been to 10 destinations: jaccard(B, C) = 1/10 = 0.10.

- A and C have three destinations in common (Grand Canyon, Paris, and Venice). Collectively, they have been to seven destinations: jaccard(A, C) = 3/7 = 0.43.

Among these three, A and C are the most similar. As the proprietor, you might suggest that C visit some of the places that A has visited, such as the Amazon and Machu Picchu. Or you might try to arrange a group tour, inviting both of them to somewhere they both have not been to, such as Uluru, Australia.

Cosine similarity

Cosine similarity measures the alignment of two sequences of numerical characteristics. The name comes from the geometric interpretation in which the numerical sequence is the entity's coordinates in space. The data points on the grid (the other type of "graph") in Figure 6-9 illustrate this interpretation.

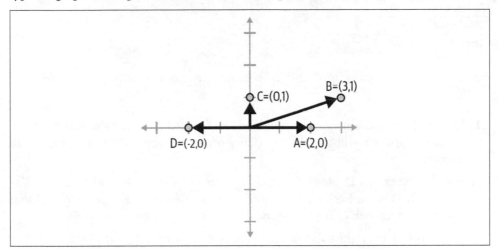

Figure 6-9. Geometric interpretation of numeric data vectors

Point A represents an entity whose feature vector is (2,0). B's feature vector is (3,1). Now we see why we call a list of property values a "vector." The vectors for A and B are somewhat aligned. The cosine of the angle between them is their similarity score. If two vectors are pointed in exactly the same direction, the angle between them is 0; the cosine of their angle is 1. cos(A,C) is 0 because A and C are perpendicular; the vectors (2,0) and (0,2) have nothing in common. cos(A,D) is –1 because A and D are pointed in opposite directions. So, cos(x,y) = 1 for two perfectly similar entities, 0 for two perfectly unrelated entities, and –1 for two perfectly anticorrelated entities.

Suppose you have scores across several categories or attributes for a set of entities. The scores could be ratings of individual features of products, employees, accounts, and so on. Let's continue the example of Bucket List Travel Advisors. This time, each customer has rated their enjoyment of a destination on a scale of 1 to 10, so we have numerical values, not just yes/no, shown in Table 6-3.

Table 6-3. Dataset for cosine similarity example

Destination	A	B	C
Amazon Rainforest, Brazil	8		
Grand Canyon, USA	10	6	8
Great Wall, China	5		8

Destination	A	B	C
Machu Picchu, Peru	8	7	
Paris, France	9		4
Pyramids, Egypt		7	
Safari, Kenya		10	
Taj Mahal, India			10
Uluru, Australia		9	
Venice, Italy	7	10	

Here are steps for using this table to compute cosine similarity between pairs of travelers:

1. List all the possible neighbors and define a standard order for the list so we can form vectors. We will use the top-down order in Table 6-3, from Amazon to Venice.

2. If each vertex has D possible neighbors, this gives us vectors of length D. For Table 6-3, D = 10. Each element in the vector is either the edge weight, if that vertex is a neighbor, or the null score, if it isn't a neighbor.

3. Determining the right null score is required to ensure that your similarity scores mean what you want them to mean. If a 0 means someone absolutely hated a destination, it is wrong to assign a 0 if someone has not visited a destination. A better approach is to *normalize* the scores. You can either normalize by entity (traveler), by neighbor/feature (destination), or by both. The idea is to replace the empty cells with a default score. You could set the default to be the average destination, or you could set it a little lower than that, because not having visited a place is a weak vote against that place. For simplicity, we won't normalize the scores; we'll just use 6 as the default rating. Then traveler A's vector is $Wt(A) = [8, 10, 5, 8, 9, 6, 6, 6, 6, 7]$.

4. Then, apply the cosine similarity:

$$cosine(a, b) = \frac{Wt(a) \cdot W(b)}{\| Wt(a) \| \ \| Wt(b) \|}$$

$$= \frac{\Sigma_{i=1}^{D} Wt(a)_i Wt(b)_i}{\sqrt{\Sigma_{i=1}^{D} Wt(a)_i^2} \sqrt{\Sigma_{i=1}^{D} Wt(b)_i^2}}$$

$Wt(a)$ and $Wt(b)$ are the neighbor connection weight vectors for a and b, respectively. The numerator goes element by element in the vectors, multiplying the weight from a by the weight from b, then adding together these products. The more that the weights align, the larger the sum we get. The denominator is a scaling factor, the Euclidean length of vector $Wt(a)$ multiplied by the length of vector $Wt(b)$.

Let's look at one more use case, people who rate movies, to compare how Jaccard and cosine similarity work. In Figure 6-10, we have two persons, A and B, who have each rated three movies. They have both rated two of the same movies, *Black Panther* and *Frozen*.

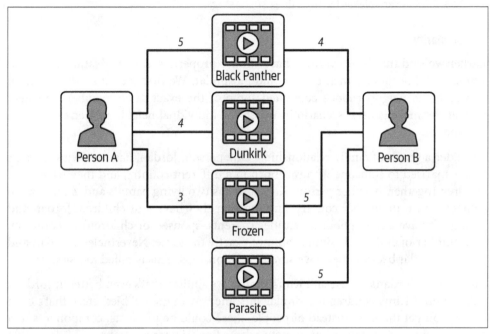

Figure 6-10. Similarity of persons who rate movies

If we only care about what movies the persons have seen and not about the scores, then Jaccard similarity is sufficient and easier to compute. This would also be your choice if scores were not available or if the relationships were not numeric. The Jaccard similarity is (size of overlap) / (size of total set) = 2 / 4 = 0.5. That seems like a middling score, but if there are hundreds or thousands of possible movies they could have seen, then it's a very high score.

If we want to take the movie ratings into account to see how similar A's and B's taste are, we should use cosine similarity. Assuming the null score is 0, then A's neighbor score vector is [5, 4, 3, 0] and B's is [4, 0, 5, 5]. For cosine similarity, the numerator is [5, 4, 3, 0] · [4, 0, 5, 5] = (5)(4)+(4)(0)+(3)(5)+(0)(5) = 35. The denominator = $\sqrt{5^2 + 4^2 + 3^2 + 0^2}\sqrt{4^2 + 0^2 + 5^2 + 5^2} = \sqrt{50}\sqrt{66} = 57.446$. The final result is 0.60927. This again seems like a reasonably good score—not strong similarity, but much better than a random pairing.

Use Jaccard similarity when the features of interest are yes/no or categorical variables.

Use cosine similarity when you have numerical variables. If you have both types, you can use cosine similarity and treat your yes/no variables as having values 1/0.

Role similarity

Earlier we said that if two vertices have similar properties, similar relationships, and similar neighborhoods, then they should be similar. We first examined the situation in which the neighborhoods contained some of the exact same members, but let's look at the more general scenario in which the individual neighbors aren't the *same*, just similar.

Consider a graph of family relationships. One person, Jordan, has two living parents and is married to someone who was born in a different country, and they have three children together. Another person, Kim, also has two living parents and is married to someone born in another country, and together they have four children. Jordan and Kim don't have any neighboring entities (parents, spouses, or children) in common. The number of children is similar but not exactly the same. Nevertheless, Jordan and Kim are similar because they have similar relationships. This is called *role similarity*.

Moreover, if Jordan's spouse and Kim's spouse are similar, that's even better. If Jordan's children and Kim's children are similar in some way (ages, hobbies, etc.), that's even better. You get the idea. Instead of people, these could be products, components in a supply chain or power distribution network, or financial transactions.

> Two entities have similar roles if they have similar relationships to entities, which themselves have similar roles.

This is a recursive definition: A and B are similar if their neighbors are similar. Where does it stop? What is the base case where we can say for certain how much two things are similar?

SimRank

In their 2002 paper, Glen Jeh and Jennifer Widom proposed SimRank,[2] which measures similarity by having equal-length paths from A and B both reach the same individual. For example, if Jordan and Kim share a grandparent, that contributes to their SimRank score. The formal definition of SimRank is:

---

2 Glen Jeh and Jennifer Widom, "SimRank: A Measure of Structural-Context Similarity," *KDD '02: Proceedings of the Eighth ACM SIGKDD International Conference on Knowledge Discovery and Data Mining* (July 2002): 538–543, *https://dl.acm.org/doi/10.1145/775047.775126*.

$$simrank(a, b) = \frac{C}{|In(a)In(b)|} \Sigma_{u \in In(a)} \Sigma_{v \in In(b)} \, simrank(In(u), In(v))$$

$$simrank(a, a) = 1$$

$In(a)$ and $In(b)$ are the sets of in-neighbors of vertices a and b, respectively; u is a member of $In(a)$; v is a member of $In(b)$; and C is a constant between 0 and 1 to control the rate at which neighbors' influence decreases as distance from a source vertex increases. Lower values of C mean a more rapid decrease. SimRank computes an N × N array of similarity scores, one for each possible pair of vertices. This differs from cosine and Jaccard similarity, which compute a single pair's score on demand. It is necessary to compute the full array of SimRank scores because the value of SimRank(a,b) depends of the SimRank score of pairs of their neighbors (e.g., SimRank(u,v)), which in turn depends on *their* neighbors, and so on. To compute SimRank, you initialize the array so that SimRank(a,b) = 1 if $a = b$; otherwise, it is 0. Then calculate a revised set of scores by applying the SimRank equation for each pair (a,b) where the SimRank scores on the right side are from the previous iteration. Note that this is like PageRank's computation, except that we have N × N scores instead of just N scores. SimRank has a few weaknesses. It only finds similarity if two entities eventually find some vertex that is the same distance from both of them. This is too rigid for some cases. It would not work for Jordan and Kim unless our graph contained their common relatives.

RoleSim

To address these shortcomings, Ruoming Jin, Victor E. Lee, and Hui Hong introduced RoleSim[3] in 2011. RoleSim starts with the (over)estimate that the similarity between any two entities is the ratio of the sizes of their neighborhoods. The initial estimate for RoleSim(Jordan, Kim) would be 5/6. RoleSim then uses the current estimated similarity of their neighbors to make an improved guess for the next round. RoleSim is defined as follows:

$$rolesim(a, b) = (1 - \beta) \max_{M(a, b)} \frac{\Sigma_{(u, v) \in M(a, b)} rolesim(u, v)}{max(|N(u)|, |N(v)|)} + \beta$$

$$rolesim_0(a, b) = \frac{min(|N(u)|, |N(v)|)}{max(|N(u)|, |N(v)|)}$$

The parameter β is similar to SimRank's C. The main difference is the function M. $M(a,b)$ is a *bipartite matching* between the neighborhoods of a and b. This is like trying to pair up the three children of Jordan with the four children of Kim. M(Jordan, Kim) will consist of three pairs (and one child left out). Moreover, there are 24 possible matchings. For computational purposes (not actual social dynamics),

---

3 Ruoming Jin, Victor E. Lee, and Hui Hong, "Axiomatic Ranking of Network Role Similarity," *KDD '11: Proceedings of the 17th ACM SIGKDD International Conference on Knowledge Discovery and Data Mining* (August 2011): 922–930, *https://doi.org/10.1145/2020408.2020561*.

assume that the oldest child of Jordan selects a child of Kim; there are four options. The next child of Jordan picks from the three remaining children of Kim, and the third child of Jordan can choose from the two remaining children of Kim. This yields (4)(3)(2) = 24 possibilities. The max term in the equation means that we select the matching that yields the highest sum of RoleSim scores for the three chosen pairs. If you think of RoleSim as a compatibility score, then we are looking for the combination of pairings that gives us the highest total compatibility of partners. You can see that this is more computational work than SimRank, but the resulting scores have nicer properties:

1. There is no requirement that the neighborhoods of a and b ever meet.
2. If the neighborhoods of a and b "look" exactly the same, because they have the same size, and each of the neighbors can be paired up so that their neighborhoods look the same, and so on, then their RoleSim score will be a perfect 1. Mathematically, this level of similarity is called *automorphic equivalence*.

Classification and prediction algorithms

Not only can graph algorithms compute descriptive properties such as centrality or similarity, but they also can take on the predictive side of data science. One of the most in-demand uses for graph analytics employs vertex classification methods to predict whether a particular transaction is fraudulent. We'll wrap up our chapter by looking at a few algorithms for predictive tasks relevant to graphs: predicting the class of a vertex and predicting the future success or the present existence of a relationship.[4] We often associate prediction with guessing the future, but an equally important application is trying to predict facts about the current world, acknowledging that our database doesn't know everything.

Humans navigate the world by constantly performing entity classification. Every time we encounter something we have not seen before, our brains try to assign it to one of the categories of things we already know. We even classify people, which affects how we perceive them. In our minds, we have thousands of categories of items, each defined by some key characteristics. We then subconsciously perform the duck test: if it looks like a duck, swims like a duck, and quacks like a duck, it's a duck. If we take a more quantitative approach and say that we are trying to find the most matches between the properties of some known category and this new item, we have just described Jaccard similarity.

The natural way to perform classification and prediction in a graph is to leverage graph-based similarity. Compute the similarity between the vertex in question and

---

4 In the academic literature for graph data science, these two tasks are usually known as *node classification* and *link prediction*.

other vertices by applying a formula like cosine or Jaccard similarity to their neighborhoods. If we have previously performed some modeling, so that we have representative exemplars for each class, then we only need to compare to the exemplars. Training a machine learning model is one way to obtain these exemplars. If we haven't yet performed this modeling, we can still perform classification. We just need to look at more data to discover what categories are out there and what their characteristics are. A popular approach is *k-nearest neighbors*, or kNN for short.

Here is the basic workflow for kNN:

1. Compute similar scores between the query vertex and other vertices that have a known class. If an item's class is known, we say it is *labeled*. If there are too many labeled vertices, we can select a random sample of them.

2. Select the k most similar vertices, where 1 < k < N.

3. Count the occurrences of each category among the k-nearest vertices. Pick the category that occurs the most often.

For example, if among the 10 persons most similar to Kim, 7 prefer *Star Trek* to *Star Wars*, we predict that Kim prefers *Star Trek*.

There is no universally ideal value of k. Values that are too small are too sensitive to noise. Values that are too big are ignoring the importance of nearness. One heuristic is $k = \sqrt{N}$. Another is to perform the prediction for a range of values and then to pick the most frequent prediction among the many predictions.

In Figure 6-11, the query vertex is in the center, and the distance between a vertex and the center represents the distance (inverse similarity) between that vertex and the query vertex. Vertices that are shaded have a known class. We have two classes: dark and light. If k = 6, then two of those six are dark, and the other four are light. Therefore, we predict that the class of the query vertex is light.

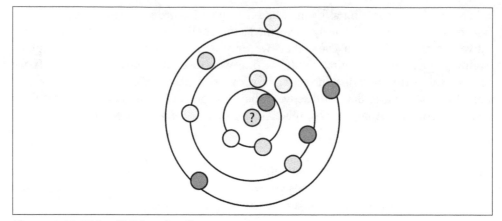

Figure 6-11. Using kNN to classify a vertex

Link prediction can also make use of graph-based similarity. This task is usually more complicated than node classification. First, we are dealing with two vertices (the endpoints) instead of one. Moreover, the link might be directional. For the general case, we hypothesize, "There is probably an edge of type L from vertex A to vertex B, if there is usually an edge of type L from vertices similar to A to vertices similar to B." We can apply cosine or Jaccard similarity to our vertices, and then count how often we see edges between pairs of similar vertices. The task is simpler if the two endpoints are the same type of vertex: then we only need to study one type of vertex.

Different types of relationships may correlate to different types of similarity. For example, suppose we are trying to predict a friendship relationship. Friendship is often characterized by *homophily*: persons who have a lot in common tend to like one another. Jaccard similarity might be appropriate. If homophily is an important characteristic, we can skip the step where we look for existing examples of edges and just make our prediction based on the two vertices being sufficiently similar. For other types of relationships, such as knowing one another or doing business together, two vertices belonging to the same community might be a good predictor of eventually having a direct relationship.

Besides Jaccard and cosine, here are some ways to measure vertex similarity in the service of link prediction:

Common neighbors
Count the number of neighbors in common. Is this number high?

Total neighbors
Count the number of neighbors in common, for neighborhoods to a depth of D hops. Is this number high?

Same community

Are the two vertices already in the same community?

Using raw counts can be problematic. How much is enough? Jaccard similarity normalizes the counts by dividing the count of common neighbors by the total number of distinct neighbors among them. Another way to normalize is to think about how many neighbors each of the common neighbors has. Suppose A and B are both friends with C. If C is friends with only three persons, then your two friendships are very significant to C. If C has one thousand friends, then it's not that significant that they have C in common. Adamic and Adar proposed a similarity index[5] that scales the contribution of each common neighbor by the inverse log of that neighbor's neighborhood size. The smaller the neighborhood, the bigger the contribution to similarity:

$$S(A,B) = \Sigma\_(u \in N(A) \cap N(B)) \, 1/(log \, N(u))$$

All of these similarity algorithms are available in TigerGraph's GDS Library in the Topological Similarity category.

Chapter Summary

In this chapter, we articulated a definition of graph analytics, discussed the computational requirements for graph analytics, and did an in-depth review of graph algorithms, the toolset for graph analytics. Graph analytics is making observations and drawing conclusions *on* connected data and *about* connected data. Graph analytics can give you more insight into your data than would be possible or practical with conventional tabular analytics.

Graph algorithms are handy tools for addressing standard analytical tasks. Major categories of graph algorithms for analytics include shortest path, centrality, community, similarity, node classification, and link prediction. As with any craft, using graph algorithms as tools requires some study and practice to know how to make the best use of them.

---

5 Lada A. Adamic and Eytan Adar, "Friends and Neighbors on the Web," *Social Networks* 25, no. 3 (July 2003): 211–230, *https://doi.org/10.1016/S0378-8733(03)00009-1*.

CHAPTER 7

Better Referrals and Recommendations

This chapter will demonstrate how graph analytics can retrieve information from a network to make better referrals and recommendations, using two real-world use cases. In the first use case, we will build a referral network between patients and healthcare specialists. We will see how to determine which doctors are the most influential and how their interrelations form communities. The second use case is about making a better recommendation engine using features based on the connections and affinities among customers, context factors, products, and features. By the end of this chapter, you should be able to:

- Understand how graph connections provide context
- Apply multiple techniques for analyzing context in order to make recommendations and referrals
- Know how to model and analyze a referral network
- Know how to model and analyze a recommendation engine using graphs
- Explain the meaning of a high PageRank score using the concepts of referral and authority

Case 1: Improving Healthcare Referrals

Today's healthcare industry has evolved to include many specialties and specialists. This has advanced the state of the art in many areas and given patients the potential to receive expert care. When a patient's situation is beyond the routine care offered by a general practitioner, the general practitioner may refer the patient to a specialist. There may be subsequent referrals to other specialists. In many healthcare systems, a patient does not have the authority to see a specialist without a referral; a formal referral from one doctor to another is required in order to manage healthcare costs and efficiency.

Understanding referral behavior is important to doctors, their patients, healthcare provider organizations, and insurance companies. Healthcare specialists who want to grow their businesses and client bases must build and maintain a strong level of referrals. According to market research in 2020, there is annual leaked revenue of $900,000 per physician alone due to missed referrals.[1] In this regard, medical practitioners are similar to lawyers, physical trainers, home decorators, and many other service providers who in part rely on referrals to build their businesses. Patients may want to know if a referral is due to quality of care or some economic factor. Insurers can study the referral data to see if there is a suspicious pattern that may constitute a form of fraud. Is a provider steering referrals to another provider beyond what is medically necessary?

To answer these questions, we need to be able to see the big picture and analyze multiple layers of doctors making referrals to other doctors in what can be a chain of referrals, or sometimes even a loop. The industry talks about referral *networks*. The structure of these provider-patient referral networks lends itself quite well to graph analysis.

Solution: Form and Analyze a Referral Graph

The goal of a referral network is to ensure the healthcare quality of the patient by sending them to the correct specialty practices via their doctors. A referral network achieves this through streamlined communication among patients, doctors, and healthcare specialists that is transparent and efficient for all stakeholders.

Understanding the dynamics in a referral network is valuable to both the individual participants and an organization like a health insurance provider that wants to manage the network as a whole. An in-depth analysis of a referral network can reveal inefficiencies in the system. For example, a doctor might routinely refer patients with specific symptoms to a particular specialist, not realizing that the specialist tends to refer those patients again to another specialist. Today's medical providers are busy dealing with the patient issues immediately in front of them and may not see the more holistic system-level view. A doctor or administrator who has access to analysis of the referral network could identify these patterns and adjust their referral protocols in light of the data.

1 "Importance of Physician Referral Network in Healthcare," JournoMed, August 18, 2020, *https://journomed.com/importance-of-physician-referral-network-in-healthcare*.

In general, there are three reasons why doctors refer their patients to other healthcare specialists: first, to seek the advice of the specialist on the diagnosis or treatment; second, to add the specialist to a team of healthcare providers for the patient; and third, to transfer the patient when the original doctor is not the right fit because of experience gaps or other personal factors. In a referral network, vertices represent doctors, patients, and healthcare specialists. A patient's referral by a doctor to a healthcare specialist is represented as a directed edge. Making the right referrals at the right time is an important part of providing good quality and efficient health care. We can analyze the resultant directed network to identify important doctors and specialists.

Implementing a Referral Network of Healthcare Specialists

TigerGraph has a starter kit that models a healthcare referral network. We use this starter kit to explore and analyze the referral network of healthcare specialists, patients, and doctors. You can install it following the steps from Chapter 3.

The Healthcare Referral Network Starter Kit

Deploy a new TigerGraph Cloud instance, selecting "Healthcare – Referral Networks, Hub & Community Detection" as the starter kit. After successful installation, you can load the data following the steps listed in the section "Load data and install queries for a starter kit" on page 50 in Chapter 3.

Graph Schema

The Healthcare Referral Network Starter Kit includes more than 11K vertices and more than 40K edges. There are five different vertex types and five directed edge types.[2] The schema of this starter kit is shown in Figure 7-1.

---

2 Actually, in this schema, each directed edge also has a corresponding reverse edge, so there are 10 edge types.

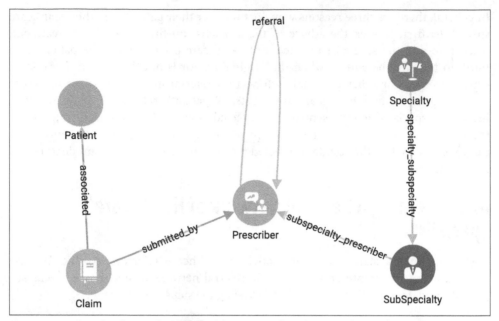

Figure 7-1. Graph schema for the Healthcare - Referral Networks, Hub & Community Detection Starter Kit (see a larger version of this figure at https://oreil.ly/gpam0701)

We describe the five vertex types in Table 7-1. A **Prescriber** is a doctor or nurse practitioner who performs medical service and then submits a **Claim** associated with a **Patient**. Each **Prescriber** has a **Specialty** and **Subspecialty**.

Four of the five edge types are very straightforward; the **referral** edge type deserves some special attention. A **Prescriber** may make a **referral** to another **Prescriber** so that the **Patient** can receive additional care. However, if you look at the Graph statistics table on the Load Data page, you will see that there are zero referral edges! The source data does not specify any referrals. One of the queries we will run will use the data in the graph to *infer* referrals. Link inference, also known as link prediction, is one of the most valuable capabilities offered by graph analytics.

Table 7-1. Vertex types in the Healthcare Referral graph model

Vertex type	Description
Prescriber	A medical practitioner who can make diagnoses and prescribe medicines
Claim	A description of billable medical services performed by the Prescriber and associated with a Patient
Patient	A person who receives medical care
Specialty	A branch of medical practice focused on a category of biological systems, disorders, treatments, or patients
Subspecialty	A subcategory of a Specialty

Queries and Analytics

The Healthcare Referral Network Starter Kit contains numerous queries. We will focus on four queries that showcase how graph analytics techniques can provide insights into healthcare referral network behavior. The following is a brief description of these four queries. Then we'll dive into more details of how each query works.

Get common patients
> Given two doctors, find all patients that these doctors have in common.

Infer the referral network
> The source data does not explicitly specify referrals. This analysis infers referrals by looking for situations where a **Patient** had a **Claim** submitted by one **Prescriber** and then another **Claim** submitted by a different **Prescriber** within a limited amount of time.

Find influential doctors
> It's easy to see which doctors receive the most referrals, but which doctors are the most *influential*? Influence is a more subtle concept than just the number of referrals. There are multiple ways to define *influence*. This analysis uses the PageRank algorithm's concept of influence to find the most influential **Prescribers**.

Find referral communities
> Looking at the referral graph as a social network, what communities do we see? That is, which **Prescribers** are closely affiliated with other **Prescribers** due to referral relationships? This analysis looks not only at the presence of one-to-one relationships but also at how groups of providers might be closely affiliated.

Get common patients

The query get_common_patients takes two **Prescriber** vertices as input parameters and finds each **Patient** that has a **Claim** with these two doctors. For example, Figure 7-2 illustrates the query output if we used the suggested inputs of prescribers Douglas Thomas and Helen Su. The query not only discovers that they have five patients in common but also shows why the patients are seeing the doctors. Note that we are not requiring that this reflect a referral relationship. A person could be seeing the two doctors for unrelated reasons, such as an ulcer and a broken bone. Nevertheless, this information is helpful for several reasons. Providers can compare the number of common patients to what they expect. They can also look at the overall characteristics of the set of common patients. Is there anything noteworthy or unusual about the demographics or health profiles of these common patients? Are there indirect referrals in which there is no referral edg, but the patient would have received better care if a direct referral had been made?

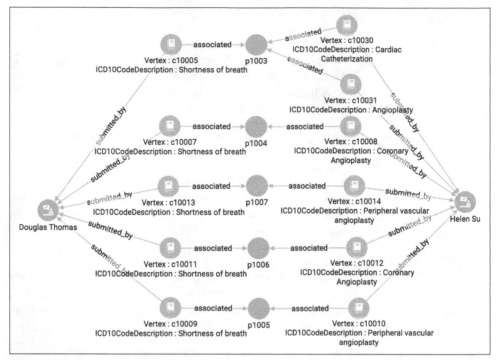

Figure 7-2. Common patients between doctors Douglas Thomas and Helen Su (see a larger version of this figure at https://oreil.ly/gpam0702)

The `get_common_patients` query is implemented in six steps. The first four steps find the common patients, and the last two steps gather the connecting vertices and edges so that we can display the connectivity. You may find it helpful to refer to this figure as we walk through the computation steps.

The first step is to collect all the claims associated with the first **Prescriber** by traversing over the `submitted_by` edge type. To remember which vertices we've traversed to, we mark `@visited` to `true` for each visited **Claim**:

```
claims1 = SELECT t
   FROM Pre1:s -(<submitted_by:e)- Claim:t
   ACCUM t.@visited += true;
```

In our example, if Douglas Thomas is Prescriber 1, then `claims1` will include vertices c10005, c0007, c0009, c10011, and c10013. It could include more than these. Those other vertices will get filtered out in a later stage.

Then, in the next step we find the linked **Patient** elements for each **Claim**. Again, we use @visited to mark the vertices that we use. In this case, these are **Patient** vertices:

```
patients1 = SELECT t
    FROM claims1:s -(associated>:e)- Patient:t
    ACCUM t.@visited += true;
```

Continuing with our example of Douglas Thomas, this step would find **Patient** p1003, p1004, p1005, p1006, and p1007. Again, it might find more, but these will be filtered out later.

In the third step, we do the same as in the first step, but now we collect the **Claim** elements for the second **Prescriber**. This would find the six claims in the lower part of Figure 7-2:

```
claims2 = SELECT t
    FROM Pre2:s -(<submitted_by:e)- Claim:t
    ACCUM t.@visited += true;
```

In the fourth step we do the same as in the second step, but now we start traversing from the **Claim** elements found in the third step, and we use a WHERE condition to include only the **Patient** vertices that have been visited before. Any **Patient** that has been visited already must be a patient of the first **Prescriber**, so we know this **Patient** is a common patient. This is the filtering stage that we mentioned before:

```
common_patient = SELECT t
    FROM claims2:s -(associated>:e)- Patient:t
    WHERE t.@visited == true;
PRINT common_patients;s
```

In the fifth step, we select each **Claim** from common **Patient** elements and collect their edges using the **associated** edge type. We store these edges in @@edges_to_dis play. We will gather more edges in the last step:

```
claims = SELECT t
    FROM common_patients:s -(<associated:e)- Claim:t
    WHERE t.@visited == true
    ACCUM @@edges_to_display += e;
PRINT claims;
```

Finally, we collect all edges between the **Claim** elements found in the fifth step and the two **Prescriber** elements. We store those edges in @@edges_to_display and print them:

```
claims = SELECT s
    FROM claims:s -(submitted_by>:e)- :t
    ACCUM @@edges_to_display += e;
PRINT @@edges_to_display;
```

Infer the referral network

The source data does not explicitly include **referral** edges, so we create a query to infer when there was a referral and then insert a **referral** edge into the graph. If a patient visited Prescriber 1 at Time A and then visited Prescriber 2 a little while later at Time B, it may be due to a referral. The query parameter max_days sets the upper limit for the number of days between two doctor visits that will be considered a referral. The query has a default value of 30 days.

There are a couple of reasons why this time sequence might *not* be due to a referral:

- Both Prescriber 1 and Prescriber 2 are treating aspects of the same condition of the patient, but Prescriber 1 did not make the suggestion to see Prescriber 2.
- The visit to Prescriber 2 is unrelated to the visit to Prescriber 1.

To make these distinctions between true and false referrals would require more information than we have in our dataset.

The query infer_all_referrals merely calls infer_referrals, once for each **Prescriber** vertex. infer_referrals does the real work:

```
SumAccum<INT> @@num_referrals_created;

all_prescribers = SELECT s FROM Prescriber:s
    ACCUM
        @@num_referrals_created += infer_referrals(s, max_days);

PRINT @@num_referrals_created;
```

Figure 7-3 shows an example of the graph traversal flow in the infer_referrals query. There are four hops to get from input_prescriber D1 to another **Prescriber** D2. These correspond to the four SELECT statements described in Figure 7-3.

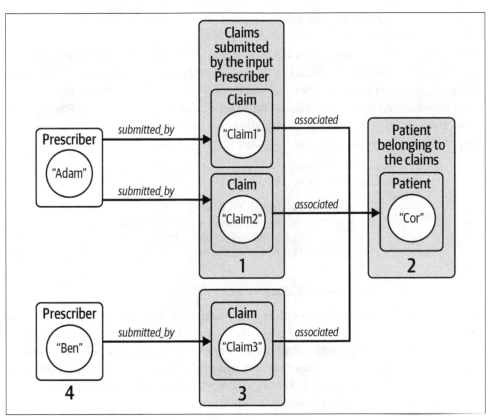

Figure 7-3. Graph traversal example for `infer_referrals` *query*

The `infer_referrals` query takes two input parameters: `input_prescriber`, a vertex of type **Prescriber**; and the integer value `max_days`. Starting from `input_pre scriber`, the query selects all **Claim** elements related to the input prescriber by traversing the edge type **submitted_by**. From there, it finds all **Patient** vertices that belong to that **Claim** set by selecting the edge type **associated**. In Figure 7-3, these two steps correspond to going from Adam (the input prescriber) to **Patient** Cor.

Notice that patient Cor has multiple claims from a single prescriber (Adam). The date of a claim is a key factor in deciding whether there is a referral or not, so we need to pay attention to each individual date. The following GSQL code snippet shows the first two hops from `input_prescriber` to their patients, including collecting the dates of each patient's claims in a `@date_list` accumulator:

```
Start = {input_prescriber};

my_claims = SELECT t FROM Start:s -(<submitted_by:e)- :t
    POST-ACCUM t.@visited = true;
my_patients = SELECT t FROM my_claims:s -(associated>:e)- :t
```

```
// A Patient may have multiple claims; save each date
ACCUM t.@date_list += s.rx_fill_date;
```

Now we want to find the claims made by other prescribers for these patients. The clause WHERE t.@visited == false in the following code ensures that these other claims are different from the ones we looked at before. We then compare the date of a claim encountered in this step against the dates of claims in the Patient's @date_list. If the time difference is less than max_days, we mark this new claim as a referral (earlier in the query, we converted max_days to max_seconds):

```
other_claims = SELECT t FROM my_patients:s -(<associated:e)- :t
    WHERE t.@visited == false
    ACCUM
            FOREACH date IN s.@date_list DO
            CASE WHEN datetime_diff(date, t.rx_fill_date)
                    BETWEEN 0 AND max_seconds THEN
                t.@is_referred_claim = true
            END
        END
    HAVING t.@is_referred_claim == true;
```

Next, we find the **Prescriber** vertices associated with the marked claims and use an INSERT statement to create the edges. For informational purposes, we count the number of inserted edges with the @@num_referrals_created accumulator. In GSQL, graph updates are not committed until the end of the query. Therefore, it would not work to count the number of **referral** edges within this query directly. We could only perform such a count in a subsequent query:

```
other_prescribers = SELECT t FROM other_claims:s -(submitted_by>:e)- :t
    POST-ACCUM
        INSERT INTO referral VALUES(input_prescriber, t, 1),
        @@num_referrals_created += 1;
```

Lastly, we RETURN @@num_referrals_created, sending data back to the query that called this one. The caller query (infer_all_referrals) adds together each returned value for each **Prescriber** to compute the total number of edges created for the entire graph.

Subqueries in GSQL

A query can be defined as a subquery by using RETURNS (<data_type>) in the header and RETURN <value> at the end of the query. Besides returning a value, a subquery can have graph modification side effects (e.g., inserting edges). PRINT statements in subqueries do not print to the console; an alternative is to write to a file with PRINTLN or LOG. See TigerGraph's GSQL Language Reference (*https://oreil.ly/Q7U-D*) for more details.

Find influential doctors

This query finds the most influential specialists. An influential specialist is considered an authority. They not only receive a lot of referrals but also work on the important cases. If they were to drop out of the graph suddenly, the impact would be significant. Analysis of relative influence can help doctors understand their relative importance and see if they can improve it. Healthcare administrators can take a holistic look to see if they can reduce overdependence on individuals and provide more balanced care to patients while reducing costs. Epidemiologists, pharmaceutical companies, and medical equipment vendors may also want to know which doctors are the most influential.

Fortunately for us, a well-known graph algorithm measures influence in this way, considering both the number and relative importance of incoming edges. The *PageRank algorithm*, developed by Google founders Larry Page and Sergey Brin, ranks a web page based on how many other pages are linking it and the rank of these other pages. We can look at the influence of doctors in a referral network in a similar way. A doctor's influence increases if they receive more referrals or if the influence of those referrers increases.

An implementation of the PageRank algorithm (`tg_pagerank`) is included in Tiger-Graph's GDS Library. The algorithm is included in this starter kit for convenience, but installing library algorithms into your database instance is a simple process. Unlike other GSQL algorithms we have seen that were written for a specific graph schema in a specific starter kit, this algorithm is general purpose. It has 10 input parameters (shown in Table 7-2), but 8 of them have default values. We only need to set the first 2. In our case, we set v_type = **Prescriber** and e_type = **referral**.

 Inside GraphStudio, the GSQL GDS Library is available in the New Query window. With a graph selected, choose "Write Queries" in the left sidebar, then click the green ⊕ button to add a new query to the list of installed and saved queries. Click "Choose from library" in the new window that appears. Hover over the question mark icon next to any query for a brief explanation of its purpose.

Table 7-2. Input parameters for tg_pagerank library algorithm

Parameter	Default value	Description
v_type		Name of vertex type to use.
e_type		Name of edge type to use.
max_change	0.001	Stop iterating when the interim PageRank scores are stable, changing less than 0.001.
max_iter	25	Stop iterating if we have computed interim PageRank scores this many times.
damping	0.85	Relative importance of neighbors versus random movement (between unconnected vertices). Some random movement is needed for stability.

Parameter	Default value	Description
top_k	100	Number of top scores to print in the output.
print_accum	TRUE	Print the output in JSON format.
result_attr	FALSE	Store the results as vertex attributes.
file_path	*empty string*	Write the results in tabular format to this file.
display_edges	FALSE	Include edges of interest in the output. If the algorithm is run on GraphStudio, selecting this option causes a better visual display.

The next three parameters after e_type are specific to PageRank. The last five parameters are general purpose and appear in many or most GSQL algorithms in the GDS Library. They deal with the way the query output is printed to the console and/or exported to a file. result_attr is a way to store the PageRank results in the graph as a vertex attribute so that later queries can make use of this algorithm's results in their own calculations. The display_edges parameter specifies whether the output should include edges that are helpful to visualize the results. For example, if the get_common_patients query were to add this parameter, it would specify whether steps 5 and 6 should execute.

If you run PageRank with parameter settings v_type = **Prescriber**, e_type = **refer ral**, and top_k = 5, you should get the following output:

```
[ {
    "@@top_scores_heap": [
        {"Vertex_ID": "pre16", "score": 2.72331},
        {"Vertex_ID": "pre61", "score": 2.5498},
        {"Vertex_ID": "pre58","score": 2.20136},
        {"Vertex_ID": "pre52","score": 2.08101},
        {"Vertex_ID": "pre69","score": 1.89883}
    ]
} ]
```

Find a referral community

This query detects communities within a referral network. A community is a set of vertices that are highly connected to one another while having sparse relationships with the rest of the graph. In a referral network, communities arise through dense connections among doctors, patients, and healthcare providers when they interact with one another. They form a group together because of their many interactions with one another. Detecting communities can help doctors to identify the spread of their referrals within a network and make better referrals for their patients. Healthcare managers can investigate the communities to evaluate the local healthcare systems.

A widely popular graph algorithm to detect communities is the Louvain algorithm, which we mentioned in Chapter 6. This algorithm, developed by Vincent Blondel of the University of Louvain, chooses graph communities by trying to optimize[3] the relative density of edges inside a community, known as *modules*, versus the edges outside the modules. A key feature of the Louvain method is that it does not have a fixed number of communities to detect as an input parameter, making it advantageous for practical applications like those where the number of communities to detect is not known at the outset. It starts with detecting small modules and then groups them together into larger modules whenever that improves the modularity score.

The Louvain algorithm (`tg_louvain`) is included in the Healthcare – Referral Networks, Hub & Community Detection Starter Kit. It has eight input parameters (shown in Table 7-3). The vertex type (**Prescriber**) and edge type (**referral**, in both forward and reverse directions) have been hardcoded into the query. There is no need to adjust any of the parameters, though you might experiment with increasing the `output_level`.

Table 7-3. Input parameters for `tg_louvain` library algorithm

Parameter	Default value	Description
`iter1`	10	Maximum iterations for move.
`iter2`	10	Maximum iterations for merge.
`iter3`	10	Maximum iterations for refine.
`split`	10	Number of data batches, to reduce peak memory consumption. `split=1` processes the whole graph at once. `split=10` processes the graph in 10 batches.
`output_level`	0	If 0: JSON output is statistics about communities. If 1: also output the community IDs indexed by cluster size. If 2: also output the membership of each community.
`print_accum`	TRUE	Print the output in JSON format.
`result_attr`	FALSE	Store the results as vertex attributes.
`file_path`	*empty string*	Write the results in tabular format to this file.

Run the query with default settings. With more than 11,000 vertices, it is difficult to visualize the results, so we will examine the JSON output. The first three sections of the JSON output are shown belows. The first section tells us that the algorithm grouped the vertices into 17 communities. The second section says the largest community has 11,055 members. The next largest community has only 10 members. The third section says that the community with `id = 0` is the one with 11,055 members, community 68157440 has 6 members, and so on. Because this is a heuristic algorithm, you might get slightly different community sizes and qualities. The community IDs may certainly differ:

---

3 No known algorithm is guaranteed to find the most optimal solution without expending compute resources that grow exponentially with the data size. Louvain efficiently finds a "good" answer in a time-efficient way.

```
[
    {"num_of_clusters": 17},
    {"@@largest_clusters": [
        {"csize": 11055,"number": 1},
        {"csize": 10,"number": 1},
        {"csize": 9,"number": 1},
        {"csize": 8,"number": 4},
        {"csize": 7,"number": 3},
        {"csize": 6,"number": 2},
        {"csize": 4,"number": 4},
        {"csize": 3,"number": 1}
      ]
    },
    {
      "@@cluster_sizes": {
        "0": 11055,
        "68157440": 6,
        "68157441": 8,
        "71303168": 9,
        "71303169": 10,
        "71303170": 8,
        "72351746": 3,
        "72351747": 7,
        "73400320": 8,
        "75497473": 4,
        "77594625": 6,
        "77594628": 8,
        "79691776": 4,
        "81788928": 4,
        "84934657": 7,
        "84934658": 4,
        "88080385": 7
      }
    }
]
```

Case 2: Personalized Recommendations

Consumers today often have too many choices. They have trouble knowing what is available and reaching a decision, and vendors have trouble making sure that they are noticed and meeting the consumers' needs. Recommendation engines have become increasingly crucial for guiding users through this jungle of offerings. Recommendation engines aim to prevent users from information overload and provide them with more personalized information, making the solution's user experience more efficient. An online retailer like Amazon may have hundreds of thousands of separate products in the same category. Online retailers offering many products benefit from a recommendation engine because it helps shoppers find products of interest more quickly and easily. Repeat business also comes from customers who are satisfied with a personalized experience that other retailers do not offer.

Traditional recommendation engines provide suggestions of products, content, or services to users based on their historical behavior and the behavior of similar users. There are a few problems with this approach, however. First, new users do not have a history yet, so we cannot make correct suggestions to them at the beginning. This is known as the cold start problem. Second, when only looking into the user's historical behavior, we are limited to suggesting the same type of content repeatedly. The user might miss out on other products, content, and services the vendor offers. Finally, making highly personalized recommendations is not easily scalable, because as the user base and the level of detail grow, the number of persons, products, and factors to consider will grow as well, requiring exponentially more comparisons over time.

To combat these issues, we need a recommendation engine that maintains and processes up-to-date information in near real time. It must also not rely on batch processing. Another requirement is to be fast and scalable to millions of users and products.

Solution: Use Graph for Multirelationship-Based Recommendations

Making recommendations to users of an application is, in essence, discovering connections or similarities. Purchasing a product is a connection between a consumer and a product, and there are also connections among a consumer, a product, and their respective features. If two persons have similar tastes, that similarity is a type of connection, and products that are often purchased together likewise share a connection. These connections arise once users interact with the application, and recommendation is a form of analyzing these connections. Collectively, these connections form a graph. By modeling the data as a graph, we can query right on the graph-structured data without making large join operations on batch data. Therefore, a graph is a natural and flexible way to represent these connections. Organizing the relationships in such a way makes adding, modifying, and removing data easy and the application highly scalable.

Another benefit of using graphs for a recommendation engine is to prevent a cold start for the user. Because a graph model is a single interconnected system, we can populate the starting user experience with a mix of recommendation techniques: content associated with the new user's demographic information; content-based, collaborative filtering; and vendor promotion. In a graph, these techniques can be implemented using pattern matching and similarity scoring. Moreover, adding more data, adding more relationships, and revising the recommendation scheme is straightforward.

Implementing a Multirelationship Recommendation Engine

TigerGraph offers a starter kit to demonstrate how graph analytics can derive customer product recommendations. The starter kit can be installed by following the steps in Chapter 3.

The Recommendation Engine 2.0 Starter Kit

Deploy a new TigerGraph Cloud instance, selecting "Recommendation Engine 2.0 (Hyper-Personalized Marketing)" as the starter kit. Launch it and load the data following the steps in the section "Load data and install queries for a starter kit" on page 50 in Chapter 3.

Graph Schema

Figure 7-4 shows the graph schema of this starter kit, which contains six vertex types and seven edge types.

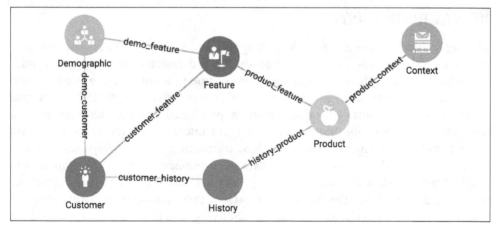

Figure 7-4. Graph schema for the Recommendation Engine 2.0 (see a larger version of this figure at https://oreil.ly/gpam0704)

Table 7-4 describes the vertex types. A **Demographic** vertex refers to the demographic properties of a **Customer**. A **Customer** is a natural person who has an account in our web shop. Furthermore, each **Customer** has a **History** of buying a **Product**. A **Feature** can be a characteristic of a **Demographic**, **Customer**, or a **Product** vertex. With **Context**, we add a contextual layer to our queries with time constraints or weather conditions.

Table 7-4. Vertex types in the Recommendation Engine 2.0 graph model

Vertex type	Description
Customer	A natural person
Demographic	A demographic property of a **Customer**
History	A buying history of a **Customer**
Product	A product
Feature	A feature of a **Customer**
Context	A contextual constraint

In our simplified example, each **Context** vertex has an ID value, which is a word or phrase that describes its characteristic. In a real-world example, the schema would probably categorize the data into different types of context, such as location, date, weather, and so on, but we have lumped them all together into one attribute.

Some of the edge types have weight attributes. The **product_feature** edge type has an attribute simply called `weight`. A high `weight` means that feature is an important aspect of that product. The **customer_feature** edge type has an attribute called `affinity`. A high affinity means there is a strong association between that feature and the customer's desires. We can use these weights to compute how strongly a customer will prefer a product, that is, to make a feature-based recommendation. A standard approach is to multiply the **product_feature** `weight` by the **customer_feature** `affinity`.

The graph in this starter kit is intentionally very small to make it easy to follow the calculations. The entire graph is shown in Figure 7-5. From top to bottom, the vertex types are **Customer**, **Demographic**, **Feature**, **Product**, and **Context**.

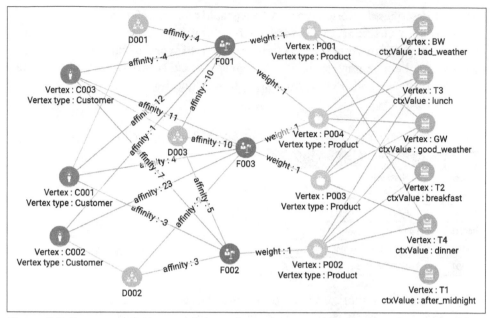

Figure 7-5. Recommendation graph (see a larger version of this figure at https://oreil.ly/gpam0705)

Queries and Analytics

The Recommendation Engine 2.0 Starter Kit includes three queries that show how recommendation engines can be improved using graph analytics. They allow us to select top-ranked products while considering the **Context** and **Feature** elements of the **Customer**.

Recommend by features and context
Return the `top_k` products for `source_customer` while taking into account `weather` and `time_of_day`.

Recommend products by customer and context
Recommend the highest-rated product for a customer while taking into account the weather and the time of the day.

Get top demographic
Display the demographic with the highest average affinity among its customers and features related to the demographic.

Recommend by features and context

Given a set of context conditions and a customer, the `recommend_by_features_and_context` query returns the products that satisfy the context conditions and have the strongest match between their features and the features preferred by the customers. This query takes four input parameters. The first parameter, `source_customer`, names the **Customer** whose top-rated products we would like to know. Then with `weather` and `time_of_day` we specify the **Context** of our selection, and with `top_k` we set how many top-rated products we want to return.

The query begins by initializing the vertex set `start` to `source_customer`. Next, we count how many context filters the user wants to apply. If the user does not want to filter by an input factor (`time_of_day` or `weather`), then the user should just leave that input parameter blank. The following code counts the number of activated context filters:

```
IF time_of_day != "" THEN min_filters = min_filters + 1; END;
IF weather != "" THEN min_filters = min_filters + 1; END;
```

Next, we find those products that satisfy our context filters. We start by initializing `candidate_products` to be all products and `filtered_context` to be all contexts. Then, if `min_filters` is not zero, it means that the **Context** has been set, so we execute our first SELECT statement to narrow down `filtered_context` to only the elements that match `time_of_day` or `weather`:

```
IF min_filters != 0 THEN
    filtered_context = SELECT c FROM Context:c
    WHERE c.id == weather OR c.id == time_of_day; // filter for context
```

We use another SELECT statement to refine `candidate_products` down to only those that link to all of our `filtered_context`:

```
candidate_products = SELECT p
    FROM filtered_context:c -(product_context:pc)- Product:p
    ACCUM p.@filters += 1        // count # matching filter properties
    HAVING p.@filters >= min_filters; // must match all context filters
```

The ACCUM clause counts how many context matches each product makes. The HAVING clause filters the final selection to only include products that match on all the specified context parameters. Referring to Figure 7-5, if we set parameters `weather` = "BW" and `time_of_day` = "T2", then `candidate_products` will be {P004}, the only product that connects to both `filtered_context` vertices.

Now we can compute the overall recommendation score between the customer and products. We use a two-hop path to find connections between our given **Customer** and the candidate **Product** vertices, with **Feature** serving as an intermediary. For each selected product that connects to a feature of interest, we multiply the **product_feature** weight by **customer_feature** affinity and add that to the accumulator @max_score.

Adding the contributions of all the relevant features to compute a total score would be a valid approach, but that is not what we are actually doing here. @max_score is defined as a `MaxAccum`, so it preserves the highest value that it is given. In other words, we look for the single most important feature and use only that one for scoring.[4] Then we use `@max_score` along with the SQL-like `ORDER BY` and `LIMIT` clauses to select the `top_k` products with the highest recommendation scores:

```
recomm_products = SELECT p
    FROM start:s -(customer_feature:cf)- Feature:f
        -(product_feature:pf)- candidate_products:p
    ACCUM p.@max_score += pf.weight*cf.affinity  // compute score
    ORDER BY p.@max_score DESC
    LIMIT top_k;
```

Suppose we set `weather` = `"GW"` and `time_of_day` = `"T2"`. Then `candidate_products` will be {P004, P002}, as highlighted in Figure 7-6. (Since "GW" connects to every product, it has no filtering effect.) If `source_customer` = `C002`, there is only one `Customer-Feature-Product` path to **candidate_products**, with weight 23.

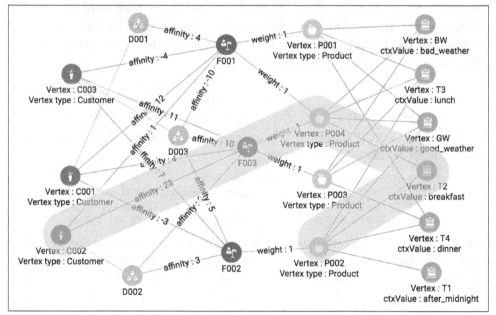

Figure 7-6. Graph paths for recommendation by features and context (see a larger version of this figure at https://oreil.ly/gpam0706)

To see the scores, switch to the JSON output. Now suppose we set `source_customer` = `C001`, `weather` = `GW`, `time_of_day` = `T2`, and `top_k` = 2. Think about what

---

4 You could easily modify the scoring scheme by changing this accumulator type from a `MaxAccum` to a `SumAccum` (total affinity) or `AvgAccum` (average affinity).

paths you can see from C001 to GW and T2 in Figure 7-6 that lead to the following recommendation scores:

```
{
  "attributes": {
    "@max_score": 12,
  },
  "v_id": "P004",
  "v_type": "Product"
},
{
  "attributes": {
    "@max_score": -3,
  },
  "v_id": "P002",
  "v_type": "Product"
}
```

Recommend products by customer and context

Given a set of context conditions and a set of customers, this query returns the product that satisfies the context conditions and that has the strongest match between its features and the features preferred by the customers. The basic task of this query is very similar to that of our first query, recommend by features and context, but there are some interesting differences. The first difference is that this query accepts a list of any context values (input_context_set) rather than asking for one weather condition and one time condition. The second difference is that it can process multiple input customers (input_customer_set) instead of a single one. Both of these changes make it more universal. A third difference is that it returns only one product. That is because this query shows a visual representation of all the connections to **Customer** and **Context** vertices that led to the recommendation. If it selected the top k products, then the visual representation would not be as easy to interpret.

The query starts by defining a tuple type and several accumulators. The first four definitions are to help with sorting products by their average affinity to the customers. A HeapAccum will automatically sort the tuples given to it. After we have our HeapAccum, we will need to convert it to a vertex set for further processing:

```
TYPEDEF TUPLE<VERTEX<product> v, DOUBLE avg_score> Product_Score_Tuple;
AvgAccum @product_avg_score;
HeapAccum<Product_Score_Tuple>(1, avg_score DESC) @@top_product_heap;
SetAccum<VERTEX<product>> @@top_product_vertex_set;
```

 A heap is a more scalable way to get the top k elements from a very large list because the heap has a fixed and usually small size. While ORDER BY and LIMIT are syntactically simpler, they will build a temporary table of all the elements to be sorted.

The last seven accumulators are simply to collect the vertices and edges to display. While we choose to have separate containers for each type, you could merge them into just one vertex set and one edge set:

```
SetAccum<VERTEX<customer>> @@final_customer_vertex_set;
SetAccum<VERTEX<feature>> @@final_feature_vertex_set;
SetAccum<VERTEX<product>> @@final_product_vertex_set;
SetAccum<VERTEX<context>> @@final_context_vertex_set;
SetAccum<EDGE> @@final_context_feature_edge_set;
SetAccum<EDGE> @@final_product_feature_edge_set;
SetAccum<EDGE> @@final_product_context_edge_set;
```

We start with selecting all the **Product** vertices that share a **Feature** with a **Customer** vertex in customer_vertex_set and that also link to one of the input **Context** vertices in context_vertex_set. In a graph query language like GSQL, you perform this selection by searching for paths that make these connections. Figure 7-7 shows the graph schema previously seen in Figure 7-4, with the search path and the specified vertex sets highlighted.

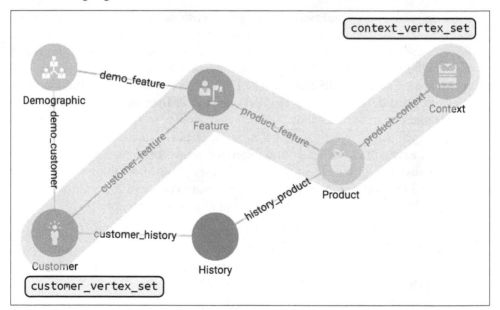

Figure 7-7. Graph path to select products that have features valued by certain customers and that satisfy certain context constraints (see a larger version of this figure at https:// oreil.ly/gpam0707)

There are two syntax options to describe this path in GSQL: as three one-hop paths separated by commas or as one multihop path. While the multihop path is usually more elegant, the separate paths can give you more control over how the query is executed, if performance tuning is required. Note how the multihop FROM clause corresponds exactly to the highlighted path in the figure:

```
product_vertex_set = SELECT p
    FROM customer_vertex_set:c -(customer_feature:cf)- feature:f
    -(product_feature:pf)- product:p
    -(product_context:pctx)- context_vertex_set:ctx
```

Each **Customer-Feature-Product** path has a score: cf.affinity * pf.weight. We compute all the path scores and accumulate them in AvgAccum accumulators (@product_avg_score) to get an average score for each product. We then insert each product with its score into a HeapAccum (@@order_product_heap), which sorts them. Since we set the size of our heap to 1, we end with the single highest-scoring product:

```
ACCUM p.@product_avg_score += (cf.affinity * pf.weight)
POST-ACCUM
    @@order_product_heap += Order_Product_Tuple(p, p.@product_avg_score);
```

In one SELECT statement, we have performed our recommendation analysis.

The purpose of the final SELECT statement is to visualize the elements that we want to display in a graph. We traverse the same paths that we did before, using an almost identical FROM clause, with one change: we include only our top product instead of all products. We add all elements from the vertex types we've visited in the @@final_customer_vertex_set, @@final_feature_vertex_set, @@final_product_vertex_set, and @@final_context_vertex_set accumulators, and then print those accumulators:

```
product_vertex_set = SELECT p
    FROM customer_vertex_set:c -(customer_feature:cf)- Feature:f
     -(product_feature:pf)- product_vertex_set:p
     -(product_context:pctx)- context_vertex_set:ctx
    ACCUM @@final_context_feature_edge_set += cf,
     @@final_product_feature_edge_set += pf,
     @@final_product_context_edge_set += pctx
    POST-ACCUM @@final_customer_vertex_set += c
    POST-ACCUM @@final_feature_vertex_set += f
    POST-ACCUM @@final_product_vertex_set += p
    POST-ACCUM @@final_context_vertex_set += ctx;
```

Figure 7-8 shows the output when the input customers are C002 and C003 and the input contexts are BW (bad weather) and T3 (lunch). The weights that determined this selection are shown.

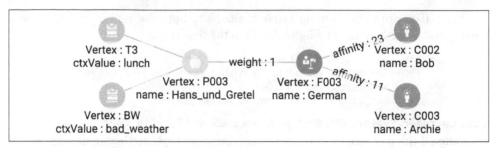

Figure 7-8. Example query result for `recomm_by_customer_and_context` *(see a larger version of this figure at https://oreil.ly/gpam0708)*

Get top demographics

The query called `display_top_demographic` finds the **Demographic** element that has the highest average affinity score among its members and displays the **Customer** and **Feature** elements that are connected to this **Demographic**. The intuition here is that a **Demographic** with high affinity should have members that are similar to one another, and therefore you should be able to make better predictions about their preferences. The structure of this query is very similar to that of recommend products by customer and context. We score each **Demographic** element according to its average feature-based affinity to its connected **Customer** elements. This tells us if we have a **Demographic** group that is strongly bound versus a group that is only loosely bound.

Unlike the previous query, this one does not have input parameters since it is calculating the top **Demographic** of the entire dataset without any given **Context**. We start with defining a tuple type and accumulators to score and sort **Demographic** vertices:

```
TYPEDEF TUPLE<VERTEX<demographic> v, DOUBLE score> Top_Demographic_Tuple;
AvgAccum @demographic_avg_score;
HeapAccum<Demographic_Score_Tuple>(1, score DESC) @@top_product_heap;
SetAccum<VERTEX<Demographic>> @@top_demographic_vertex_set;
```

We also define six accumulators to collect the vertices and edges to display.

We use `SELECT` – `FROM` to find the paths that connect **Demographic** to **Customer** via **Feature**. Figure 7-9 illustrates this selection.

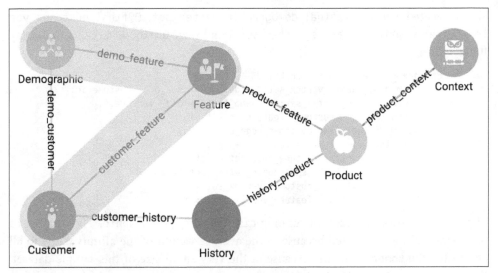

*Figure 7-9. Graph paths that connect **Demographic** to **Customer** via **Feature**. After finding the paths, we score them by multiplying their edge weights. (See a larger version of this figure at https://oreil.ly/gpam0709.)*

Then we use an ACCUM statement to calculate the average demographic score for each element in **Demographic** by multiplying the attributes of cf.affinity with df.affinity and adding that score in @@demographic_avg_score. We create a Top_Demographic_Tuple for each **Demographic** and add that to @@top_product_heap:

```
demographic_vertex_set = SELECT d
    FROM Demographic:d -(demo_feature:df)- Feature:f
      -(customer_feature:cf)- Customer:c
      // Score each demographic by its avg affinity to customers
    ACCUM d.@demographic_avg_score += (cf.affinity * df.affinity)
    // Pick the top scoring demographic
    POST-ACCUM @@top_product_heap += Demographic_Score_Tuple(
                                     d, d.@demographic_avg_score);
```

A few lines are needed to convert the heap to a simple vertex set:

```
WHILE (@@top_product_heap.size() > 0) DO
    @@top_demographic_vertex_set += @@top_product_heap.pop().v;
END;
demographic_vertex_set = { @@top_demographic_vertex_set }; // top product
```

The goal of the second SELECT statement is to display the found top **Demographic** and its connected **Customer** and **Feature** elements. We would like to also display the edges directly connecting **Customer** to **Demographic**, so the path traversal in the FROM clause is a bit longer this time. During these traversals, we store all the edges in @@final_demo_customer_edge_set, @@final_demo_feature_edge_set, and @@final_context_feature_edge_set using accumulators. With POST-ACCUM we store all the visited vertices `@@final_demographic_vertex_set`, `@@final_customer_ver` `tex_set`, and `@@final_feature_vertex_set`. Finally, we use these variables to display the graph:

```
demographic_vertex_set = SELECT d
    FROM demographic_vertex_set:d -(demo_customer:dc)- customer:c,
        demographic_vertex_set:d -(demo_feature:df)- feature:f,
        customer:c -(customer_feature:cf)- feature:f
    ACCUM @@final_demo_customer_edge_set += dc,
        @@final_demo_feature_edge_set += df,
        @@final_context_feature_edge_set += cf
    POST-ACCUM @@final_demographic_vertex_set += d
    POST-ACCUM @@final_customer_vertex_set += c
    POST-ACCUM @@final_feature_vertex_set += f;
```

Figure 7-10 shows the result of running `display_top_demographic`. The `Old_Cruis` `ers` demographic is selected because of the average weight of the affinity paths to all connected **Customer** elements. Because of the very small size of this sample dataset, there is only one connected **Customer**.

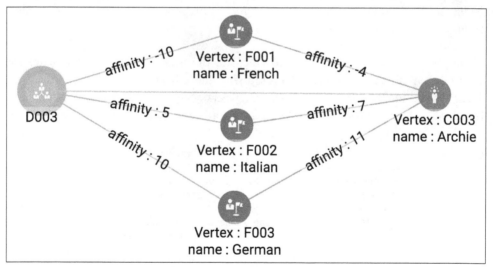

Figure 7-10. Output of the `display_top_demographic` query (see a larger version of this figure at https://oreil.ly/gpam0710)

Chapter Summary

In this chapter, we have looked into graph techniques to identify important vertices in a network. With a real-world use case, we have defined a referral network of doctors, patients, and specialists to demonstrate how analyzing its structure can help doctors make the proper referrals more efficiently.

We have also demonstrated how we can use a network of contextual information to improve customer recommendations. Our proposed solution includes a network of customers, demographics, features, and products. We have seen that analyzing the connections between these entities makes the recommendation more natural and scalable. This approach also helps us to avoid the cold start problem, which we often encounter using traditional database data structures.

In the next chapter, we will demonstrate the use of graph analytics in the field of cybersecurity. We will show how we can detect and mitigate cyberattacks against firewalls and block devices used in DDoS attacks.

CHAPTER 8

Strengthening Cybersecurity

In this chapter, we will describe how graphs can strengthen a cybersecurity system. We will demonstrate how graph analytics can identify root causes of a reported alert, detect bypassing of a firewall, and discover anomalous behavior such as flooding and footprinting. We will also show how graphs can find connections to suspicious IP addresses that may be responsible for attacks. After finishing this chapter, you should be able to:

- Understand how to apply graph concepts within the cybersecurity space
- Build graph queries to trace microservices
- Build graph queries to detect statistical anomalies

The Cost of Cyberattacks

We rely on technology constantly challenged by cyberattacks that aim to damage, disrupt, or maliciously control our IT infrastructure or our sensitive data. According to a Ponemon Institute survey in 2019, 66% of small to medium enterprises had experienced a cyberattack within the past 12 months.[1] These cyberattacks have become a daily threat to the functioning of our society. For example, leading up to the US presidential election of 2016, Russian hackers coordinated attacks on members of the Democratic Party to steer the election's outcome. According to the US National Security Agency (NSA), email accounts of more than 300 people affiliated with Hillary Clinton's campaign as well as those of other Democratic Party organizations were attacked.[2] These attacks led to information leaks that sought to harm Clinton's

---

1 Ponemon Institute, *2019 Global State of Cybersecurity in Small and Medium-Sized Businesses*, 2019, *https://www.cisco.com/c/dam/en/us/products/collateral/security/ponemon-report-smb.pdf*.

election campaign. In a more recent example, from February 2022, a hacker group executed a large-scale cyberattack on NVIDIA, one of the world's largest semiconductor chip companies. The attackers leaked credentials and employee information online. The perpetrators claimed they had access to more than one terabyte of company data, which they would release if NVIDIA did not meet their ransom demands.

Cyberattacks can damage governmental and commercial organizations as well as individuals, leading to political disruptions and financial implications. According to research into the costs of data breaches conducted by the Ponemon Institute and IBM, the average cost of a single data breach is $3.86 million globally. The US tops this chart with an average cost of $8.64 million for a single breach. A key challenge to minimizing these damages is identifying the breach as soon as possible. Researchers claim that organizations can save $1.12 million when a breach is detected within less than 200 days. However, they also suggest that the time to detect and contain a data breach is still, on average, up to 315 days for a malicious breach.[3] The average cost of a data breach is expected to be $5 million in 2023.[4]

Understanding how attackers operate is essential to building effective cybersecurity systems. The Common Attack Pattern Enumerations and Classifications (CAPEC)[5] initiative provides a standard set of categories and descriptions of cyberattack patterns that analysts, developers, and IT architects can use to enhance defenses. CAPEC divides these attack patterns into nine categories. For example, Abuse Existing Functionality is an attack pattern where the adversary manipulates the functionality of an application to achieve a malicious output not originally intended or depletes a resource to influence functionality. Collect and Analyze Information attack patterns focus on gathering, collecting, and stealing information. Methods used in this category include active querying and passive observation. The example case from the 2016 US presidential election falls under this category. Inject Unexpected Items includes attack patterns that focus on the ability to control or disrupt the behavior of an application. These attack patterns install and execute malicious code by exploiting an input on the target application.

---

2 Mark Mazzetti and Katie Benner, "12 Russian Agents Indicted in Mueller Investigation," *New York Times*, July 13, 2018, *https://www.nytimes.com/2018/07/13/us/politics/mueller-indictment-russian-intelligence-hacking.html*.

3 IBM Security, "Cost of a Data Breach Report 2020," 2020, *https://www.ibm.com/downloads/cas/QMXVZX6R*.

4 Acronis, *Acronis Cyber Protection Operation Center Report: Cyberthreats in the Second Half of 2022 – Data Under Attack*, 2022, *https://dl.acronis.com/u/rc/White-Paper-Acronis-Cyber-Protect-Cloud-Cyberthreats-Report-Year-End-2022-EN-US-221212.pdf*.

5 "CAPEC List Version 3.9," CAPEC, last updated October 21, 2021, *https://capec.mitre.org/data/index.html*.

Problem

A key challenge is monitoring the information flow so that vulnerabilities are visible and attacks are reported quickly. Suppose a microservice triggers another microservice that raises an alert. In that case, the system must be able to support deep-link analytics to trace the root cause or pattern matching for detecting anomalous behavior. With the growing volume of data stored, processed, and modified, it becomes more difficult to efficiently manage and extract relevant information from the data in real time.

The information above reveals that cybersecurity attack detection:

- Must process a large volume of data
- Must identify threats and trigger alerts as fast as possible
- Must assist in finding the original point of failure
- Is an urgent and growing business need remaining unmet at many enterprises

Solution

Cybersecurity aims to ensure confidentiality, integrity, and availability of information and to protect networks, devices, and data from unauthorized access or criminal use.[6] Graphs are a natural fit for modeling digital systems and detecting attacks because the internet itself, with its infrastructure and devices, is an interconnected network. It is the medium through which cyberattacks are made. An attack pattern can be analyzed as a chain of events, or a path within the graph consisting of individual processes. A process can be an object or interaction between different objects, depending on what we want to model.

Often, a large number of attacks are the work of relatively few perpetrators. This is the case with DDoS attacks. In a graph model, this translates to a hub structure. A graph-based cybersecurity system can seek out and analyze unexpected hubs.

We must consider four aspects when building a cyberattack defense system based on graphs. First, the data that we collect in our organization is a network in itself, but we must model its processes, assets, and operations as a unified real-time graph. Second, we must monitor key operations and vulnerable places in our graph. Therefore, we can use known attack patterns to express those within our graph and build our defense around them. Third, the graph can assist us when an actual attack occurs. It can help to identify where the attack takes place in the graph and trace both upstream to the source and downstream to the effects. Lastly, we collect historical data from

---

6 "What Is Cybersecurity?" Cybersecurity & Infrastructure Security Agency, February 1, 2021, *https://www.cisa.gov/news-events/news/what-cybersecurity*.

our organization and merge it with data from a third party, such as an anonymized dataset from McAfee or Norton, and feed that into machine learning models to predict future attacks.

A cybersecurity system must be able to integrate multiple data sources and process them in real time. For example, we need to integrate service information to know which microservice is called throughout our operations or server information to know where our applications are deployed and see the status of our virtual machines. Another common data source to include is user information regarding permission and authorizations. Graphs can integrate these many data types into a single view, where services, databases, and users are linked with an interconnected cybersecurity solution.

Implementing a Cybersecurity Graph

Using one of TigerGraph Cloud's starter kits, we will show how to implement a cyberattack detection system.

The Cybersecurity Threat Detection Starter Kit

Using TigerGraph Cloud, deploy a new cloud instance and select "Cybersecurity Threat Detection" as the starter kit. Once this starter kit is installed, load the data following the steps listed in the section "Load data and install queries for a starter kit" on page 50 in Chapter 3.

Graph Schema

The Cybersecurity Threat Detection Starter Kit schema has nine vertex types, with **Event** as the central vertex type. In total there are 1,325 vertices and 2,692 edges. The schema of this starter kit is shown in Figure 8-1.

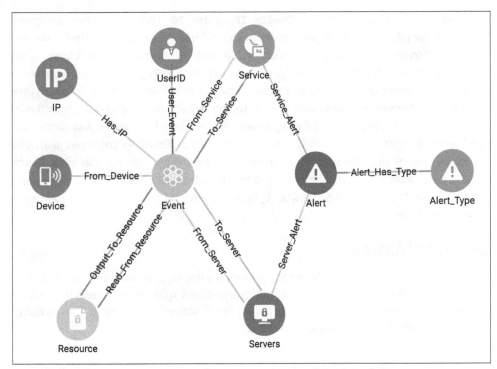

Figure 8-1. Graph Schema for the Cybersecurity Threat Detection Starter Kit (see a larger version of this figure at https://oreil.ly/gpam0801)

There are six types of events: authentication, firewall, login, request, read, and write. If an event is caused by a person or network device, it may be associated with a **UserID**, **Device**, or **IP** address. The **Event** may be an action that involves a **Service**, **Servers**, or a **Resource**. A **Service** or **Servers** can report an **Alert**, which has an **Alert_Type**. These vertex types are described in Table 8-1.

Table 8-1. Vertex types in the Cybersecurity Threat Detection graph model

Vertex type	Description
Event	An event triggered by an action in the system
IP	An IP address involved in an **Event**
UserID	A user ID referring to a user involved in an **Event**
Service	A microservice that performs the action of an **Event**
Alert	An alert triggered by a **Service** on a **Server**
Alert_Type	The alert type of an **Alert**
Server	A server on which an **Event** occurs
Resource	A resource used in an **Event**
Device	A device used in an **Event**

An **Event** can be associated with a **Device**, **IP**, or **UserID**. The associations are represented by the edge types **From_Device**, **Has_ip**, and user_event, respectively. We use two edge directions to indicate the relationships between **Event** and **Services**. If we want to know which **Services** belong to an **Event**, we use **To_Service**, or if we want to know the **Event** that belongs to the **Service**, we use **From_Service**. Similarly, we can find the **Server** elements that belong to the **Event** and vice versa, respectively, with the edges **To_Server** and **From_Server**. With edges **Output_To_Resource** and **Read_From_Resource**, respectively, we can find which **Event** is triggered with the **Resource** and which **Resource** are involved in an **Event**. We use **Service_Alert** and **Server_Alert** to indicate which **Service** and **Servers** are related to the reported **Alert**. And to find the **Alert_Type** for each **Alert**, we use the edge type **Alert_Has_Type**.

Queries and Analytics

The queries included in this starter kit present a sample of several different cyberattack patterns that can be detected using graph-based queries and analytics. Three of them correspond to attack pattern categories described by CAPEC: functionality bypassing, footprinting, and fingerprinting.

Detect bypassing of a firewall
Detect users who read from a resource that is protected by a firewall but who are somehow evading the firewall.

Suspicious IP detection
Given an IP address, find all connections to banned IP addresses within a given number of hops.

Flooding detection
Detect anomalies based on an unusually high number of requests to a service. Return the user who is responsible for the flooding event.

Footprinting detection
Detect anomalies based on an unusually high number of calls to an endpoint of a service in a short period of time. Return the user who is responsible for the footprinting event.

Tracing the source of an alert
Track down which user elements and IP addresses cause an alert for a corrupted file.

Some of these queries will display paths from events or IPs of interest back to the targeted related entities. Other queries are most easily understood by looking at the tabular results.

Detect bypassing of a firewall

A functionality bypass attack accesses services while bypassing functionality intended to provide system protection.[7] If access to a certain resource is protected by a firewall, then every read access should be preceded by a successful firewall event, as illustrated in Figure 8-2 (reading from right to left). The `firewall_bypass_detection` query detects users or IP addresses that somehow evaded firewall protection and read a protected resource. It uses both graph traversal and set algebra to group users into four different categories. We start with selecting all the **Resource** elements for which `Firewall_required == TRUE`. From those resources, we first traverse to all read **Event** vertices. This corresponds to the first hop shown in Figure 8-2.

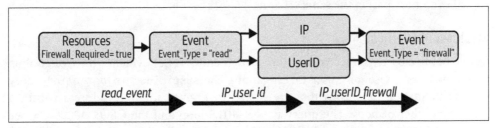

Figure 8-2. Traversal path and first two user sets for `firewall_bypass_detection` query

Then we identify four sets of users. In this case, we will consider both **UserID** and **IP** addresses as "users." The first set of users is simply everyone linked to the read events to firewall-protected resources:

```
ip_userid = SELECT t // set of all users accessing the events
    FROM read_events:s -((Has_IP|User_Event):e)- :t
    ACCUM t.@read_time += s.Start_Date;
```

The second set is the subset of those users who are also linked to a firewall event:

```
ip_userid_firewall = SELECT s  // set of all users accessing with firewall
    FROM ip_userid:s -((Has_IP|User_Event):e)- :event
    WHERE event.Event_Type == "firewall"
    ACCUM s.@firewall_time += event.Start_Date;
```

The third set is those users who read without also engaging in a firewall event. We can obtain this set by subtracting the second set from the first set:

```
ip_userid_no_firewall = ip_userid MINUS ip_userid_firewall;
```

---

7 "CAPEC-554: Functionality Bypass," CAPEC, last updated October 21, 2021, *https://capec.mitre.org/data/defi nitions/554.html*.

Our fourth and final set of users is those who had both a read and a firewall event (second set), but the read event took place prior to the firewall event, meaning that the firewall was bypassed:

```
ip_userid_bypass_firewall = SELECT s
    FROM ip_userid_firewall:s
    WHERE s.@read_time.size() > s.@firewall_time.size();
```

Table view is the best option for viewing these results. You'll find nine IDs in the `IP_userID_no_firewall` category and one IP in the `IP_userID_bypass_firewall` group. In a real use case, a user could have many read and firewall events over time, so timestamps, session IDs, or some other mechanism should be used to determine which events are part of the same session.

Suspicious IP detection

While being closely connected to an undesired entity is not evidence of wrongdoing, it is a justified cause for closer investigation. The `suspicious_ip_detection` query detects banned IP addresses that are linked to a given input IP address within a certain number of hops. The query uses a `WHILE` loop and the GSQL `ACCUM` clause's natural orientation for breadth-first search to efficiently discover shortest paths. It returns the number of banned IP addresses within a given number of hops and the number of the shortest paths to those banned IP addresses.

The query has three parameters: `input_ip` is the IP address to investigate, `depth` is how many hops away from `input_ip` we would like to travel (the default is 3), and `display_paths` is a Boolean indicator to specify whether to visualize the paths to the banned IP addresses:

```
CREATE QUERY suspicious_ip_detection(VERTEX<IP> input_ip, INT depth=3,
    BOOL diplay_paths=FALSE) {
```

The implementation follows a classic breadth-first unweighted shortest path search method. Each vertex has two accumulators to track information about shortest paths from `input_ip` to itself. We initialize a vertex set (called `start`) to be `input_ip` and initialize its accumulator `@num_shortest_paths` to 1 (because there is one path from `input_ip` to itself). Then, using a `WHILE` loop that iterates depth times, we repeat the following.

First we travel from `start` to all neighboring vertices that have not been visited. We know a vertex t has not been visited before if `t.@num_shortest_paths == 0`:

```
start = SELECT t                    // (1) Step to unvisited neighbors
    FROM start:s -(:e)- :t
    WHERE t.@num_shortest_paths == 0
```

Second, we account for shortest paths. When we arrive at a previously unvisited neighbor vertex t, it must have been along a shortest path. Therefore we update t's count of shortest paths to itself (`t.@num_shortest_paths`) and its collection of edges to display these paths (`t.@edge_list`):

```
ACCUM                              // (2) record # shortest paths
    t.@num_shortest_paths += s.@num_shortest_paths,
    t.@edge_list += e,
    t.@edge_list += s.@edge_list
```

Third, we check if the neighbor is tagged as a banned IP. If it is, we update three global accumulators. First, we add that neighbor to `@@nearby_ban ned_IPs`. Second, we add the number of shortest paths to t (`t.@num_short est_paths`) to `@@num_paths_to_banned_IPs`. Third, we append the paths themselves (`t.@edge_list`) to `@@paths_to_banned_IPs`:

```
POST-ACCUM CASE WHEN t.banned == TRUE THEN
    // (3) Track the banned IPs. Tally the paths to banned IPs
    @@nearby_banned_IPs += t,
    @@num_paths_to_banned_IPs += t.@num_shortest_paths,
    @@paths_to_banned_IPs += t.@edge_list
```

We then update the vertex set `start` to be the target set t. We repeat the three steps above, this time starting the traversal from our newly visited vertices of the previous round. We perform depth rounds to ensure that we move that many steps away from our input IP address, or until we run out of unvisited vertices (`WHILE start.size() > 0 LIMIT depth DO`).

Using the suggested inputs `input_ip` = 188.117.3.237 and `depth` = 4, we find 18 suspicious IPs, as shown in Figure 8-3. A higher depth will find even more, but the greater distance may decrease the likelihood of malfeasance.

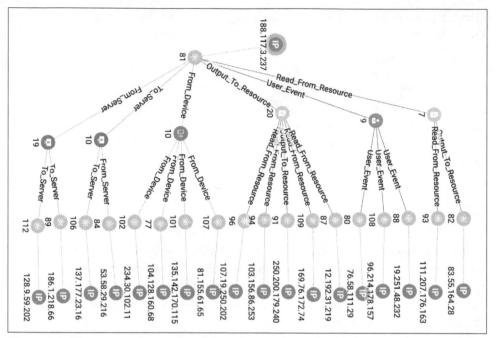

Figure 8-3. IPs connected to a given banned IP, within a depth of 4 (see a larger version of this figure at https://oreil.ly/gpam0803)

Flooding detection

The next two queries focus on detecting anomalies that may be a cyberattack. A *flooding* attack makes a large number of service requests to a target in an attempt to overwhelm it.[8] The `flooding_detection` query detects if one service receives many more requests than usual. This query is a good example of how GSQL's support for algorithmic programming and accumulators makes it easy to calculate statistics such as mean and standard deviation, and then to perform filtering based on those values.

The query includes one parameter, `n_sigma`, where `sigma>` refers to standard deviation. The default value is 3.0, which means that an IP is considered an outlier if its number of login events is more than three standard deviations above the mean. This parameter lets users easily tune the alert threshold.

The overall flow of this query consists of four single hops, where we eventually count the number of service requests per IP and compare it against the mean among all other IPs to determine if it is an outlier. Figure 8-4 shows a sample graph and how the events would be aggregated by the query.

---

8 "CAPEC-125: Flooding," CAPEC, last updated October 21, 2021, *https://capec.mitre.org/data/defini tions/125.html*.

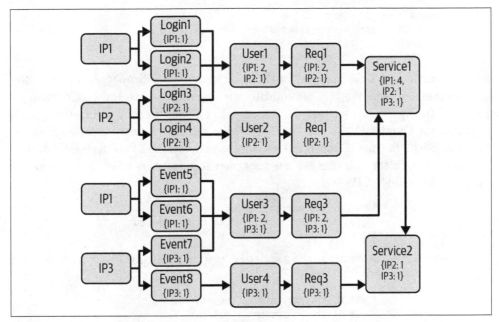

Figure 8-4. Accumulation in the `flooding_detection` query

In the first hop, we select all the login events per IP address by traversing from **IP** to **Event** via **Has_IP** edges. The clause WHERE event.Event_Type == "login" filters the selection to only include login events. Then we count the number of logins per IP address: @count_map += (i->1). The i->1 in this statement means that we add 1 for each occurrence by an IP address i. In the next few hops, we will transfer or regroup the counts from this step to compute the subtotal by user, request event, and service:

```
login_events = SELECT event
    FROM IPs:i -(Has_IP)- :event
    WHERE event.Event_Type == "login"
    ACCUM event.@count_map += (i->1);
```

In the second hop, we link the number of login events to the users. This is done by traversing from login_events to **User** over **User_Events** edges. We use user.@count_map += le.@count_map to group the previously counted events by user. In Figure 8-4, we see that User1 has two login events from IP1:

```
users = SELECT user
    FROM login_events:le -(User_Event)- :user
    ACCUM user.@count_map += le.@count_map;
```

In the third hop, we link to the request events of the users that we found in the second hop. The clause WHERE event.Event_Type == "request" checks that we are including only request events. Then we copy our previous counts to the request events:

```
events = SELECT event
    FROM users:u -(User_Event:e)- :event
    WHERE event.Event_Type == "request"
    ACCUM event.@count_map += u.@count_map;
```

In the fourth and final hop, we link the request events from the previous hop to **Service** elements. We also accumulate our ongoing counts and group them by **Service**. In Figure 8-4, we see that Service1 has a total of four login events from IP1, two via User1 and two via User3. Now we can compute the final statistics to determine whether the IP has triggered an unusual volume of requests. We do this in three steps. In the first step, we use AvgAccum accumulators to easily calculate the mean count among all IPs:

```
FOREACH (ip,cnt) in s.@count_map DO
    s.@mean += cnt    // @mean is an AvgAccum
END,
```

In the second step, we compute the standard deviation (using the @mean from the first pass):

```
FOREACH (ip,cnt) in s.@count_map DO
    s.@stdev += pow(cnt - s.@mean, 2)
END,
s.@stdev = sqrt(s.@stdev/(s.@count_map.size()-1)),
```

Lastly, we check for outliers by comparing each login count with the mean and standard deviation. If the count is larger than the mean plus the product of n_sigma (our threshold value set in the parameter) and the standard deviation, then the IP's login behavior is an outlier:

```
CASE WHEN s.@stdev != 0 THEN
    // calculate the outlier
    FOREACH (ip,cnt) in s.@count_map DO
        CASE WHEN cnt-s.@mean > n_sigma*s.@stdev THEN
            @@outlier_list += Result_Tuple(
                                ip,s,cnt,s.@mean,s.@stdev)
        END
    END
END
```

For simplicity, we did not include the time aspect of each login and request event. In a real-life scenario, a login event must precede its associated request event, and the request events must occur within a small enough time window to be considered an attack. In this example, we kept it simple and only demonstrated how graphs can obtain event triggers over the entire network to calculate individual statistics.

Running the query with n_sigma = 3 finds IP 216.61.220.149 listed twice in the table view, once for high use of service 11 and once for service 12.

Footprint detection

Another type of cyberattack is footprinting. Footprinting calls many endpoints of a service in a short time in an attempt to understand its configuration, behavior, and vulnerabilities.[9] The footprinting_detection query demonstrates how we can detect users carrying out these operations. The implementation is very similar to the flooding detection query in the sense that it computes the mean, standard deviation, and outlier to detect **Users** with anomalous behavior.

This query has three parameters: n_sigma sets the threshold for determining an outlier, and start_date and end_date determine the time window in which we want to detect footprinting.

First, we select all **Events** that are of type "request" and that occurred between start_date and end_date:

```
events = SELECT s
    FROM events:s
    WHERE s.Start_Date > start_date AND s.Start_Date < end_date
        AND s.Event_Type == "request";
```

Then, we record all the endpoint requests by each user. We do this by traversing from **Events** to **User** using the **User_Event** edge type. We add every endpoint that the user has called to event.@api_map. Because the maps are attached to each event, each event will have a single map entry:

```
events = SELECT event
    FROM events:event -(User_Event)- :user
    ACCUM event.@api_map += (user -> event.Endpoint); // make map
```

Then we traverse from **Events** to **Service** to group the endpoint requests by service:

```
services = SELECT s
    FROM events:ev -(To_Service)- :s
    ACCUM s.@api_map += ev.@api_map
```

We then compute outlier statistics as we did in the flooding detection query. There is a small difference here between the flooding detection and footprinting detection queries. The flooding detection's MapAccum value type is SumAccum<INT>. It is already a sum. In footprinting detection, the MapAccum value type is SetAccum<STRING>: a collection of names of endpoints. To compute a mean, we need to know how many endpoints are in each set, thus cnt.size():

```
FOREACH (user,cnt) IN s.@api_map DO
    s.@mean += cnt.size()
END,
```

---

9 "CAPEC-169: Footprinting," CAPEC, last updated October 21, 2021, *https://capec.mitre.org/data/defini tions/169.html.*

The standard deviation and outlier computations are exactly analogous to the computations in the flooding detection query. Running the query with the default input values shows that user 1 has unusually high use of services 13 and 14.

Tracing the source of an alert

In our last example, an alert has already been raised, and we follow a path in the graph to track down the users and their IP addresses that may have caused an alert. The path we will follow is illustrated in Figure 8-5. We start from the most recent **Alert** of a particular **Alert_Type** that was raised and then trace backward to its cause. From the **Alert**, we follow links to the **Service** that raised the **Alert**. If the **Alert_Type** is data corruption of a file, the **Alert** would be noticed during a file read **Event**, so we trace back to that. A write **Event** would have caused the corruption, so we trace back to that. Finally, we trace back to the **UserID** and the **IP** that performed that write. The overall flow of this query is eight hops in a straight line. With traditional relational databases, this would be eight joins, which is prohibitively slow. In contrast, we can obtain this insight in real time by traversing the graph model directly.

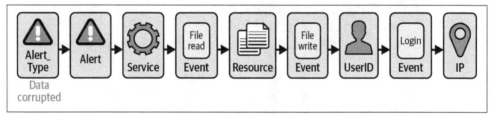

Figure 8-5. Path traversal to file the source of an alert

The `alert_source_tracing` query has three input parameters: `alert_type` is the type of alert to trace; `num_days` is the number of days to look back starting from the moment the alert was raised; and `top_ip` is the quantity of IP addresses the query will return:

```
CREATE QUERY alert_source_tracking(STRING alert_type="Data Corrupted",
    INT num_days=8, INT top_ip=20) {
```

The two MaxAccum accumulators `@latest_alert_time` and `@latest_read_time` compute and record the times of the most recent alert and the most recent read events responsible for the alerts, respectively. `SumAccum<INT> @count` counts the number of write events per user or IP, so that we know which IP addresses are the most prolific. The `ListAccum<EDGE> @path_list` collects all the edges needed to represent the paths from the input `alert_type` back to the **IP** vertices that seem to have triggered those alerts.

We group the eight hops into four two-hop stages. In the first stage, we get **Alerts** of the given `alert_type` and then trace back to the affected **Service**. Each **Alert**'s date is added to its **Service**'s `@latest_alert_time` accumulator. Because it is a MaxAccum, it automatically retains the most recent alert date. We add the edges that we traverse for these two hops to `@path_list` accumulators at the endpoints of our traversal so far:

```
service = SELECT serv
    FROM alert_types:s -(Alert_Has_Type:e1)- :alert
                        -(Service_Alert:e2)- :serv
    ACCUM
        serv.@latest_alert_time += alert.Alert_Date,
        serv.@path_list += e1, serv.@path_list += e2;
```

In the second stage, we traverse back from these services to files that were read and that triggered the alert. We traverse two more hops to go from these **Services** back to the file **Resource** via a read **Event**. We only consider events that were reasonable triggers for the alert, occurring within one day before the alert:

```
resource = SELECT res
    FROM service:s -(From_Service:e1)- :event
                   -(Read_From_Resource:e2)- :res
    WHERE datetime_diff(s.@latest_alert_time,event.Start_Date)
        BETWEEN 0 AND 3600*24
        AND event.Event_Type == "read"
```

After selecting the appropriate file read events, we perform two tasks. First, we record the time of the most recent read to each file:

```
    res.@latest_read_time += event.Start_Date,
```

Second, we transfer the partial paths from the first hop to the **Resource** vertices and extend the paths with the edges that connect **Service** to **Resource**:

```
    res.@path_list += s.@path_list,
    res.@path_list += e1, res.@path_list += e2;
```

In the third stage, we trace back from those files to users who wrote to those files. This double-hop traversal is structurally similar to the stage two traversal. This stage starts from **Resource** vertices to **User** vertices using the **Output_To_Resource** and **User_Event** edges. It accepts events that are writes and that occurred up to `num_days` days before the latest read. In addition, we increment `user.@count` to store the number of times the user has written to the file, and we again transfer and extend the paths:

```
users = SELECT user
    FROM resource:s -(Output_To_Resource:e1)- :event
                    -(User_Event:e2)- :user
    WHERE datetime_diff(s.@latest_read_time, event.Start_Date)
        BETWEEN 0 AND 3600*24*num_days
```

```
        AND event.Event_Type == "write"
    ACCUM user.@count += 1, // Tally writes per user
      user.@path_list += s.@path_list,
      user.@path_list += e1, user.@path_list += e2;
```

In this final stage of the query, we trace back from those user vertices, through login events, ending at the IP addresses that caused the alert. We start our traversal from the **User** vertices and perform a double hop using **User_Event** and **Has_IP** edges. We use accumulators to transfer and extend the paths one more time. The paths now have length 8, from **Alert_Type** to **IP**. We also compute the number of times a user has written to the file per IP address. Finally, we sort the list of IPs by write count and only take the top_ip addresses to return:

```
login_IP = SELECT ip
    FROM users:s -(User_Event:e1)- :event
                -(Has_IP:e2)- :ip
    WHERE event.Event_Type == "login"
    ACCUM ip.@count += s.@count, // Tally user-writes per IP
      ip.@path_list += s.@path_list,
      ip.@path_list += e1, ip.@path_list += e2
    ORDER BY ip.@count DESC
    LIMIT top_ip;
```

Using the default input values (alert_type = "Data Corrupted", num_days = 7, and top_ip = 3), we find that the top IP sources of file corruption have 31, 18, and 11 events, respectively, of a user writing to an eventually corrupted file, within the time window. The visual display of the paths explains how we arrived at these sums.

Chapter Summary

In this chapter, we have shown how graphs can strengthen cybersecurity. Cyberattacks follow patterns, and these patterns can be represented as a graph query. We demonstrated detection queries for three types of attacks, a risk-assessment query that measures the proximity to banned IPs, and a source-tracing query to see who and what caused an alert.

CHAPTER 9

Analyzing Airline Flight Routes

Graph algorithms are an essential tool for performing graph analytics. While one can study the algorithms themselves from a textbook, a practitioner needs to gain hands-on experience using a graph algorithm library and applying algorithms to real-world use cases. This chapter will use graph algorithms to analyze a global airline flight route network. We will apply three categories of algorithms: shortest path, centrality, and community detection.

After completing this chapter, you should be able to:

- Install and run TigerGraph GDS algorithms
- Set required and optional parameters for algorithms
- Modify a GSQL algorithm or other query to make a customized version
- Use the Explore Graph feature to display selected vertices and edges, including creating an attribute filter
- Understand the application of shortest path, centrality, and community algorithms to a routing network

Goal: Analyzing Airline Flight Routes

Schiphol Airport in Amsterdam is located in the relatively small country of the Netherlands. Despite the Netherlands having only 17 million residents, its biggest airport is a top-tier hub for transferring over 25 million passengers and 1.6 million tonnes of cargo in 2021.[1] To achieve such a feat, airports like Schiphol face the challenge of scheduling hundreds of aircraft for thousands of flights. Schiphol Airport had almost 500 million air transport movements in 2019, just prior to the COVID-19 pandemic. An airport is a time-sensitive business that operates under complex logistical constraints such as flight connectivity for each route. The goal of an airport is to maximize the total profit by scheduling these routes in the most cost-efficient way.

Once airlines have established their flight schedules, passengers then have the task of choosing the routes that make the most sense for them. For some routes, fliers will be able to choose from multiple options. Fliers may want a route that makes the fewest connections, or they may want the shortest route. Today, fliers can use online search tools that can incorporate the benefits and costs of each flight, such as the shortest route. Just as the PageRank algorithm was the start for Google's web search utility, shortest path algorithms were the core for airline flight search tools. Some fliers seek additional analysis of the flight network. Persons who fly to a wide range of destinations on a regular basis, such as salespersons and consultants, may want to know which airports are the best hubs.

Some industries may benefit from finding communities of connected airports where there are actually *fewer* connections to the larger network of airports as a whole. For example, a wildlife photography tour agency may be interested in selling package tours in a remote area. If that area is less connected to large hubs, it is likely to be more remote and therefore more popular with photographers looking to get "off the beaten track." Ideally, that remote region would have its own local community of flight routes to facilitate travel to different locations. Another example might be a consultant for an airline company looking for underserved routes. A graph of what communities are relatively isolated from the rest of the world could be a starting point for suggestions for new routes to open up.

Solution: Graph Algorithms on a Flight Route Network

Flight traffic forms a network of airports connected by flights. Therefore, graph analytics is a natural way to visualize and analyze routes and their influence on airport business. We can use directional graphs to incorporate the departure location and the destination of each flight and use edge attributes to include costs such as distance, time, or carbon exhaust. Just by forming the graph, we can easily make basic observations such as the number of incoming or outgoing flights from an airport. However, by using graph algorithms, we can perform more complex analyses such as identifying the most influential airports and the most cost-efficient paths.

---

1 "Our Most Important Traffic and Transport Figures," Schiphol, accessed May 24, 2023, *https://www.schi phol.nl/en/schiphol-group/page/traffic-review*.

We can define the most efficient route for our use case using edge attributes. For example, if we are looking for the shortest route, we can include the flight distance as an attribute. In other cases, where we are looking for the cheapest flight, we can include the price of each flight between airports, or we can include CO_2 emissions on each edge attribute if we are interested in finding the most sustainable flight option.

Implementing an Airport and Flight Route Analyzer

Now we show some of these graph algorithms in action, using another TigerGraph Cloud Starter Kit.

The Graph Algorithms Starter Kit

Using TigerGraph Cloud, deploy a new cloud database instance and select "Graph Algorithms - Centrality Algorithms" as the use case. Once this starter kit is installed, load the data following the steps listed in the section "Load data and install queries for a starter kit" on page 50 in Chapter 3.

Graph Schema and Dataset

The dataset represents actual airports and flight routes circa 2014 obtained from OpenFlights.org.[2] There is only one vertex type, **Airport**, with attributes for ID, name, city, country, IATA code,[3] latitude, and longitude. An additional attribute called score is included as a generic placeholder to store the result of an algorithm. For example, if we were to run PageRank on the graph, that would generate a PageRank score for each vertex. We could store those values in this attribute. We have data for 7,935 airports. Having a single vertex type makes this graph ideal for direct analysis with standardized graph algorithms, most of which assume a graph with a single vertex type.

The two edge types, **flight_route** and **flight_to**, come from the same source file *routes.dat*, a list of scheduled commercial service from one airport to another. The table has a row for each airline that offers nonstop service from one city to another, regardless of frequency. The **flight_to** edges are directed. The **flight_route** edges are undirected, meaning there is nonstop service between these cities, but ignoring the direction. There are 19,268 **flight_route** edges and 37,606 **flight_to** edges, almost twice the number of **flight_route** edges, meaning nonstop service is usually

---

2 "Airline, Airport and Route Data," OpenFlights.org (*http://openflights.org*), accessed May 24, 2023, *https://openflights.org/data.html*.

3 The International Air Transport Association assigns each major airport a three-letter code, such as AMS for Amsterdam Schiphol Airport or CDG for Paris Charles de Gaulle Airport. The vertex attribute ID is an internal number used only in this dataset.

bidirectional. The simplicity of the schema in Figure 9-1 is a good reminder of the difference between schema complexity (here, one vertex type and two edge types) and data complexity (about 8,000 vertices and 57,000 edges).

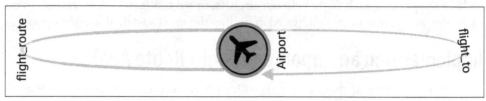

Figure 9-1. Schema for flight route dataset (see a larger version of this figure at https://oreil.ly/gpam0901)

Installing Algorithms from the GDS Library

One of the beauties of graph algorithms is that they have standard definitions and will work on any graph that meets their conditions. For example, a shortest path algorithm for unweighted edges should work on *any* graph. As of May 2023, the TigerGraph GDS (Graph Data Science) Library contains more than 55 algorithms, available on GitHub.[4] They are offered in two formats to let users choose convenience over performance: schema-free and template.

Schema-free algorithms are written as open source GSQL queries where the vertex type, edge type, and relevant attributes of vertices or edges are runtime parameters. They only need to be installed once, and then they are ready to be used for any graph. Template algorithms are written in proto-GSQL. The user does not perform an explicit install operation. Template algorithms are executed using CALL instead of INSTALL and RUN. If a CALL statement specifies schema details (vertex type, edge type, and attributes) that have not been CALLed before, then the database installs an optimized version of the template query with those schema details hardcoded. CALL then runs this schema-specific algorithm. If a CALL statement uses schema details that have been used before, then the database skips installation and just runs the installed algorithm. Table 9-1 compares the two types.

Table 9-1. Comparing schema-free and template algorithms

	Schema-free algorithms	Template algorithms
Installation	Once	Once for each combination (vertex type, edge type, graph attributes) used in a CALL
Runtime performance	Somewhat slower, may use more memory	Optimized: faster and less memory

---

4 "tigergraph / gsql-graph-algorithms," GitHub, accessed May 24, 2023, *https://github.com/tigergraph/gsql-graph-algorithms*.

	Schema-free algorithms	Template algorithms
Commands	INSTALL, RUN	CALL
User customization	Simple, just like GSQL queries	Indirect, due to template nature

We will use schema-free algorithms. Follow these steps to install the schema-free algorithms we will use to analyze the flight route network:

1. On the Write Queries page of GraphStudio, look for and click the Add New Query button (a dark circle with a + symbol) at the bottom of the GSQL queries pane.

2. A panel will pop up.

3. Click CHOOSE FROM LIBRARY.

A new panel with a list of algorithm categories appears. Click on the arrow to the right of Centrality. Select the boxes next to Betweenness Centrality and Closeness Centrality. Also select Community → Connected Components and Path → Shortest Path. Then click INSTALL. Installation will take a few minutes.

Queries and Analytics

This starter kit covers three categories of graph algorithms, which all provide useful answers and analyses about flight routes. In addition, there are a few utility queries that help to prepare the data in order to inspect the individual records.

Utility queries
Calculate flight distances

- The original dataset does not tell us the distances traveled. This query uses latitude and longitude to calculate the length of a direct flight between two airports.[5]

Search for vertex

- Not every airport in the dataset has an IATA code. To identify an airport, we may need to search based on the city or airport name. This query provides a general vertex search function.

Path algorithms
Many travelers want to find the routes with the fewest connections, shortest distance traveled, or lowest cost. The Shortest Path algorithm will find the route from one vertex to another having the fewest segments. The Shortest Path,

---

5 In real-life situations, flights often take slightly indirect routes to benefit from wind currents or to avoid restricted airspace.

Weighted algorithm works with data where each edge has a numeric weight that could represent a real-world factor like time, distance, or dollars. It finds the path from one vertex to another that has the least total weight.

Centrality algorithms

This kit uses Closeness Centrality and Betweenness Centrality to rank the routing importance of airports in two different ways.

Community detection algorithms

In a routing network, there are more routing options available to travel within one community than to travel between communities. We run the Strongly Connected Component algorithm to see what it reveals about the worldwide airline route network.

Calculate route length

The first step when using this starter kit is to run the `calculate_route_length` query. This query calculates the length in miles of each route, using the latitudes and longitudes of the airports. The query uses the haversine formula to account for the curvature of the earth. The arc length of each route is then stored in each vertex's attribute called `miles`.

When running the query, you need to specify the edge type. Run the query twice: once with edge type **flight_to**, and another time with edge type **flight_route**. Were you to run this query in a GSQL command line shell, the commands and output would be like the following:

```
RUN QUERY calculate_route_length("flight_to", True)
[
  {
    "@@dontChangeList": [],
    "@@numChanged": 37606
  }
]

RUN QUERY calculate_route_length("flight_route", True)
[
  {
    "@@dontChangeList": [],
    "@@numChanged": 38535
  }
]
```

Measure and analyze centrality

Which airports have the most connecting flights? Which airports would be the best base of operations for a person or company who wants to travel conveniently to anywhere? If this is what you want to know, use a centrality algorithm. Centrality is a measure of the importance of a vertex based on its relative position in a network. There are several ways to define centrality; as of October 2022, the TigerGraph GDS algorithm library had 12. We will try two of them, closeness and betweenness, comparing their definitions and their results.

The closeness centrality score of a vertex v is the inverse of the average of shortest path distances from v to other vertices in the graph. For example, in a four-vertex graph, if the shortest path distances from v to the other three vertices are 1, 1, and 2, then closeness$(v) = 1/(1+1+2) = 0.25$. In an airline route network, a high closeness centrality score for an airport means it has a large number of nonstop and one-stop routes to other airports. A small regional airport generally has low closeness centrality because of the low number of destinations directly reachable from it.

In the query selection pane, click on the `tg_closeness_cent` algorithm query. Table 9-2 lists the full set of parameters. Many of these parameters are standard features of TigerGraph GDS algorithms, so we'll spend a little time reviewing them here.

Table 9-2. Parameter for tg_closeness_cent algorithm

Parameter	Description	Default
SET<STRING> v_type	Vertex types to use	(empty set of strings)
SET<STRING> e_type	Edge types to use	(empty set of strings)
SET<STRING> rev_e_type	Reverse edge types to use	(empty set of strings)
INT max_hops	If >=0, look only this far from each vertex	10
INT top_k	Output only this many scores (scores are always sorted highest to lowest)	100
BOOL wf	Whether to use Wasserman-Faust normalization for multicomponent graphs	True
BOOL print_results	If true, output JSON to standard output	True
STRING result_attr	If not empty, store centrality values in FLOAT format to this vertex attribute	(empty string)
STRING file_path	If not empty, write output to this file in CSV format	(empty string)
BOOL display_edges	If true, include the graph's edges in the JSON output so that the full graph can be displayed	False

The first three parameters (`v_type`, `e_type`, `rev_e_type`) specify which vertices and edges of the graph the algorithm should run on. Some algorithms are designed for directed edges, some for undirected edges. It's important to check the documentation[6] to see which type of edge is preferred or permitted. Reverse edges may or may not exist in a graph; they are an option available to the schema designer.

The next three parameters (`max_hops`, `top_k`, `wf`) are specific to `closeness_central ity`, though `max_hops` and `top_k` appear in several other algorithms. For closeness centrality, vertices further away than the `max_hops` limit will not be considered in the computation of average distance. `top_k` is available for algorithms that produce results that can be treated as a ranking. The `wf` parameter enables a modified measure of closeness centrality that normalizes scores in the case of a graph that is composed of disconnected subgraphs of different sizes.

The last four parameters (`print_results`, `result_attr`, `file_path`, `display_edges`) are standard parameters for the user to specify how they want the results to be delivered. The default is to stream JSON text to the standard output.

Run `tg_closeness_cent` with `v_type` = `Airport`, `e_type` = **`flight_to`**, and `rev_e_type` = `reverse_flight_to`. The other parameters can be left at their default values.

The results show that the top 10 airports are FRA, CDG, LHR, DXB, AMS, LAX, JFK, YYZ, IST, and ORD, which decode to Frankfurt, Charles de Gaulle (Paris), London Heathrow, Domodedovo (Moscow), Amsterdam, Los Angeles, John F. Kennedy (New York), Toronto, Istanbul, and O'Hare (Chicago). These airports are widely recognized as the busiest and more important hub airports in the world, so the results seem logical.

We next calculate betweenness centrality. The betweenness centrality of a vertex is defined as the number of shortest paths that pass through it, divided by the total number of shortest paths of the graph. An example of high betweenness is the Panama Canal. It is a part of the sea journey between ports on the Atlantic Ocean and ports on the Pacific Ocean, giving it high betweenness centrality even though Panama itself is less often the start or end of a journey. Gas stations are also often placed at intersections with high betweenness centrality. Though they are typically not the start or end of a journey, it's useful for gas stations to be along the routes of many travelers, each of whom has a different start and end route.

Next, run `tg_betweenness_cent` with the same parameter settings you used for `tg_closeness_cent`. It takes longer to run because betweenness centrality considers paths from anywhere to anywhere, whereas closeness centrality considers only one hub vertex.

---

6 "TigerGraph Graph Data Science Library," TigerGraph, accessed May 24, 2023, *https://docs.tiger graph.com/graph-ml/current/intro*.

All algorithms are not created equal. Check your algorithm library's documentation for guidance on the expected time and resources to run an algorithm.

For betweenness, the top 10 airports are Domodedovo, Peking (Beijing), Chicago O'Hare, Istanbul, Bogota, Denver, Atlanta, Manila, Bueno Aires, and Dallas–Fort Worth. These results are quite different and perhaps surprising. Remember that betweenness gives a high score to bottlenecks or gateways like the Panama Canal. We can speculate that Bogota and Buenos Aires are important gateway airports for regional airports in South America. Manila may play a similar role for the Philippines and Southeast Asia.

Moreover, the standard betweenness algorithm considers all shortest paths to be equally important, so getting from LAX (Los Angeles) to JFK (New York) has the same importance as getting from SXE (Sale, Australia) to QGQ (Attu, Greenland). We did not take passenger volume or number of flights into consideration. If we had this data, we would then want to modify the algorithm to compute a weighted betweenness score. Since TigerGraph GDS algorithms are written in GSQL, they can be modified by a GSQL user. In the next section, we will try our hand at customizing algorithms.

Find shortest paths

First we will use the shortest path algorithm for unweighted edges; this will tell us which airline routes have the fewest stops. Then we will run the shortest path algorithm for positive edge weights, which will tell us which routes travel the fewest miles. Of course, there can be multiple paths that have the same path length. Some algorithms find *a* shortest path, and some find *all* shortest paths. In a weighted graph, it takes only a little more bookkeeping to find the set of shortest paths from one starting point to *every* other vertex as it does to find the shortest path to just one destination vertex. This is because, for a weighted graph, every edge in the graph must be traversed in order to be certain that the algorithm has found the absolute shortest path. Therefore, the shortest path algorithms in the library are the one-source-all-destinations variety.

We need to know the ID for the source vertex. Unfortunately, it is difficult to select an airport ID system that uses names that everyone knows. City names are insufficient, because some cities have multiple airports, and while many travelers know IATA codes like LAX, this database extends to smaller airports that do not have IATA codes. The OpenFlights.org data tables use numerical IDs of their own devising. For example, the ID for LAX is 3484. As a compromise, our graph database concatenates the IATA code with the OpenFlights.org ID, so our ID for LAX is LAX-3484.

To help users find an airport's ID, the starter kit includes a query called _search_for_vertex. It has three parameters: a vertex type, the name of an attribute of that vertex type, and the value you are looking for. The query returns the IDs and names of all matching vertices. For example if we wanted to find the ID for Cleveland's main airport, we would run the following query:

```
RUN QUERY _search_for_vertex("Airport","city","Cleveland")
```

We get three matching airports. Cleveland Hopkins International Airport is the major one, so let's use CLE-3486. Looking at GraphStudio's table view, you will see output like Table 9-3.

Table 9-3. Search results for airports located in Cleveland

v_id	v_type	Result.id	Result.name
HDI-8793	Airport	HDI-8793	Hardwick Field
CLE-3486	Airport	CLE-3486	Cleveland Hopkins International Airport
BKL-8544	Airport	BKL-8544	Burke Lakefront Airport

Now run the shortest path algorithm, tg_shortest_ss_no_wt, with these arguments:

```
source = CLE-3486
v_type = Airport
e_type = flight_to
```

Look at either the JSON or tabular output. It's a lot of data (remember we have nearly eight thousad airports), and many of the airport IDs are unfamiliar. Table 9-4 shows one of the shortest paths. While the data may be correct and useful for a database, it's not very human friendly.

Table 9-4. Example of shortest path from CLE to another airport

v_id	v_type	ResultSet.@min_dis	ResultSet.@path_list
ZQZ-10940	Airport	4	["CLE-3486", "YYZ-193", "TPE-2276", "SJW-6347", "ZQZ-10940"]

In the next section, we will modify the algorithm to give us more readable output and to only show results a certain distance from the source vertex using edge weights.

Modify a GSQL algorithm to customize the output

Let's make two changes to customize the output. First, click on the Save As icon on the menu bar above the GSQL code window. Name the copied algorithm *tg_short-*

est_ss_modified. We will output only those paths that are no more than three hops long, and we will add the city name as another field in the output. We make edits in four places:

1. Find the line:

   ```
   ListAccum<VERTEX> @path_list;
   ```

   Insert another line below it:

   ```
   ListAccum<STRING> @city_list;
   ```

   This defines data structures to hold lists of cities.

2. About 10 lines below that, find the line:

   ```
   s.@path_list = s;
   ```

   Insert this line above it:

   ```
   s.@city_list = s.city,
   ```

   It's important to insert this line above, in order to get the right punctuation. That is, we want to end up with:

   ```
   s.@city_list = s.city, // Added
   s.@path_list = s;
   ```

3. Find the other line that updates `@path_list`:

   ```
   t.@path_list = s.@path_list + [t],
   ```

   Insert another line below it:

   ```
   t.@city_list = s.@city_list + [t.city],
   ```

4. Find the line near the end that prints the paths:

   ```
   PRINT ResultSet[ResultSet.@min_dis, ResultSet.@path_list];
   ```

   Modify and extend it so that it becomes:

   ```
   PRINT ResultSet[ResultSet.@min_dis, ResultSet.@path_list,
     ResultSet.@city_list]
   WHERE ResultSet.@path_list.size() <= 3;
   ```

Save and install this algorithm. Run it with the same input parameters as before. Now you should see some recognizable paths, such as the examples in Table 9-5.

Table 9-5. Examples of shortest paths with the addition of city names

v_id	v_type	ResultSet.@city_list	ResultSet.@min_dis	ResultSet.@path_list
LAR-5746	Airport	["Cleveland", "Denver", "Laramie"]	2	["CLE-3486", "DEN-3751", "LAR-5746"]
BQK-5725	Airport	["Cleveland", "Atlanta", "Brunswick"]	2	["CLE-3486", "ATL-3682", "BQK-5725"]

Let's now run the shortest path algorithm for positive weights. This version is better for travelers who want to minimize the distance traveled. If our weights were CO_2 exhaust instead of miles, we would be minimizing carbon emissions.

While there may be an algorithm already in the starter kit, let's go to the GitHub repository for the algorithm library and look for the latest version. In a web browser, go to *https://github.com/tigergraph/gsql-graph-algorithms/blob/ master/algorithms*. From there, drill down several categories and subcategories— *Path → shortest_path → weighted → positive → traceback*—to eventually find *tg_shortest_ss_pos_wt_tb.gsql*.

If you do not already have the *tg_shortest_ss_pos_wt_tb* query in GraphStudio, then click the Create Query (+ symbol) button in the GraphStudio query selection pane. Name the new query *tg_shortest_ss_pos_wt_tb*. Copy the text from *tg_short- est_ss_pos_wt_tb.gsql* in the GitHub repository and use it to replace the existing query text in GraphStudio. Save and install the query. Run the algorithm with the following settings:

```
Vertex_id = CLE-3486
v_type = Airport
e_type = flight_to
wt_attr = miles
wt_type = INT
output_limit = 10000
```

One might think that fewest miles would correlate well with fewest connections, but in the results you will see some paths that have 8 and even 10 hops. To narrow down the results, let's make one edit to the algorithm: only display paths that have a cost value under 3,000 (representing a total trip distance shorter than three thousand miles). That will limit the results to North America.

Find the lines that print the output:

```
PRINT tmp[tmp.@min_path_heap.top().cost as cost, tmp.@path_list as p];
```

Add a WHERE clause (and move the semicolon) to change each of them to:

```
PRINT tmp[tmp.@min_path_heap.top().cost as cost, tmp.@path_list as p]
    WHERE tmp.@min_path_heap.top().cost < 3000;
```

These shorter results still have some long paths. For example, one can go from Cleveland to ZKE (the small town of Kashechewan, Ontario, reachable only by airport and seasonal ice road) in five hops, via YYZ (Toronto), YTS (Timmins), YMO (Moosonee), and YFA (Fort Albany), all in just 820 miles. This five-hop route is a fairly straight path going north. It requires multiple hops because the northern towns are very small with limited air service.

Find and analyze communities

We expect the global airport network to be highly interconnected, but there are parts of the world that are served only by smaller regional airports. Will a community detection algorithm point these out to us?

In a directed graph, a strongly connected component (SCC) is the maximal set of vertices such that every vertex can reach every other vertex in the component. In an airline route network, if an airline offers direct service between two airports in both directions, then meeting the SCC requirement is easy. In some areas where there is less demand, the direct service is not bidirectional. That is where we may find a break, separating the graph into separate SCCs.

Run `tg_scc` with the following parameter settings:

```
v_type_set = Airport
e_type_set = flight_to
rev_e_type_set = reverse_flight_to
top_k_dist = 100
print_limit = 10000
result_attr = score
```

`top_k_dist` determines how many communities to output, and `output_limit` is how many individual vertices to output. The community ID of each vertex will be stored on the vertex attribute called `score`.

Switch the output to tabular results. There are two tables to display. The table for `@@cluster_dist_heap`, shown in Table 9-6, tells us that the largest community includes 3,354 airports. Then there is one community with 10 airports, one with 8, three with 4 airports, three with 2 airports, and 4,545 singleton airports.

Table 9-6. Airport community sizes and counts

csize	num
3,354	1
10	1
8	1
4	3
2	3
1	4,545

The output also includes a full list of all the vertices along with their community IDs. All vertices with the same community ID are members of the same community. Scanning the list of eight thousand vertices is not convenient, so let's make another algorithm modification to get friendlier output.

Use Save As to create a copy of the algorithm query called `tg_scc_modified`. Make the following three edits:

1. In the top section containing the `Accum` declarations, add the declaration below:

```
MapAccum<INT, ListAccum<VERTEX>> @@cluster_member_map;
```

This data structure will record the list of vertices belonging to each community.

2. Near the end, in the output results section and just after several `clear()` statements, find the following block:

```
v_all = SELECT s
  FROM v_all:s
  POST-ACCUM
    @@cluster_size_map += (s.@sum_cid -> 1);
```

Insert one additional line in the `POST-ACCUM` clause, and add the five-line `FOREACH` block afterward:

```
v_all = SELECT s
  FROM v_all:s
  POST-ACCUM
    @@cluster_member_map += (s.@sum_cid -> s), //added
    @@cluster_size_map += (s.@sum_cid -> 1);
FOREACH (cid, member_list) IN @@cluster_member_map DO
  IF member_list.size() == 1 OR member_list.size() > 50 THEN
    @@cluster_member_map.remove(cid);
  END;
END;
```

The line in the `POST-ACCUM` block builds the list of member lists, and the `FOREACH` block removes the lists that are too small or too big for our interest.

3. Find the line:

```
    PRINT @@cluster_dist_heap;
```

Add the following line after it:

```
    PRINT @@cluster_member_map; // added
```

Save and install the `tg_scc_modified algorithm` query. Run it with the following settings. This time, we will exclude the list of individual vertices:

```
    v_type_set = Airport
    e_type_set = flight_to
    rev_e_type_set = reverse_flight_to
    top_k_dist = 100
    print_limit = 10000
print_results = false
result_attr = score
```

Look at the Table View results for `@@cluster_member_map`. The results show a community 1048630 with four members: ["AKB-7195", "DUT-3860", "KQA-6134", "IKO-7196"] and community 3145861 with eight members: ["CXH-5500", "LKE-6457", "WSX-8173", "RCE-8170", "FBS-8174", "LPS-6136", "YWH-4106", "DHB-9540"]. The community ID values that you see might differ, but the group membership should be consistent.

Let's visualize a community with 10 members and their flight connections. Note the community ID: 1048774. Go to the Explore Graph page.

You should be on the Search vertices (magnifying glass icon) work screen. Follow these steps:

1. In the Search configuration pane, next to **Airport**, click the filter icon to open an "Add attribute filter" popup window.

2. In the Condition drop-down menu, select Expression1 == Expression2.

3. For Expression1, set Operand = Attribute and Attribute name = score.

4. For Expression2, set Operand = Real number and value = 1048774. Your window should now look like Figure 9-2.

5. Click ADD.

6. Back on the search configuration pane, make sure the number of vertices next to the Pick vertices button is at least 10.

7. Click the Pick vertices button.

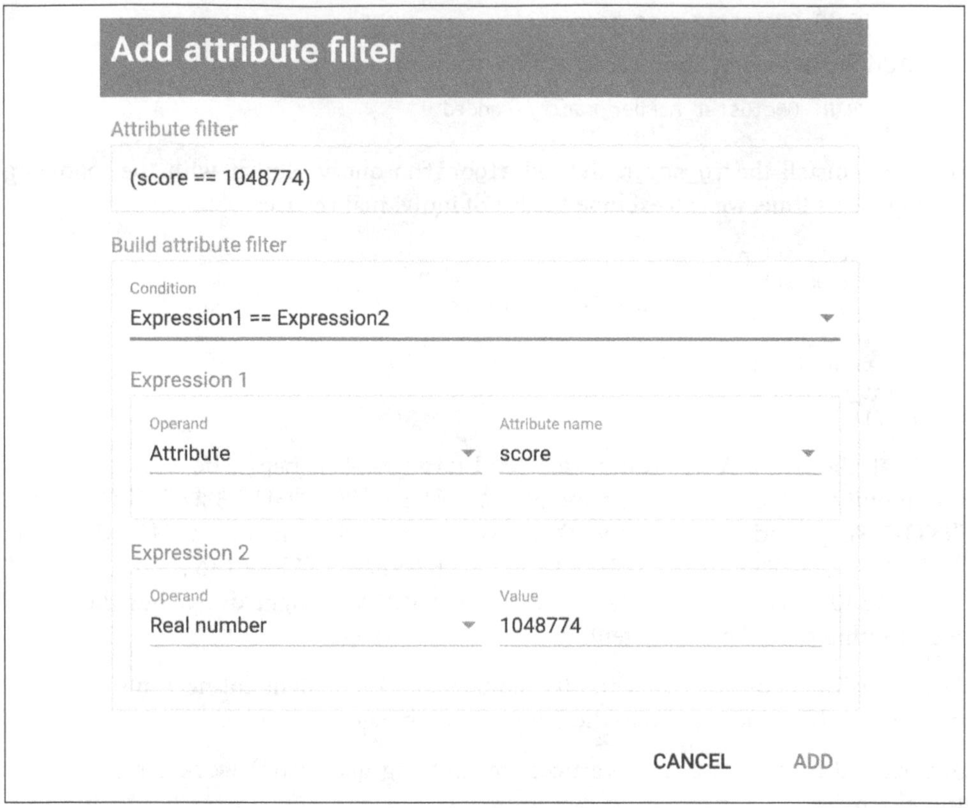

Figure 9-2. Adding a filter to select the vertices that belong to community 1048774

In the exploration mode vertical menu, click the second icon, the one for "Expand from vertices." In the list of edge types, unselect **flight_route**, so that we only include **flight_to** edges. Make sure the number of edges per vertex is at least 10. Click the Expand button.

You should now see edges between the vertices. To tidy up the display, click the layout mode button in the lower right corner of the graph display pane. Choose force. You should now see a starlike shape, as in Figure 9-3. We'd like to know more about these vertices, so click the Setting (gear-shaped) button in the menu at the top. With the **Airport** vertex type selected, check the boxes for city and country, and then click APPLY at the bottom. This adds labels in the graph view for city and country.

We can see that this network of flights is confined to New Caledonia, a collection of islands in the South Pacific. The hub is Noumea, which is the capital. Furthermore, when we performed the "Expand from vertices" step, if there had been any flights to airports outside of New Caledonia, they would have shown up. Apparently there are no such flights in our database. This may not reflect reality. The OpenFlights.org dataset may be missing some flights, but it nevertheless proved to be an interesting vehicle to see how graph algorithms can be used to reveal facts and insights.

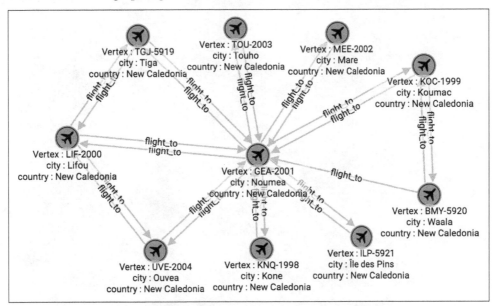

Figure 9-3. Community of isolated flight routes covering New Caledonia (see a larger version of this figure at https://oreil.ly/gpam0903)

Chapter Summary

In this chapter, we looked at the ways a network of airlines can be examined with graph algorithms. We used built-in GSQL algorithms included in the GDS Library to perform pathfinding, centrality calculation, and community detection operations. In addition, we modified existing query algorithms to filter the data and to give us more readable and useful results. Finally, we explored more of the functionality in the Explore Graph window of GraphStudio, creating a visually appealing graph diagram with easy-to-read labels in seconds.

PART III

Learn

CHAPTER 10

Graph-Powered Machine Learning Methods

After completing this chapter, you should be able to:

- List three basic ways that graph data and analytics can improve machine learning
- Point out which graph algorithms have proved valuable for unsupervised learning
- Extract graph features to enrich your training data for supervised machine learning
- Describe how neural networks have been extended to learn on graphs
- Provide use cases and examples to illustrate graph-powered machine learning
- Choose which types of graph-powered machine learning are right for you

We now begin the third theme of our book: Learn. That is, we're going to get serious about the core of machine learning: model training. Figure 10-1 shows the stages of a simple machine learning pipeline. In Part 1 of this book, we explored the Connect theme, which fits the first two stages of the pipeline: data acquisition and data preparation. Graph databases make it easy to pull data from multiple sources into one connected database and to perform entity resolution.

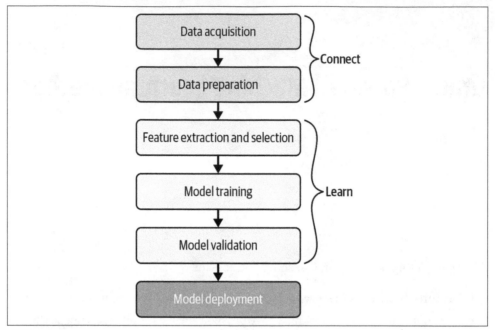

Figure 10-1. Machine learning pipeline

In this chapter, we'll show how graphs enhance the central stages in the pipeline: feature extraction and all-important model training. Features are simply the characteristics or properties of your data entities, like the age of a person or the color of a sweater. Graphs offer a whole new realm of features that are based on how an entity connects to other entities. The addition of these unique graph-oriented features provides machine learning with better raw materials with which to build its models.

This chapter has four sections. The first three sections each describe a different way that graphs enhance machine learning. First, we will start with unsupervised learning with graph algorithms, as it is similar to the techniques we discussed in Part 2: Analyze. Second, we will turn to graph feature extraction for supervised and unsupervised machine learning. Third, we culminate with model training directly on graphs, for both supervised and unsupervised approaches. This includes techniques for clustering, embedding, and neural networks. The fourth section reviews the various methods in order to compare them and to help you decide which approaches will meet your needs.

Unsupervised Learning with Graph Algorithms

Unsupervised learning is the sibling of supervised learning and reinforcement learning, who together form the three major branches of machine learning. If you want your AI system to learn how to do a task, to classify things according to your categories, or to make predictions, you want to use supervised learning and/or reinforcement learning. Unsupervised learning, however, has the great advantage of being self-sufficient and ready to go. Unlike supervised learning, you don't need to already know the right answer for some cases. Unlike reinforcement learning, you don't have to be patient and forgiving as you stumble through learning by trial and error. Unsupervised learning simply takes the data you have and reports what it learned.

An unsupervised learning algorithm can look at your network of customers and sales and identify your actual market segments, which may not fit simple ideas of age and income. An unsupervised learning algorithm can point out customer behavior that is an outlier, or far from normal, by determining "normal" from your data and not from your preconceptions. For example, an outlier can point out which customers are likely to churn (that is, discontinue using your product or service).

The first way we will learn from graph data is by applying graph algorithms to discover patterns or characteristics of our data. In Chapter 6, we gave a detailed overview of five categories of algorithms. In this section, we'll discuss which of these algorithms are a good fit for unsupervised learning. We'll also introduce another graph analytics task: frequent pattern mining.

Learning Through Similarity and Community Structure

Among the five algorithm categories presented in Chapter 6, the last one—classification and prediction—is commonly considered by data scientists to be in the machine learning domain. Classification, in particular, is usually supervised learning. Prediction comes in all flavors. As we previously pointed out, both of those tasks hinge on some means of measuring similarity. Similarity algorithms, then, are key tools for machine learning.

If you find all the vertices that have high Jaccard similarity, it might not feel like you're doing machine learning. You could take it one step further: was the number of similar vertices that you found much higher or much lower than what you expected? You could base your expectation on the typical number of connections that a vertex has and the likelihood that two random vertices will have a neighbor in common. Characteristics such as these can tell you important things about your graph and the real-world things that it represents. For example, suppose a large corporation maps out its employees and various job-related data in a graph. A manager could search to see if there are other employees with job qualifications similar to those of the manager's current team. What do the results say about cross-training, resiliency, and redundancy in the workforce?

When a graph's structure is determined by lots of individual players rather than by central planning, its community structure is not known a priori; we have to analyze the graph to discover the structure. The structure is a reflection of the entities and their mutual relationships, so learning the structure tells us something about the entities and their dynamics. The modularity-based algorithms like Louvain and Leiden are fine examples of self-learning: determining community membership by looking at the graph's own relative densities of connections. The recursively defined SimRank and RoleSim measures also fit the self-learning trait of unsupervised learning. Then isn't PageRank also a form of unsupervised learning?

These algorithms are also quite valuable. Many financial institutions have found that applying centrality and community algorithms to graphs of transactions has helped them to better identify financial crimes.

Finding Frequent Patterns

As we've said in this book, graphs are wonderful because they make it easy to discover and analyze multiconnection patterns based on connections. In Part 2: Analyze, we talked about finding particular patterns, and we will return to that topic later in this chapter. In the context of unsupervised learning, this is the goal:

> Find any and all patterns that occur frequently.

Computer scientists call this the *frequent subgraph mining* task, because a pattern of connections is just a subgraph. This task is particularly useful for understanding natural behavior and structure, such as consumer behavior, social structures, biological structures, and even software code structure. However, it also presents a much more difficult problem. "Any and all" patterns in a large graph means a vast number of possible occurrences to check. The saving grace is the threshold parameter T. To be considered frequent, a pattern must occur at least T times. Selecting a good value for T is important. We want it high enough to filter out small, insignificant patterns—the more we filter, the less overall work we need to do—but not so high as to exclude interesting patterns. Choosing a good threshold can be a machine learning task in itself.

There are many advanced approaches to attempt speeding up frequent subgraph mining, but the basic approach is to start with one-edge patterns, keep the patterns that occur at least T times, and then try to connect those patterns to make bigger patterns:

1. Group all the edges according to their type and the types of their endpoint vertices. For example, **Shopper-(bought)-Product** is a pattern.

2. Count how many times each pattern occurs.

3. Keep all the frequent patterns (having at least T members) and discard the rest. For example, we keep `Shopper-(lives_in)-Florida` but eliminate `Shopper-(lives_in)-Guam` because it is infrequent.

4. Consider every pair of groups that have compatible vertex types (e.g., groups 1 and 2 both have a **Shopper** vertex), and see how many individual vertices in group 1 are also in group 2. Merge these individual small patterns to make a new group for the larger pattern. For example, we merge the cases where the same person in the frequent pattern `Shopper-(bought)-Blender` was also in the frequent pattern `Shopper-(lives_in)-Florida`.

5. Repeat steps 2 and 3 (filtering for frequency) for these newly formed larger patterns.

6. Repeat step 4 using the expanded collection of patterns.

7. Stop when no new frequent patterns have been built.

There is a complication with counting (step 2). The complication is *isomorphism*, that is, how the same set of vertices and edges can fit a template pattern in more than one way. Consider the pattern A-(friend_of)-B. If Jordan is a friend of Kim, which implies that Kim is a friend of Jordan, is that one instance of the pattern or two? Now suppose the pattern is "find pairs of friends A and B, who are both friends with a third person, C." This forms a triangle. Let's say Jordan, Kim, and Logan form a friendship triangle. There are six possible ways we could assign Jordan, Kim, and Logan to the variables A, B, and C. You need to decide up front whether these types of symmetrical patterns should be counted separately or merged into one instance, and then make sure your counting method is correct.

Graph algorithms can perform unsupervised machine learning on graph data. Key takeaways from this section are as follows:

- Graph algorithms in several categories fit the self-learning idea of unsupervised learning: similarity, community detection, centrality, prediction, and frequent pattern mining.

- Unsupervised learning has the benefit of providing insight without the requirement of prior classifications. Unsupervised learning can also make observations relative to the data's own context.

Extracting Graph Features

In the previous section, we showed how you can use graph algorithms to perform unsupervised machine learning. In most of those examples, we analyzed the graph as a whole to discover some characteristics, such as communities or frequent patterns.

In this section, you'll learn how graphs can provide additional and valuable features to describe and help you understand your data. A *graph feature* is a characteristic that is based on the pattern of connections in the graph. A feature can be either local—attributed to the neighborhood of an individual vertex or edge—or global—pertaining to the whole graph or a subgraph. In most cases, we are interested in vertex features: characteristics of the neighborhood around a vertex. That's because vertices usually represent the real-world entities we want to model with machine learning.

When an entity (an instance of a real-world thing) has several features and we arrange those features in a standard order, we call the ordered list a *feature vector*. Some of the methods we'll look at in this section provide individual features; others produce entire sets of features. You can concatenate a vertex's entity properties (the ones that aren't based on connections) with its graph features obtained from one or more of the methods discussed here to make a longer, richer feature vector. We'll also look at a special feature vector called an *embedding*, which summarizes a vertex's entire neighborhood.

These features can provide insight as is, but one of their most powerful uses is to enrich the training data for supervised machine learning. Feature extraction is one of the key phases in a machine learning pipeline (refer back to Figure 10-1). For graphs, this is particularly important because traditional machine learning techniques are designed for vectors, not for graphs. So in a machine learning pipeline, feature extraction is also where we transform the graph into a different representation.

In the sections that follow, we'll look at three key topics: domain-independent features, domain-dependent features, and the exciting developments in graph embedding.

Domain-Independent Features

If graph features are new to you, the best way to understand them is to look at simple examples that would work for any graph. Because these features can be used regardless of the type of data we are modeling, we say they are *domain independent*. Consider the graph in Figure 10-2. We see a network of friendships, and we count occurrences of some simple domain-independent graph features.

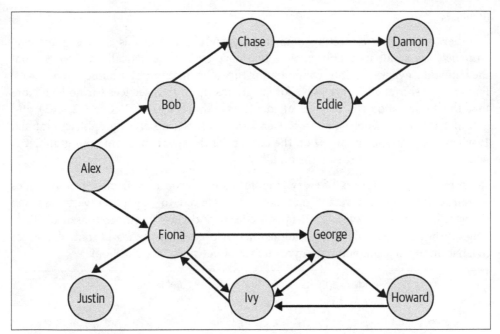

Figure 10-2. Graph with directed friendship edges (see a larger version of this figure at https://oreil.ly/gpam1002)

Table 10-1 shows the results for four selected vertices (Alex, Chase, Fiona, Justin) and four selected features.

Table 10-1. Examples of domain-independent features from the graph of Figure 10-2

	Number of in-neighbors	Number of out-neighbors	Number of vertices within two forward hops	Number of triangles (ignoring direction)
Alex	0	2 (Bob, Fiona)	6 (B, C, F, G, I, J)	0
Chase	1 (Bob)	2 (Damon, Eddie)	2 (D, E)	1 (Chase, Damon, Eddie)
Fiona	2 (Alex, Ivy)	3 (George, Ivy, Justin)	4 (G, I, J, H)	1 (Fiona, George, Ivy)
Justin	1 (Fiona)	0	0	0

You could easily come up with more features, by looking farther than one or two hops, by considering generic weight properties of the vertices or edges, and by calculating in more sophisticated ways: computing average, maximum, or other functions. Because these are domain-independent features, we are not thinking about the meaning of "person" or "friend." We could change the object types to "computers" and "sends data to." Domain-independent features, however, may not be the right choice for you if there are many types of edges with very different meanings.

Graphlets

Another option for extracting domain-independent features is to use graphlets.[1] *Graphlets* are small subgraph patterns that have been systematically defined so that they include every possible configuration up to a maximum number of vertices. Figure 10-3 shows all 72 graphlets for subgraphs up to five vertices (or nodes). Note that the figure shows two types of identifiers: shape IDs (G0, G1, G2, etc.) and graphlet IDs (1, 2, 3, etc.). Shape G1 encompasses two different graphlets: graphlet 1, when the reference vertex is on the end of the three-vertex chain, and graphlet 2, when the reference vertex is in the middle.

Counting the occurrences of every graphlet pattern around a given vertex provides a standardized feature vector that can be compared to any other vertex in any graph. This universal signature lets you cluster and classify entities based on their neighborhood structure for applications such as predicting the world trade dynamics of a nation[2] or link prediction in dynamic social networks like Facebook.[3]

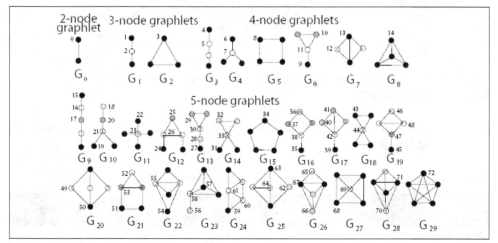

Figure 10-3. Graphlets up to five vertices (or nodes) in size[4] (see a larger version of this figure at https://oreil.ly/gpam1003)

---

1 Graphlets were first presented in Nataša Pržulj, Derek G. Corneil, and Igor Jurisi, "Modeling Interactome: Scale-Free or Geometric?" *Bioinformatics* 20, no. 18 (December 2004): 3508–3515, *https://doi.org/10.1093/bioinformatics/bth436*.

2 Anida Sarajlić, Noël Malod-Dognin, Ömer Nebil Yaveroğlu, and Nataša Pržulj, "Graphlet-Based Characterization of Directed Networks," *Scientific Reports* 6 (2016), *https://www.nature.com/articles/srep35098*.

3 Mahmudur Rahman and Mohammad Al Hasan, "Link Prediction in Dynamic Networks using Graphlet," in *Machine Learning and Knowledge Discovery in Databases*, Proceedings, Part I, ed. Paolo Frasconi, Niels Landwehr, Giuseppe Manco, Jilles Vreeken (Riva del Garda, Italy: European Conference, ECML PKDD: 2016), 394–409.

A key rule for graphlets is that they are the *induced* subgraph for a set of vertices within a graph of interest. Induced means that they include *all* the edges that the base graph has among the selected set of vertices. This rule causes each particular set of vertices to match at most one graphlet pattern.

For example, consider the four persons Fiona, George, Howard, and Ivy in Figure 10-2. Which shape and graphlet do they match, if any? It's shape G7, because those four persons form a rectangle with one cross-connection. They do not match shape G5, the square, because of that cross-connection between George and Ivy. While we're talking about that cross-connection, look carefully at the two graphlets for shape G7, graphlets 12 and 13. Graphlet 13's source node is located at one end of the cross-connection, just as George and Ivy are. This means graphlet 13 is one of their graphlets. Fiona and Howard are at the other corners of the square, which don't have the cross-connection. Therefore they have graphlet 12 in their graphlet portfolios.

There is obviously some overlap between the ad hoc features we first talked about (e.g., number of neighbors) and graphlets. Suppose a vertex A has three neighbors, B, C, and D, as shown in Figure 10-4. However, we do not know about any other connections. What do we know about vertex A's graphlets?

1. It exhibits the graphlet 0 pattern three times. Counting the occurrences is important.

2. Now consider subgraphs with three vertices. We can define three different subgraphs containing A: (A, B, C), (A, B, D), and (A, C, D). Each of those threesomes satisfies either graphlet 2 or 3. Without knowing about the connections among B, C, and D (the dotted-line edges in the figure), we cannot be more specific.

3. Considering all four vertices, we might be tempted to say they match graphlet 7. Since there might be other connections between B, C, and D, it might actually be a different graphlet. Which one? Graphlet 11 if there's one peripheral connection, graphlet 13 if it's two connections, or graphlet 14 if it's all three possible connections.

---

4 Tijana Milenković and Nataša Pržulj, "Uncovering Biological Network Function via Graphlet Degree Signatures," *Cancer Informatics* 6, no. 10 (April 2008), *https://www.researchgate.net/publica tion/26510215_Przulj_N_Uncovering_Biological_Network_Function_via_Graphlet_Degree_Signatures.*

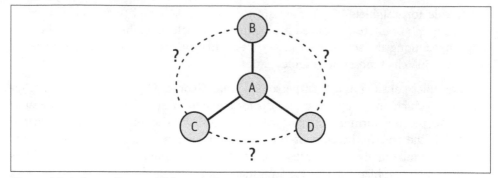

Figure 10-4. Immediate neighbors and graphlet implications

The advantage of graphlets is that they are thorough and methodical. Checking for all graphlets up to five-node size is equal to considering all the details of the source vertex's four-hop neighborhood. You could run an automated graphlet counter without spending time and money to design custom feature extraction. The disadvantage of graphlets is that they can require a lot of computational work, and it might be more productive to focus on a more selective set of domain-dependent features. We'll cover these types of features shortly.

Graph algorithms

Here's a third option for extracting domain-independent graph features: graph algorithms! In particular, the centrality and ranking algorithms that we discussed in Part 2: Analyze work well because they systematically look at everything around a vertex and produce a score for each vertex. Figure 10-5 and Figure 10-6 show the PageRank and closeness centrality[5] scores, respectively, for the graph presented earlier in Figure 10-2. For example, Alex has a PageRank score of 0.15, while Eddie has a PageRank score of 1. This tells us that Eddie is valued by his peers much more than Alex. Eddie's ranking is due not only to the number of connections but also to the direction of edges. Howard, who like Eddie has two connections and is at the far end of the rough "C" shape of the graph, has a PageRank score of only 0.49983 because one edge comes in and the other goes out.

---

5 These algorithms were introduced in Part 2: Analyze.

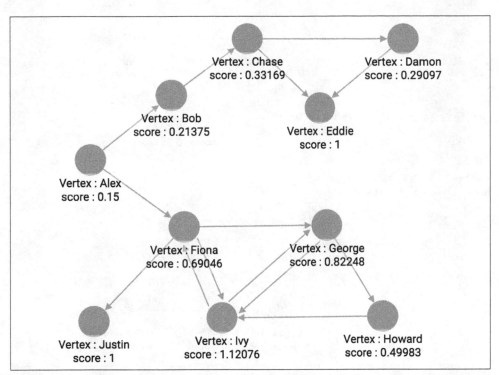

Figure 10-5. PageRank scores for the friendship graph (see a larger version of this figure at https://oreil.ly/gpam1005)

The closeness centrality scores in Figure 10-6 tell a completely different story. Alex has a top score of 0.47368 because she is at the middle of the C. Damon and Howard have scores at or near the bottom—0.11111 and 0.22222, respectively—because they are at the ends of the C.

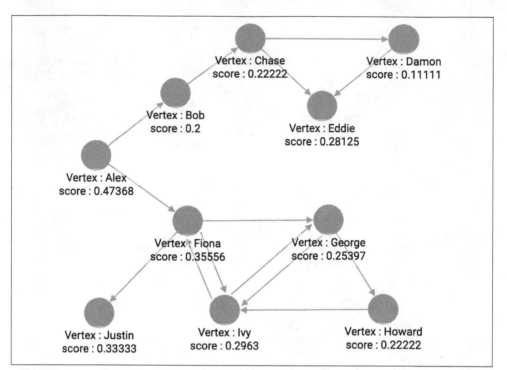

Figure 10-6. Closeness centrality scores for the friendship graph (see a larger version of this figure at https://oreil.ly/gpam1006)

The main advantage of domain-independent feature extraction is its universality: generic extraction tools can be designed and optimized in advance, and the tools can be applied immediately on any data. Its unguided approach, however, can make it a blunt instrument.

Domain-independent feature extraction has two main drawbacks. Because it doesn't pay attention to what types of edges and vertices it considers, it can group together occurrences that have the same shape but have radically different meanings. The second drawback is that it can waste resources computing and cataloging features that have no real importance or no logical meaning. Depending on your use case, you may want to focus on a more selective set of domain-dependent features.

Domain-Dependent Features

A little bit of domain knowledge can go a long way toward making your feature extraction smarter and more efficient.

When extracting domain-dependent features, the first thing you want to do is pay attention to the vertex types and edge types in your graph. It's helpful to look at a display of your graph's schema. Some schemas break down information hierarchically

---

into graph paths, such as `City-(IN)-State-(IN)-Country` or `Day-(IN)-Month-(IN)-Year`. This is a graph-oriented way of indexing and pregrouping data according to location or date. This is the case in a graph model for South Korean COVID-19 contact-tracing data,[6] shown in Figure 10-7. While `city-to-country` and `day-to-year` are each two-hop paths, those paths are simply baseline information and do not hold the significance of a two-hop path like `Patient-(INFECTED_BY)-Patient-(INFECTED_BY)-Patient`.

You can see how the graphlet approach and other domain-independent approaches can provide confusing results when you have mixed edge types. A simple solution is to take a domain-semi-independent approach by considering only certain vertex types and edge types when looking for features. For example, if looking for graphlet patterns, you might want to ignore the `Month` vertices and their connecting edges. You might still care about the year of birth of patients and the (exact) day on which they traveled, but you don't need the graph to tell you that each year contains 12 months.

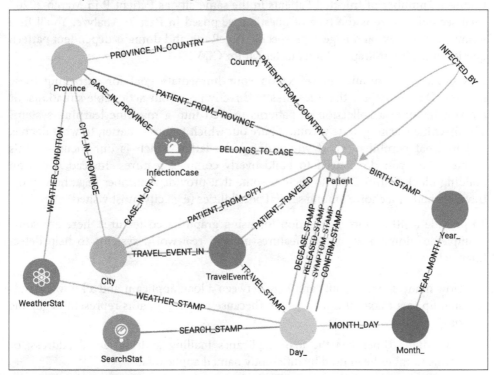

Figure 10-7. Graph schema for South Korean COVID-19 contact-tracing data (see a larger version of this figure at https://oreil.ly/gpam1007)

---

6 "[NeurIPS 2020] Data Science for COVID-19 (DS4C)," Kaggle, accessed May 25, 2023, *https://www.kaggle.com/datasets/kimjihoo/coronavirusdataset*.

With this vertex- and edge-type awareness, you can refine some of the domain-independent searches. For example, while you can run PageRank on any graph, the scores will only have significance if all the edges have the same or relatively similar meanings. It would not make sense to run PageRank on the entire COVID-19 contact-tracing graph because we can't rank all the different vertex types and edge types on one scale. It would make sense, however, to consider only the **Patient** vertices and **INFECTED_BY** edges. PageRank would then tell you who was the most influential Patient in terms of causing infection: patient zero, so to speak.

In this type of scenario, you also want to apply your understanding of the domain to think of small patterns with two or more edges of specific types that indicate something meaningful. For this COVID-19 contact-tracing schema, the most important facts are Infection Status (InfectionCase), Who (Patient), Where (City and TravelEvent), and When (Day_). Paths that connect these are important. A possible feature is "number of travel events made by Patient P in March 2020." A more specific feature is "number of Infected Patients in the same city as Patient P in March 2020." That second feature is the type of question we posed in Part 2: Analyze. You'll find examples of vertex- and edge-type-specific PageRank and domain-dependent pattern queries in the TigerGraph Cloud Starter Kit for COVID-19.

Let's pause for a minute to reflect on your immediate goal for extracting these features. Do you expect these features to directly point out actionable situations, or are you building a collection of patterns to feed into a machine learning system? The machine learning system could figure out which features matter, to what degree, and in what combination. If you're doing the latter, which is our focus for this chapter, then you don't need to build overly complex features. Instead, focus on building-block features. Try to include some that provide a number (e.g., how many travel events) or a choice among several possibilities (e.g., city most visited).

To provide a little more inspiration for using graph-based features, here are some examples of domain-dependent features used in real-world systems to help detect financial fraud:

- How many shortest paths are there between a loan applicant and a known fraudster, up to a maximum path length (because very long paths represent negligible risk)?

- How many times has the loan applicant's mailing address, email address, or phone number been used by differently named applicants?

- How many charges has a particular credit card made in the last 10 minutes?

While it is easy to see that high values on any of these measures make it more likely that a situation involves financial misbehavior, our goal is to select the right features and the right threshold values. Having the right tests for fraud cuts down on both false negatives (missing cases of real fraud) and false positives (labeling a situation as fraud when it really isn't). False positives are doubly damaging. They hurt the business because they are rejecting an honest business transaction, and they hurt the customer who has been unjustly labeled a crook.

Graph Embeddings: A Whole New World

Our last approach to feature extraction is graph embedding, a hot topic of recent research and discussion. Some authorities may find it unusual that we are classifying graph embedding as a type of feature extraction. Isn't graph embedding a kind of dimensionality reduction? Isn't it representation learning? Isn't it a form of machine learning itself? All of those are true. Let's first define a graph embedding.

An *embedding* is a representation of a topological object in a particular system such that the properties we care about are preserved (or approximated well). The last part, preserving the properties we care about, gets to the heart of why we use embeddings. A well-chosen embedding makes it more convenient to see what we want to see.

Here are several examples to help illustrate the meaning of embeddings:

- The Earth is a sphere, but we print world maps on flat paper. The representation of the Earth on paper is an embedding. There are several different standard representations or embeddings of the Earth as a map. Figure 10-8 shows some examples.

- Prior to the late 2010s, when someone said "graph embedding," they probably meant something like the Earth example. To represent all the connections in a graph without edges touching one another, you often need three or more dimensions. Whenever you see a graph on a flat surface, it's an embedding, as in Figure 10-9. Moreover, unless your data specifies the location of vertices, then even a 3D representation is an embedding because it's a particular choice about the placement of the vertices. From a theoretical perspective, it actually takes up to $n - 1$ dimensions to represent a graph with n vertices.

- In natural language processing (NLP), a word embedding is a sequence of scores (i.e., a feature vector) for a given word (see Figure 10-10). There is no natural interpretation of the individual scores, but a machine learning program sets the scores so that words that tend to occur near one another in training documents have similar embeddings. For example, "machine" and "learning" might have similar embeddings. A word embedding is not convenient for human use, but it is very convenient for computer programs that need a computational way of understanding word similarities and groupings.

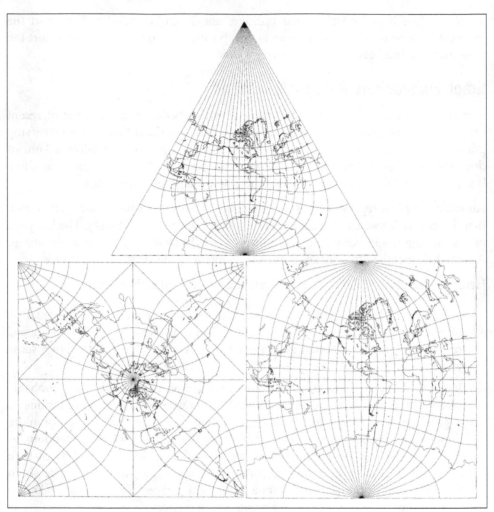

Figure 10-8. Three embeddings of the Earth's surface onto 2D space[7]

7 From John P. Snyder and Philip M. Voxland, "An Album of Map Projections," second printing (US Geological Survey Professional Paper 1453, 1994), *https://pubs.usgs.gov/pp/1453/report.pdf*.

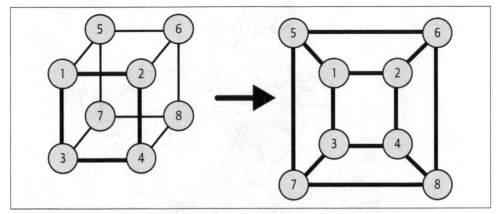

Figure 10-9. Some graphs can be embedded in 2D space without intersecting edges

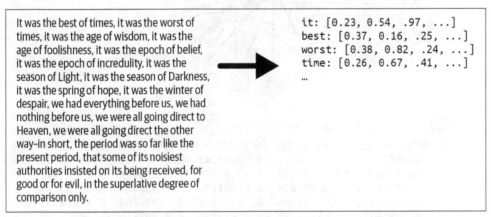

It was the best of times, it was the worst of times, it was the age of wisdom, it was the age of foolishness, it was the epoch of belief, it was the epoch of incredulity, it was the season of Light, it was the season of Darkness, it was the spring of hope, it was the winter of despair, we had everything before us, we had nothing before us, we were all going direct to Heaven, we were all going direct the other way-in short, the period was so far like the present period, that some of its noisiest authorities insisted on its being received, for good or for evil, in the superlative degree of comparison only.

```
it: [0.23, 0.54, .97, ...]
best: [0.37, 0.16, .25, ...]
worst: [0.38, 0.82, .24, ...]
time: [0.26, 0.67, .41, ...]
...
```

Figure 10-10. Word embedding

In recent years, graph embedding has taken on a new meaning, analogous to word embedding. We compute one or more feature vectors to approximate the graph's neighborhood structure. In fact, when people say "graph embedding," they often mean *vertex embedding*: computing a feature vector for each vertex in the graph. A vertex's embedding tells us something about how it connects to others. We can then use the collection of vertex embeddings to approximate the graph, no longer needing to consider the edges. There are also methods to summarize the whole graph as one embedding. This is useful for comparing one graph to another. In this book, we will focus on vertex embeddings.

Figure 10-11 shows an example of a graph (a) and portion of its vertex embedding (b). The embedding for each vertex (a series of 32 numbers) describes the structure of its neighborhood without directly mentioning any of its neighbors.

(A)

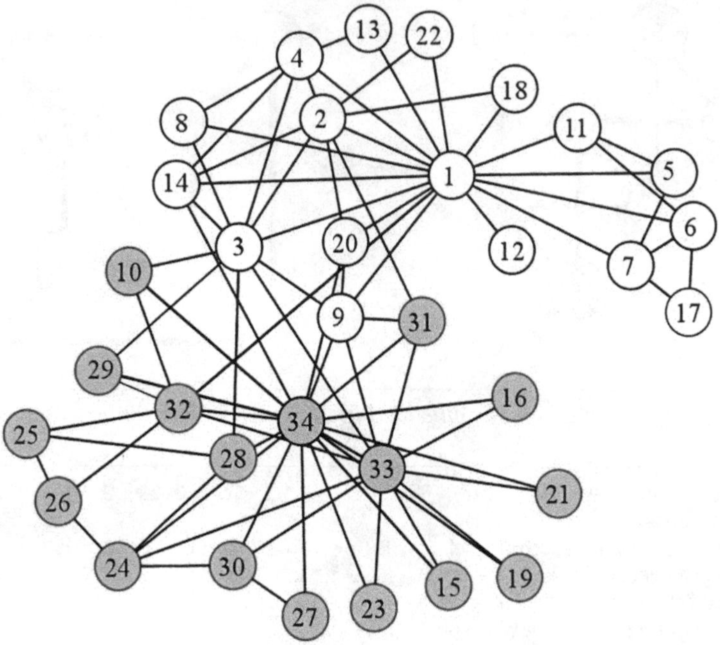

(B)

```
34 +0.31656152  +0.01232658 -0.00168657 -0.16343851 -0.03110625
   +0.00942777 +0.06975124 +0.10862143 +0.16954944 +0.04376319
   +0.08508979 +0.02639644 -0.37170425 +0.31954828 +0.18332475
   -0.37280235 +0.02704849 -0.05201775 +0.0423865  -0.21998182
   -0.06086616 -0.02641196 -0.18654257 +0.27996296 +0.14059557
   +0.2781425  -0.02252658 +0.04872169 -0.04008826 +0.20045769
   +0.01116217 +0.01404634
 1 +0.12595864  +0.04960880 -0.1426265  -0.06466998 -0.19246309
   +0.30182636 -0.06328319 +0.16227436 +0.24654388 +0.10715616
   -0.05511753 -0.04588598 -0.20784278 -0.05263712 +0.2854745
   -0.05113884 -0.0498297  +0.50398374 +0.03050438 -0.19433172
   -0.11145525 -0.13087504 -0.12485117 -0.16824125 +0.22375904
   +0.36512214 -0.02214461 +0.01254723 +0.05175329 -0.01181463
   -0.2646808  +0.08702151
```

Figure 10-11. (a) Karate club graph[8] *and (b) 64-element embedding for two of its vertices*

8 This visualized partitioning comes from "Zachary's Karate Club," Wikipedia, April 5, 2017, *https://en.wikipe dia.org/wiki/File:Zachary%27s_karate_club.png.*

Let's return to the question of classifying graph embeddings. What graph embeddings give us is a set of feature vectors. For a graph with a million vertices, a typical embedding vector would be a few hundred elements long, a lot less than the upper limit of one million dimensions. Therefore, graph embeddings represent a form of dimensionality reduction. If we're using graph embeddings to get feature vectors, they're also a form of feature extraction. As we will see, the methodology to generate an embedding qualifies as machine learning, so they are also representation learning.

Does any feature vector qualify as an embedding? That depends on whether your selected features are telling you what you want to know. Graphlets come closest to the learned embeddings we are going to examine because of the methodical way they deconstruct neighborhood relationships.

Random walk-based embeddings

One of the best-known approaches for graph embedding is to use random walks to get a statistical sample of the neighborhood surrounding each vertex v. A random walk is a sequence of connected hops in a graph G. The walk starts at some vertex v. It then picks a random neighbor of v and moves there. It repeats this selection of random neighbors until it is told to stop. In an unbiased walk, there is an equal probability of selecting any of the outgoing edges.

Random walks are great because they are easy to do and they gather a lot of information efficiently. All feature extraction methods we have looked at before require following careful rules about how to traverse the graph; graphlets are particularly demanding due to their very precise definitions and distinctions from one another. Random walks are carefree. Just go.

For the example graph in Figure 10-12, suppose we start a random walk at vertex A. There is an equal probability of one in three that we will next go to vertex B, C, or D. If you start the walk at vertex E, there is a 100% chance that the next step will be to vertex B. There are variations of random-walk rules with the possibility of staying in place, reversing your last step, jumping back to the start, or jumping to a random vertex.

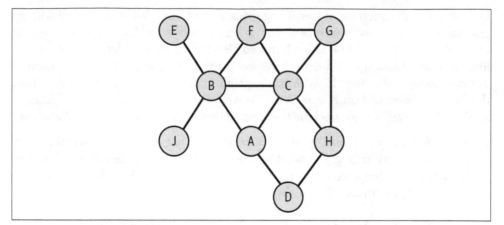

Figure 10-12. An ordinary graph for leisurely walks

Each walk can be recorded as a list of vertices, in the order in which they were visited. A-D-H-G-C is a possible walk. You can think of each walk as a signature. What does the signature tell us? Suppose that walk W1 starts at vertex 5 and then goes to 2. Walk W2 starts at vertex 9 and then goes to 2. Now they are both at 2. From here on, they have exactly the same probabilities for the remainder of their walks. Those individual walks are unlikely to be the same, but if there is a concept of a "typical walk" averaged over a sampling of several walks, then, yes, the signatures of 5 and 9 would be similar. All because 5 and 9 share a neighbor 2. Moreover, the "typical walk" of vertex 2 itself would be similar, except offset by one step.

It turns out that these random walks gather neighborhood information much in the same way that SimRank and RoleSim gather theirs. The difference is that those role similarity algorithms considered *all* paths (by considering all neighbors), which is computationally expensive. Let's take a look at two random-walk-based graph embedding algorithms that use a completely different computational method, one borrowed from neural networks.

DeepWalk

The DeepWalk algorithm[9] collects k random walks of length λ for every vertex in the graph. If you happen to know the word2vec algorithm[10], the rest is easy. Treat each vertex like a word and each walk like a sentence. Pick a window width w for the *skip-grams* and a length d for your embedding. You will end up with an embedding (latent feature vector) of length d for each vertex. The DeepWalk authors found that having walk count $k = 30$, walk length $\lambda = 40$, window width $w = 10$, and embedding

---

9 See the article by Perozzi, Al-Rfou, and Skiena *https://dl.acm.org/doi/abs/10.1145/2623330.2623732*.

10 See the article by Mikolov, Sutskever, Chen, Corrado, and Dean *https://arxiv.org/abs/1310.4546*.

length d = 64 worked well for their test graphs. Your results may vary. Figure 10-13(a) shows an example of a random walk, starting at vertex C and with a length of 16, which is 15 steps or hops from the starting point. The shadings will be explained when we explain skip-grams.

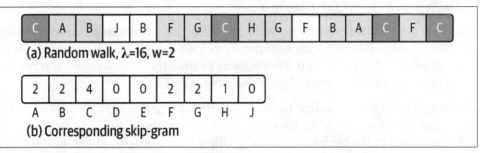

(a) Random walk, λ=16, w=2

A	B	C	D	E	F	G	H	J
2	2	4	0	0	2	2	1	0

(b) Corresponding skip-gram

Figure 10-13. (a) Random walk vector and (b) a corresponding skip-gram

We assume you don't know word2vec, so we'll give a high-level explanation, enough so you can appreciate what is happening. This is the conceptual model. The actual algorithm plays a lot of statistical tricks to speed up the work. First, we construct a simple neural network with one hidden layer, as shown in Figure 10-14. The input layer accepts vectors of length n, where n = number of vertices. The hidden layer has length d, the embedding length, because it is going to be learning the embedding vectors. The output layer also has length n.

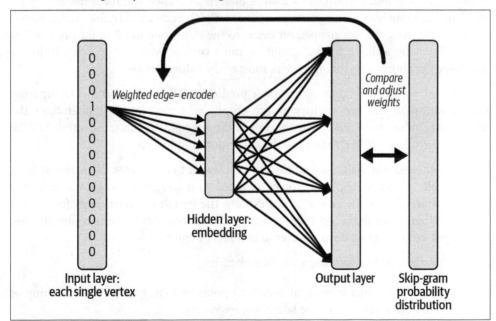

Figure 10-14. Neural network for DeepWalk

Each vertex needs to be assigned a position in the input and output layer. For example, vertex A is at position 1, vertex B is at position 2, and so on. Between the layers are two meshes of $n \times d$ connections, from each element in one layer to each element in the next layer. Each edge has a random weight initially, but we will gradually adjust the weights of the first mesh.

Start with one walk for one starting vertex. At the input, we represent the vertex using *one-hot encoding*. The vector element that corresponds to the starting vertex is set to 1; all other elements are set to 0. We are going to train this neural network to predict the neighborhood of the vertex given at the input.

Applying the weights in the first mesh to our one-hot input, we get a weighted vertex in the hidden layer. This is the current guess for the embedding of the input vertex. Take the values in the hidden layers and multiply by the weights of the second mesh to get the output layer values. You now have a length-n vector with random weights.

We're going to compare this output vector with a skip-gram representation of the walk. This is where we use the window parameter w. For each vertex in the graph, count how many times it appears within w-steps before or after the input vertex v. We'll skip the normalization process, but your final skip-gram vector expresses the relative likelihood that each of the n vertices is near vertex v in this walk. Now we'll explain the result of Figure 10-13. Vertex C was the starting point for the random walk; we've used dark shading to highlight every time we stepped on vertex C. The light shading shows every step that is within $w = 2$ steps of vertex C. Then, we form the skip-gram in (b) by counting how many times we set foot on each vertex within the shaded zones. For example, vertex G was stepped on twice, so the skip-gram has 2 in the position for G. This is a long walk on a small graph, so most vertices were stepped on within the windows. For short walks on big graphs, most of the values will be 0.

Our output vector was supposed to be a prediction of this skip-gram. Comparing each position in the two vectors, if the output vector's value is higher than the skip-gram's value, then reduce the corresponding weight in the input mesh will be lower. If the value is lower, then raise the corresponding weight.

You've processed one walk. Repeat this for one walk of each vertex. Now repeat for a second walk of each vertex, until you've adjusted your weights for $k \times n$ walks. You're done! The weights of the first $n \times d$ mesh are the length-d embeddings for your n vectors. What about the second mesh? Strangely, we were never going to directly use the output vectors, so we didn't bother to adjust its weight.

Here is how to interpret and use a vertex embedding:

- For neural networks in general, you can't point to a clear real-world meaning of the individual elements in the latent feature vector.

- Based on how we trained the network, though, we can reason backward from the skip-grams, which represent the neighbors around a vertex: vertices that have similar neighborhoods should have similar embeddings.

- If you remember the example earlier about two paths that were offset by one step, note that those two paths would have very similar skip-grams. So vertices that are close to one another should have similar embeddings.

One critique of DeepWalk is that its uniformly random walk is too random. In particular, it may wander far from the source vertex before getting an adequate sample of the neighborhoods closer to the source. One way to address that is to include a probability of resetting the walk by magically teleporting back to the source vertex and then continuing with random steps again, as shown in Zhou, Wu, and Tan (*https://oreil.ly/3YiLc*). This is known as "random walk with restart."

Node2vec

An interesting extension of the random walk is node2vec (*https://oreil.ly/GoPWK*). It uses the same skip-gram training process as DeepWalk, but it gives the user two adjustment parameters to control the direction of the walk: go farther (depth), go sideways (breadth), or go back a step. Farther and back seem obvious, but what exactly does sideways mean?

Suppose we start at vertex A of the graph in Figure 10-15. Its neighbors are vertices B, C, and D. Since we are just starting, any of the choices would be moving forward. Let's go to vertex C. For the second step, we can choose from any of vertex C's neighbors: A, B, F, G, or H.

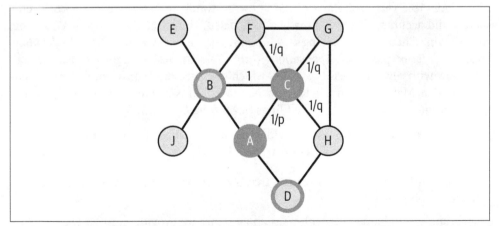

Figure 10-15. Illustrating the biased random walk with memory used in node2vec

If we remember what our choices were in our previous step, we can classify our current set of neighbors into three groups: back, sideways, and forward. We also assign a weight to each connecting edge, which represents the unnormalized probability of selecting that edge.

Back
> In our example: vertex A. Edge weight = $1/p$.

Sideways
> These are the vertices that were available in the last step and are also available in this step. They represent a second chance to visit a different neighbor of where you were previously. In our example: vertex B. Edge weight = 1.

Forward
> There are all the vertices that don't go back or sideways. In our example: vertices F, G, and H. Edge weight = $1/q$.

If we set $p = q = 1$, then all choices have equal probability, so we're back to an unbiased random walk. If $p < 1$, then returning is more likely than going sideways. If $q < 1$, then each of the forward (depth) options is more likely than sideways (breadth). Returning also keeps the walk closer to home (e.g., similar to breadth-first-search), because if you step back and then step forward randomly, you are trying out the different options in your previous neighborhood.

This ability to tune the walk makes node2vec more flexible than DeepWalk, which results in better models, in many cases, in exchange for higher computational cost.

Besides the random-walk approach, there are several other techniques for graph embedding, each with their advantages and disadvantages: matrix factorization, edge reconstruction, graph kernel, and generative models. FastRP (*https://oreil.ly/QhbWl*) and NodePiece (*https://oreil.ly/r6FZ5*) show a promising balance of real-world efficiency and accuracy. Though already a little dated, Hongyun Cai, Vincent W. Zheng, and Kevin Chen-Chuan Chang's *A Comprehensive Survey of Graph Embedding: Problems, Techniques, and Applications* (*https://oreil.ly/bIKdV*) provides a thorough overview with several accessible tables, which compare the features of different techniques. Ilya Makarov, Dmitrii Kiselev, Nikita Nikitinsky, and Lovro Subelj have a more recent survey on graph embeddings (*https://oreil.ly/3FxLA*).

Graphs can provide additional and valuable features to describe and understand your data. Key takeaways from this section are as follows:

- A graph feature is a characteristic that is based on the pattern of connections in the graph.

- Graphlets and graph algorithms such as centrality provide domain-independent features for any graph.

- Applying some domain knowledge to guide your feature extraction leads to more meaningful features.

- Machine learning can produce vertex embeddings, which encode vertex similarity and proximity in terms of compact feature vectors.
- Random walks are a simple way to sample a vertex's neighborhood.

Graph Neural Networks

In the popular press, it's not AI unless it uses a neural network, and it's not machine learning unless it uses deep learning. Neural networks were originally designed to emulate how the human brain works, but they evolved to address the capabilities of computers and mathematics. The predominant models assume that your input data is in a matrix or tensor; it's not clear how to present and train the neural network with interconnected vertices. But are there graph-based neural networks? Yes!

Graph neural networks (GNNs) are conventional neural networks with an added twist for graphs. Just as there are several variations of neural networks, there are several variations of GNNs. The simplest way to include the graph itself into the neural network is through convolution.

Graph Convolutional Networks

In mathematics, *convolution* is how two functions affect the result if one acts on the other in a particular way. It is often used to model situations in which one function describes a primary behavior and another function describes a secondary effect. For example, in image processing, convolution takes into account neighboring pixels to improve identification of boundaries and to add artificial blur. In audio processing, convolution is used to both analyze and synthesize room reverberation effects. A convolutional neural network (CNN) is a neural network that includes convolution in the training process. For example, you could use a CNN for facial recognition. The CNN would systematically take into account neighboring pixels, an essential duty when analyzing digital images.

A graph convolutional network (GCN) is a neural network that uses graph traversal as a convolution function during the learning process. While there were some earlier related works, the first model to distill the essence of graph convolution into a simple but powerful neural network was presented in 2017 in Thomas Kipf and Max Welling's "Semi-Supervised Classification with Graph Convolutional Networks" (*https://oreil.ly/b14rL*).

For graphs, we want the embedding for each vertex to include information about the relationships to other vertices. We can use the principle of convolution to accomplish this. Figure 10-16 shows a simple convolution function, with a general model at top and a more specific example at bottom.

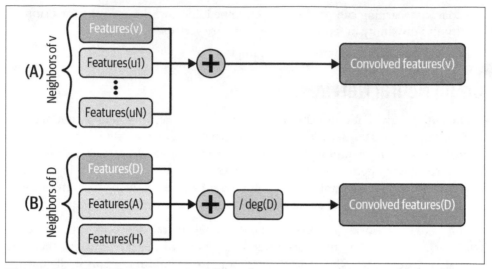

Figure 10-16. Convolution using neighbors of a vertex

In part (a) of the figure, the primary function is Features(v): given a vertex v, output its feature vector. The convolution combines the features of v with the features of all of the neighbors of v: u1, u2,…,uN. If the features are numeric, a simple convolution would be adding them. The result is the newly convolved features of v. In part (b), we set v = D from Figure 10-15. Vertex D has two neighbors, A and H. We insert one more step after summing the feature vectors: divide by the degree of the primary vertex. Vertex D has 2 neighbors, so we divide by 2. This regularizes the output values so that they don't keep getting bigger and bigger. (Yes, technically we should divide by $\deg(v) + 1$, but the simpler version seems to be good enough.)

Let's do a quick example:

```
features[0](D) = [3, 1 ,4, 1]
features[0](A) = [5, 9, 2, 6]
features[0](H) = [5, 3, 5, 8]
features[1](D) = [6.5, 6.5, 5.5, 7.5]
```

By having neighbors share their feature values, this simple convolution function performs selective information sharing: it determines what is shared (features) and by whom (neighbors). A neural network that uses this convolution function will tend to evolve according to these maxims:

- Vertices that share many neighbors will tend to be similar.

- Vertices that share the same initial feature values will tend to be similar.

These properties are reminiscent of random-walk graph embeddings.

How do we take this convolution and integrate it into a neural network? Take a look at Figure 10-17.

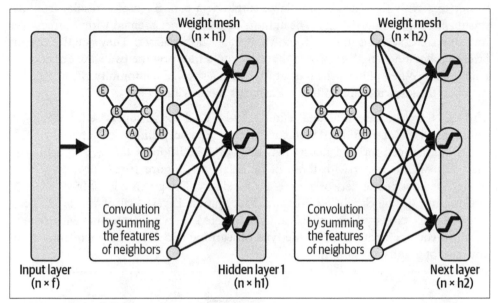

Figure 10-17. Two-layer graph convolutional network

This two-layer network flows from left to right. The input is the feature vectors for all of the graph's vertices. If the feature vectors run horizontally and we stack the vertices vertically, then we get an $n \times f$ matrix, where f is the number of features. Next, we apply the adjacency-based convolution. We then apply a set of randomized weights (similar to what we did with random-walk graph embedding networks) to merge and reduce the features to an embedding of size h1. Typically $h1 < f$. Before storing the values in the embedding matrix, we apply an activation function (indicated by the blocky "S" in a circle), which acts as a filter/amplifier. Low values are pushed lower, and high values are pushed higher. Activation functions are used in most neural networks.

Because this is a two-layer network, we repeat the same steps. The only differences are that this embedding may have a different size, where typically $h2 \leq h1$, and this weight mesh has a different set of random weights. If this is the final layer, then it's considered the output layer with the output results. By having two layers, the output embedding for each vertex takes into account the neighbors within two hops. You can add more layers to consider deeper neighbors. Two or three layers often provide the best results. With too many layers, the radius of each vertex's neighborhood becomes so large that it overlaps significantly even with the neighborhoods of unrelated vertices.

Our example here is demonstrating how a GCN can be used in unsupervised learning mode. No training data or target function was provided; we just merged features of vertices with their neighbors. Surprisingly, you can get useful results from an unsupervised, untrained GCN. The authors of GCN experimented with a three-layer untrained GCN, using the well-known Karate Club dataset. They set the output layer's embedding length of two, so that they could interpret the two values as coordinate points. When plotted, the output data points showed community clustering that matched the known communities in Zachary's Karate Club.

The GCN architecture is general enough to be used for unsupervised, supervised, semisupervised, or even reinforcement learning. The only difference between a GCN and a vanilla feed-forward neural network is the addition of the step to aggregate the features of a vector with those of its neighbors. Figure 10-18 shows a generic model for how neural networks tune their weights. The graph convolution in GCN affects only the block labeled Forward Propagation Layers. All of the other parts (input values, target values, weight adjustment, etc.) are what determine what type of learning you are doing. That is, the type of learning is decided independently from your use of graph convolution.

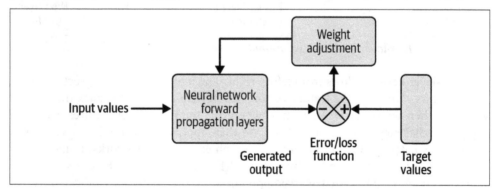

Figure 10-18. Generic model for responsive learning in a neural network

Attention neural networks use a more advanced form of feedback and adjustment. The details are beyond the scope of this book, but graph attention neural networks (GATs) can tune the weight (aka focus the attention) of each neighbor when adding them together for convolution. That is, a GAT performs a weighted sum instead of a simple sum of a neighbor's features, and the GAT trains itself to learn the best weights. When applied to the same benchmark tests, GAT outperforms GCN slightly.

Matrix Algebra Formulation

If you like to think in terms of matrices, we can express the convolution process in terms of three simple, standard matrices for any graph: the adjacency matrix A, the identity matrix I, and the degree matrix D. (Feel free to skip this section if this doesn't sound like you.)

Matrix A expresses the connectivity of the graph. Number the vertices 1 to n, and number the rows and columns similarly. The value $A(i, j) = 1$ if there is an edge from vertex i to vertex j; otherwise $A(i,j)$ is 0. The identity matrix says, "I am myself." $I(i, j) = 1$ if $i = j$; otherwise it is 0. It looks like a diagonal line from upper left to lower right. The matrix in Figure 10-19 is $(A + I)$. In each row i, the 1's tell us the convolution function for vertex i.

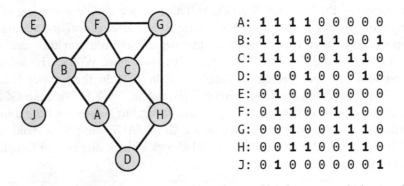

```
A: 1 1 1 1 0 0 0 0 0 0
B: 1 1 1 0 1 1 0 0 1
C: 1 1 1 0 0 1 1 1 0
D: 1 0 0 1 0 0 0 1 0
E: 0 1 0 0 1 0 0 0 0
F: 0 1 1 0 0 1 1 0 0
G: 0 0 1 0 0 1 1 1 0
H: 0 0 1 1 0 0 1 1 0
J: 0 1 0 0 0 0 0 0 1
```

Figure 10-19. A graph and matrix representing the graph's adjacency and identity: (A+I)

What about the regularization? With matrices, when we want to perform division, we instead multiply by the inverse matrix. The matrix we want is the degree matrix D, where $D(i, j) = degree(i)$ if $i = j$; otherwise it is 0. The degree matrix of the graph of Figure 10-12 is shown in the left half of Figure 10-20. At the right is the inverse matrix D^{-1}.

```
A: 3 0 0 0 0 0 0 0 0        A: ⅓ 0 0 0 0 0 0 0 0
B: 0 5 0 0 0 0 0 0 0        B: 0 ⅕ 0 0 0 0 0 0 0
C: 0 0 5 0 0 0 0 0 0        C: 0 0 ⅕ 0 0 0 0 0 0
D: 0 0 0 2 0 0 0 0 0        D: 0 0 0 ½ 0 0 0 0 0
E: 0 0 0 0 1 0 0 0 0        E: 0 0 0 0 1 0 0 0 0
F: 0 0 0 0 0 3 0 0 0        F: 0 0 0 0 0 ⅓ 0 0 0
G: 0 0 0 0 0 0 3 0 0        G: 0 0 0 0 0 0 ⅓ 0 0
H: 0 0 0 0 0 0 0 3 0        H: 0 0 0 0 0 0 0 ⅓ 0
J: 0 0 0 0 0 0 0 0 1        J: 0 0 0 0 0 0 0 0 1
```

Figure 10-20. The degree matrix D and itself inverse matrix D^{-1}

We can express the computation from layer H0 to the next layer H1 as follows:

$$H_1 = \sigma\left(D^{-1}(A + 1)H_0 W_1\right)$$

where σ is the activation function and W is the weight mesh. In Kipf and Welling's paper, they made a tweak to provide a more balanced regularization:

$$H_1 = \sigma\left(D^{-1/2}(A+1)D^{-1/2}H_0 W_1\right)$$

GraphSAGE

One limitation of the basic GCN model is that it does a simple averaging of vertex plus neighbor features. It seems we would want some more control and tuning of this convolution. Also, large variations in the number of neighbors for different vertices may lead to training difficulties. To address this limitation, William Hamilton, Rex Ying, and Jure Leskovec presented GraphSAGE in 2017 in their paper "Inductive Representation Learning on Large Graphs" (*https://oreil.ly/YTlH9*). Like GCN, this technique also combines information from neighbors, but it does it a little differently. To standardize the learning from neighbors, GraphSAGE samples a fixed number of neighbors from each vertex. Figure 10-21 shows a block diagram of GraphSAGE, with sampled neighbors.

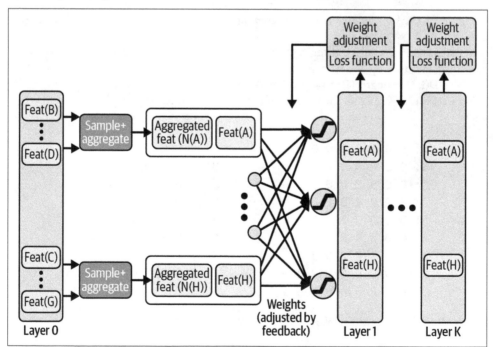

Figure 10-21. Block diagram of GraphSAGE

With GraphSAGE, the features of the neighbors are combined according to a chosen aggregation function. The function could be addition, as in GCNs. Any order-independent aggregation function could be used; long short-term memory (LSTM) with random ordering and max-pooling work well. The source vertex is not included in the aggregation as it is in GCN; instead, the aggregated feature vectors and the source vertex's feature vector are concatenated to make a double-length vector. We then apply a set of weights to mix the features together, apply an activation function, and store as the next layer's representation of the vertices. This series of sets constitutes one layer in the neural network and the gathering of information within one hop of each vertex. A GraphSAGE network has k layers, each with its own set of weights. GraphSAGE proposes a loss function that rewards nearby vertices if they have similar embeddings and rewards distant vertices if they have dissimilar embeddings.

Besides training on the full graph, as you would with GCN, you can train Graph SAGE with only a sample of the vertices and their neighborhoods. The fact that GraphSAGE's aggregation functions use equal-sized samples of neighborhoods means that it doesn't matter how you arrange the inputs. That freedom of arrangement is what allows you to train with one sample and then test or deploy with a different sample. Because it builds a model based on these generalized graph neighborhood properties, GraphSAGE performs *inductive learning*. That is, the model can be used to make predictions about new vertices that were not in the original dataset. In contrast, GCN directly uses the adjacency matrix, which forces it to use the full graph with the vertices arranged in a particular order. Training with the full data and learning a model for only that data is *transductive learning*.

Whether or not learning from a sample will work on your particular graph depends on whether your graph's structure and features follow global trends, such that a random subgraph looks similar to another subgraph of similar size. For example, one part of a forest may look a lot like another part of a forest. For a graph example, suppose you have a Customer 360 graph including all of a customer's interactions with your sales team, website, and events, their purchases, and all other profile information you have been able to obtain. Last year's customers are rated based on the total amount and frequency of their purchases. It is reasonable to expect that if you used GraphSAGE with last year's graph to predict the customer rating, it should do a decent job of predicting the ratings of this year's customers. Table 10-2 summarizes all the similarities and differences between GCN and GraphSAGE that we have presented.

Table 10-2. Comparison of GCN and GraphSAGE traits

	GCN	GraphSAGE
Neighbors for aggregation	All	Sample of n neighbors
Aggregation function	Mean	Several options
Aggregating a vertex with neighbors?	Aggregated with others	Concatenated to others
Do weights need to be learned?	Not for unsupervised transductive model	Yes, for inductive model
Supervised?	Yes	Yes
Self-supervised?	With modification	With modification
Can be trained on a sample of vertices	No	Yes

Graph-based neural networks put graphs into the mainstream of machine learning. Key takeaways from this section are as follows:

- The graph convolutional neural network enhances the vanilla neural network by averaging together the feature vectors of each vertex's neighbors with its own features during the learning process.

- GraphSAGE makes two key improvements to the basic GCN: vertex and neighborhood sampling, and keeping features of vectors separate from those of its neighbors.

- GCN learns transductively (uses the full data to learn only about that data), whereas GraphSAGE learns inductively (uses a data sample to learn a model that can apply to other data samples).

- The modular nature of neural networks and graph enhancements means that the ideas of GCN and GraphSAGE can be transferred to many other flavors of neural networks.

Comparing Graph Machine Learning Approaches

This chapter has covered many different ways to learn from graph data, but it only scratched the surface. Our goal was not to present an exhaustive survey but to provide a framework from which to continue to grow. We've outlined the major categories of and techniques for graph-powered machine learning, we've described what characterizes and distinguishes them, and we've provided simple examples to illustrate how they operate. It's worthwhile to briefly review these techniques. Our goal here is not only to summarize but also to provide you with guidance for selecting the right techniques to help you learn from your connected data.

Use Cases for Machine Learning Tasks

Table 10-3 pulls together examples of use cases for each of the major learning tasks. These are the same basic data mining and machine learning tasks you might perform on any data, but the examples are particularly relevant for graph data.

Table 10-3. Use cases for graph data learning tasks

Task	Use case examples
Community detection	Delineating social networks
	Finding a financial crime network
	Detecting a biological ecosystem or chemical reaction network
	Discovering a network of unexpectedly interdependent components or processes, such as software procedures or legal regulations
Similarity	Abstraction of physical closeness, inverse of distance
	Prerequisite for clustering, classification, and link prediction
	Entity resolution: finding two online identities that probably refer to the same real-world person
	Product recommendation or suggested action
	Identifying persons who perform the same role in different but analogous networks
Find unknown patterns	Identifying the most common "customer journeys" on your website or in your app
	Once current patterns are identified, then noticing changes
Link prediction	Predicting someone's future purchase or willingness to purchase
	Predicting that a business or personal relationship exists, even though it is not recorded in the data
Feature extraction	Enriching your customer data with graph features, so that your machine learning training to categorize and model your customers will be more successful
Embedding	Transforming a large set of features to a more compact set, for more efficient computation
	Holistically capturing a neighbor's signature without designing specific feature extraction queries
Classification (predicting a category)	Given some past examples of fraud, creating a model for identifying new cases of fraud
	Predicting categorical outcomes for future vaccine patients, based on test results of past patients
Regression (predicting a numerical value)	Predicting weight loss for diet program participants, based on results of past participants

Once you have identified what type of task you want to perform, consider the available graph-based learning techniques, what they provide, and their key strengths and differences.

Pattern Discovery and Feature Extraction Methods

Table 10-4 lists the graph algorithms and feature extraction methods we encountered both in this chapter and in Chapter 6.

Table 10-4. Pattern discovery and feature extraction methods in graphs

Task	Graph-based learning methods	Comments
Community detection	Connected components	One connection to the community is enough
	k-core	At least k connections to other community members
	Modularity optimization (e.g., Louvain)	Relatively higher density of connections inside than between communities
Similarity	Jaccard neighborhood similarity	Counts how many relationships in common, for nonnumerical data
	Cosine neighborhood similarity	Compares numeric or weighted vectors of relationships
	Role similarity	Defines similarity recursively as having similar neighbors
Find unknown patterns	Frequent pattern mining	Starts with small patterns and builds to larger patterns
Domain-independent feature extraction	Graphlets	Systematic list of all possible neighborhood configurations
	PageRank	Rank is based on the number and rank of in-neighbors, for directed graphs among vertices of the same type
	Closeness centrality	Closeness = average distance to any other vertex
	Betweenness centrality	How often a vertex lies on the shortest path between any two vertices; slow to compute
Domain-dependent feature extraction	Search for patterns relevant to your domain	Custom effort by someone with domain knowledge
Dimensionality reduction and embedding	DeepWalk	Embeddings will be similar if the vectors have similar random walks, considering nearness and role; more efficient than SimRank
	node2vec	DeepWalk with directional tuning of the random walks, for greater tuning

Graph Neural Networks: Summary and Uses

The graph neural networks presented in this chapter not only are directly useful in many cases but are also templates to show more advanced data scientists how to transform any neural network technique to include graph connectivity in the training. The key is the convolution step, which takes the features of neighboring vertices into account. All of the GNN approaches presented can be used for either unsupervised or supervised learning. Table 10-5 compares graph neural network methods.

Table 10-5. Summary of three types of graph neural networks

Name	Description	Uses
Graph convolutional network (GCN)	Convolution: average of neighbor's features	Clustering or classification on a particular graph
GraphSAGE	Convolution: average of a sample of neighbor's features	Learning a representative model on a sample of a graph, in addition to clustering or classification
Graph attention neural network (GAT)	Convolution: weighted average of neighbor's features	Clustering, classification, and model learning; added tuning and complexity by learning weights for the convolution

Chapter Summary

Graphs and graph-based algorithms contribute to several stages of the machine learning pipeline: data acquisition, data exploration and pattern discovery, data preparation, feature extraction, dimensionality reduction, and model training. As data scientists know, there is no golden ticket, no single technique that solves all their problems. Instead, you work to acquire tools for your toolkit, develop the skills to use your tools well, and gain an understanding about when to use them.

CHAPTER 11

Entity Resolution Revisited

This chapter uses entity resolution for a streaming video service as an example of unsupervised machine learning with graph algorithms. After completing this chapter, you should be able to:

- Name the categories of graph algorithms that are appropriate for entity resolution as unsupervised learning
- List three different approaches for assessing the similarity of entities
- Understand how parameterized weights can adapt entity resolution to be a supervised learning task
- Interpret a simple GSQL FROM clause and have a general understanding of ACCUM semantics
- Set up and run a TigerGraph Cloud Starter Kit using GraphStudio

Problem: Identify Real-World Users and Their Tastes

The streaming video on demand (SVoD) market is big business. Accurate estimates of the global market size are hard to come by, but the most conservative estimate may be $50 billion in 2020,[1] with annual growth rates ranging from 11%[2] to 21%[3] for the next five years or so. Movie studios, television networks, communication networks,

---

[1] "Video Streaming Market Size Worth $416.84 Billion by 2030," Grand View Research, March 2023, *https://www.grandviewresearch.com/press-release/global-video-streaming-market*.

[2] "Video Streaming (SVoD) – Worldwide," Statista, accessed May 26, 2023, *https://www.statista.com/outlook/dmo/digital-media/video-on-demand/video-streaming-svod/worldwide*.

[3] "Video Streaming Market Size Worth $416.84 Billion by 2030," Grand View Research.

and tech giants have been merging and reinventing themselves, in hopes of becoming a leader in the new preferred format for entertainment consumption: on-demand digital entertainment, on any video-capable device.

To succeed, SVoD providers need to have the content to attract and retain many millions of subscribers. Traditional video technology (movie theaters and broadcast television) limited the provider to offering only one program at a time per venue or per broadcast region. Viewers had very limited choice, and providers selected content that would appeal to large segments of the public. Home video on VHS tape and DVD introduced personalization. Wireless digital video on demand on any personal device has put the power in the hands of the consumer.

Providers no longer need to appeal to the masses. On the contrary, the road to success is microsegmentation: to offer something for everyone. The SVoD giants are assembling sizable catalogs of existing content, as well as spending billions of dollars on new content. The volume of options creates several data management problems. With so many shows available, it is very hard for users to browse. Providers must categorize the content, categorize users, and then recommend shows to users. Good recommendations increase viewership and satisfaction.

While predicting customers' interests is hard enough, the streaming video industry also needs to overcome a multifaceted *entity resolution* problem. Entity resolution, you may recall, is the task of identifying two or more entities in a dataset that refer to the same real-world entity and then linking or merging them together. In today's market, streaming video providers face at least three entity resolution challenges. First, each user may have multiple different authorization schemes, one for each type of device they use for viewing. Second, corporate mergers are common, and they require merging the databases of the constituent companies. For example, Disney+ combines the catalogs of Disney, Pixar, Marvel, and National Geographic Studios. Max brings together HBO, Warner Bros., DC Comics, and Discovery. Third, SVoD providers may form a promotional, affiliate, or partnership arrangement with another company: a customer may be able to access streaming service A because they are a customer of some other service B. For example, customers of Verizon internet service may qualify for free Disney+, Hulu, and ESPN+ service.

Solution: Graph-Based Entity Resolution

Before we can design a solution, let's start with a clear statement of the problem we want to solve.

Problem Statement

Each real-world user may have multiple digital identities. The goal is to discover the hidden connections between these digital identities and then to link or merge them together. By doing so, we will be able to connect all of the information together, forming a more complete picture of the user. In particular, we will know all the videos that a person has watched so we can get a better understanding of their personal taste and make better recommendations.

Now that we've crafted a clear problem statement, let's consider a potential solution: entity resolution. Entity resolution has two parts: deciding which entities are probably the same and then resolving entities. Let's look at each part in turn.

Learning Which Entities Are the Same

If we are fortunate enough to have training data showing us examples of entities that are in fact the same, we can use supervised learning to train a machine learning model. In this case, we do not have training data. Instead, we will rely on the characteristics of the data itself, looking at similarities and communities to perform unsupervised learning.

To do a good job, we want to build in some domain knowledge. What are the situations for a person to have multiple online identities, and what would be the clues in the data? Here are some reasons why a person may create multiple accounts:

- A user creates a second account because they forgot about or forgot how to access the first one.

- A user has accounts with two different streaming services, and the companies enter a partnership or merge.

- A person may intentionally set up multiple distinct identities, perhaps to take advantage of multiple membership rewards or to separate their behavioral profiles (e.g., to watch different types of videos on different accounts). The personal information may be very different, but the device IDs might be the same.

Whenever the same person creates two different accounts at different moments, there can be variations in some details for trivial or innocuous reasons. The person decides to use a nickname. They choose to abbreviate a city or street name. They mistype. They have multiple phone numbers and email addresses to choose from, and they make a different choice for no particular reason. Over time, more substantial changes may occur to the address, phone number, device IDs, and even the user's name.

While several situations can result in one person having multiple online identities, it seems we can focus our data analysis on only two patterns. In the first pattern, most of the personal information will be the same or similar, but a few attributes may differ. Even when two attributes differ, they may still be related. An example is the use of a nickname or a misspelling of an address. In the second pattern, much of the information is different, but one or more key pieces remain the same, such as home phone number or birthdate, and behavioral clues (such as what type of videos they like and what time of day they watch them) may suggest that two identities belong to the same person.

To build our solution, we will need to use some similarity algorithms and also a community detection or clustering algorithm to group similar entities together.

Resolving Entities

Once we have used the appropriate algorithms to identify a group of entities that we believe to be the same, what will we do about it? We want to update the database somehow to reflect this new knowledge. There are two possible ways to accomplish this: merge the group into one entity or link the entities in a special way so that whenever we look at one member of the group, we will readily see the other related identities.

Merging the entities makes sense when some online identities are considered incorrect, so we want to eliminate them. For example, suppose a customer has two online accounts because they misspelled their name or forgot that they had an account already. Both the business owner and the customer want to eliminate one account and to merge all of the records (purchase history, game scores, etc.) into one account. Knowing which account to eliminate takes more knowledge of each specific case than we have in our example.

Alternatively, one can simply link entities together. Specifically, make use of two types of entities in the graph: one representing digital identities and the other representing real-world entities. After resolution, the database will show one real-world entity having an edge to each of its digital identities, as illustrated in Figure 11-1.

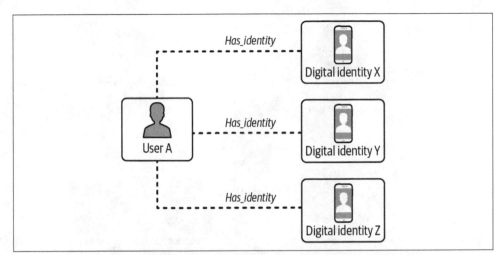

Figure 11-1. Digital entities linked to a real-world entity after resolution

Implementing Graph-Based Entity Resolution

The implementation of graph-based entity resolution we will present is available as a TigerGraph Cloud Starter Kit. As usual, we will focus on using the GraphStudio visual interface. All of the necessary operations could also be performed from a command-line interface.

The In-Database Entity Resolution Starter Kit

Using TigerGraph Cloud, deploy a new cloud instance and select "In-Database Machine Learning for Big Data Entity Resolution" as the use case. Once this starter kit is installed, load the data following the steps listed in the section "Load data and install queries for a starter kit" on page 50 in Chapter 3.

Graph Schema

Looking at the graph schema shown in Figure 11-2, you can see that **Account**, **User**, and **Video** are hub vertices, with several edges radiating from them. The other vertices represent the personal information about users and the characteristics of videos. We want to compare the personal information of different users. Following good practice for graph-oriented analytics, if we want to see if two or more entities have a feature in common (e.g., email address), we model that feature as a vertex instead of as a property of a vertex.

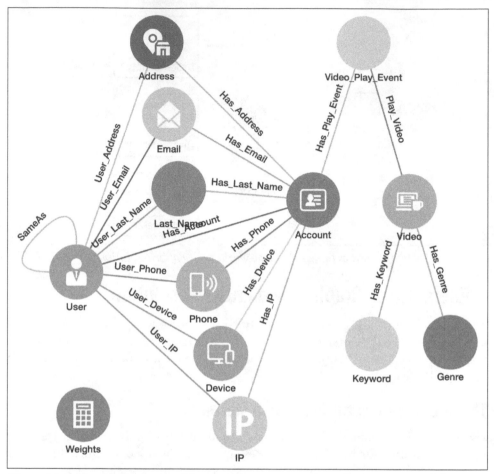

Figure 11-2. Graph schema for video customer accounts (see a larger version of this figure at https://oreil.ly/gpam1102)

Table 11-1 gives a brief explanation of each of the vertex types in the graph model. Though the starter kit's data contains much data about videos, we will not focus on the videos themselves in this exercise. We are going to focus on entity resolution of **Accounts**.

Table 11-1. Vertex types in the graph model

Vertex type	Description
`Account`	An account for a SVoD user, a digital identity
`User`	A real-world person. One `User` can link to multiple `Accounts`
`IP`, `Email`, `Last_Name`, `Phone`, `Address`, `Device`	Key attributes of an `Account`, represented as vertices to facilitate linking `Accounts`/`Users` that share a common attribute
`Video`	A video title offered by an SVoD
`Keyword`, `Genre`	Attributes of a `Video`
`Video_Play_Event`	The time and duration of a particular `Account` viewing a particular `Video`
`Weight`	Similarity model parameters

Queries and Analytics

For our entity resolution use case, we have a three-stage plan requiring three or more queries:

1. Initialization: For each **Account** vertex, create a **User** vertex and link them. **Accounts** are online identities, and **Users** represent real-world persons. We begin with the hypothesis that each **Account** is a real person.

2. Similarity detection: Apply one or more similarity algorithms to measure the similarity between **User** vertices. If we consider a pair to be similar enough, then we create a link between them, using the **SameAs** edge type shown in Figure 11-2.

3. Merging: Find the connected components of linked **User** vertices. Pick one of them to be the main vertex. Transfer all of the edges of the other members of the community to the main vertex. Delete the other community vertices.

For reasons we will explain when we talk about merging, you may need to repeat steps 2 and 3 as a pair, until the similarity detection step is no longer creating any new connections.

We will present two different methods for implementing entity resolution in our use case. The first method uses Jaccard similarity (detailed in Chapter 6) to count exact matches of neighboring vertices and treating each neighbor with equal importance. Merging will use a simple connected component algorithm. The second method is more advanced, suggesting a way to handle both exact and approximate matches of attribute values, and including weights to adjust the relative importance of relationships. Approximate matches are a good way to handle minor typos or the use of abbreviated names.

Method 1: Jaccard Similarity

For each of the three stages, well give a high-level explanation, directions for operations to perform in TigerGraph's GraphStudio, a description of what to expect as a result, and a closer look at some of the GSQL code in the queries.

Initialization

Recall in our model that an **Account** is a digital identity and a **User** is a real person. The original database contains only **Accounts**. The initialization step creates a unique temporary **User** linked to each **Account**. And for every edge that runs from an **Account** to one of the attribute vertices (**Email**, **Phone**, etc.), we create a corresponding edge from the **User** to the same set of attribute vertices. Figure 11-3 shows an example. The three vertices on the left and the two edges connecting them are part of the original data. The initialization step creates the **User** vertex and the three dotted-line edges. As a result, each **User** starts out with the same attribute neighborhood as its **Account**.

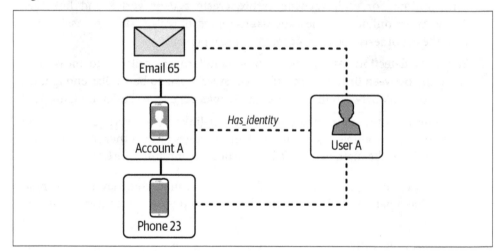

Figure 11-3. User vertex and edges created in the initialization step

Do: Run the GSQL query `initialize_users`.

This query has no input parameters, so it will run immediately without any additional steps from the user. The following block of code shows the first 20 lines of `initialize_users`. The comment at the beginning lists the six types of attribute vertices to be included:

```
CREATE QUERY initialize_users()  FOR GRAPH Entity_Resolution SYNTAX v2 {
// Create a User vertex for each Account, plus edges to connect attributes
// (IP, Email, Device, Phone, Last_Name, Address) of the Account to the User

  // Initialize each account with a user
  Accounts = SELECT s FROM Account:s
    WHERE s.outdegree("Has_Account")==0
    ACCUM
      INSERT INTO User VALUES(s.id),
      INSERT INTO Has_Account VALUES(s.id, s);

  // Connect the User to all the attributes of their account
  IPs = SELECT attr FROM Accounts:s -(Has_IP:e)- IP:attr
    ACCUM
      INSERT INTO User_IP VALUES(s.id, attr);

  Emails = SELECT attr FROM Accounts:s -(Has_Email:e)- Email:attr
    ACCUM
      INSERT INTO User_Email VALUES(s.id, attr);

  // Remaining code omitted for brevity
}
```

In the first SELECT block, for each **Account** that doesn't already have a neighboring **User**, we use INSERT statements to create a **User** vertex and a **Has_Account** edge connecting this **User** to the **Account**. The alias s refers to an **Account**; we give the new **User** the same ID as that of its paired **Account**: s.id.

The next block takes care of **IP** attribute vertices: If there is a **Has_IP** edge from an **Account** to an **IP** vertex, then insert an edge from the corresponding **User** vertex to the same **IP** vertex. The final block in the section handles **Email** attribute vertices in an analogous way. The code for the remaining four attribute types (**Device**, **Phone**, **Last_Name**, and **Address**) has been omitted for brevity.

Similarity detection

Jaccard similarity counts how many attributes two entities have in common, divided by the total number of attributes between them. Each comparison of attributes results in a yes/no answer; a miss is as good as a mile. Figure 11-4 shows an example where User A and User B each have three attributes; two of those match (Email 65 and Device 87). Therefore, A and B have two attributes in common.

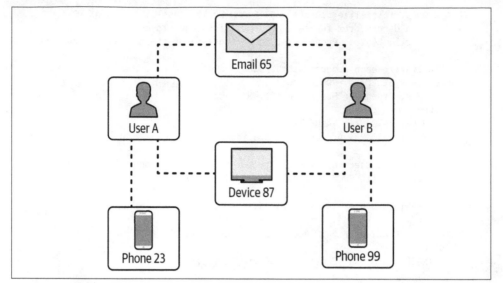

Figure 11-4. Jaccard similarity example

They have a total of four distinct attributes (Email 65, Device 87, Phone 23, and Phone 99); therefore, the Jaccard similarity is 2/4 = 0.5.

Do: Run the `connect_jaccard_sim` query with default parameter values.

This query computes this similarity score for each pair of vertices. If the score is at or above the given threshold, it creates a **Same_As** edge to connect the two **Users**. The default threshold is 0.5, but you can make it higher or lower. Jaccard scores range from 0 to 1. Figure 11-5 shows the connections for **User** vertices 1, 2, 3, 4, and 5, using Jaccard similarity and a threshold of 0.5. For these five vertices, we find communities that range in size from one vertex alone (**User** 3) to three vertices (**Users** 1 and 2).

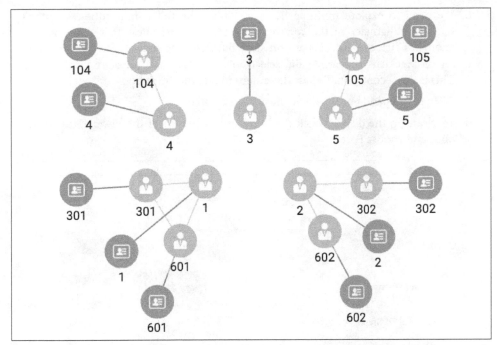

*Figure 11-5. Connections for **User** vertices 1, 2, 3, 4, and 5, using Jaccard similarity and a threshold of 0.5 (see a larger version of this figure at https://oreil.ly/gpam1105)*

How to Visualize User Communities

You can use the Explore Graph page in TigerGraph GraphStudio to create a display like the one in Figure 11-5:

1. Click the "Select vertices" icon at the top of the left-side menu (step 1 in Figure 11-6).

2. Choose the **User** vertex type. Enter the vertex ID **1** and click the Select icon. (step 2 in Figure 11-6). User 1 will appear in the display pane. Repeat for vertex IDs **2**, **3**, **4**, and **5**.

3. Shift-click the vertices so that all of them are selected (step 3, Figure 11-7).

4. Click the "Expand from vertices" icon, the next item in the left-side menu (step 4).

5. You are now presented with a checklist of all the edge types that you may wish to traverse, followed by a checklist of all the target vertex types. We want to include only the **User** and **Account** vertex types (step 5). This specifies a one-hop exploration.

6. We need to explore multiple hops, including the full communities. We don't know the diameter of the communities, but let's just guess that three hops is enough. Click the "Add expansion step" button at the bottom (step 6). Another set of checklists appear. Again, select only the **User** and **Account** vertex types. This is the second hop. Repeat these steps to set your third hop.

7. Click the Expand button above the checklists (step 7).

8. To clean up the display, click the layout menu button in the lower right corner once and choose Force.

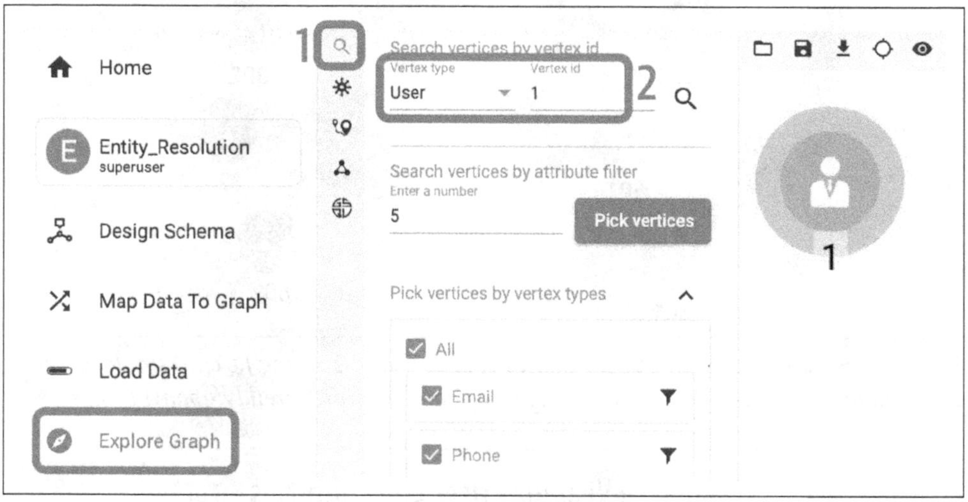

Figure 11-6. Selecting vertices on the Explore Graph page

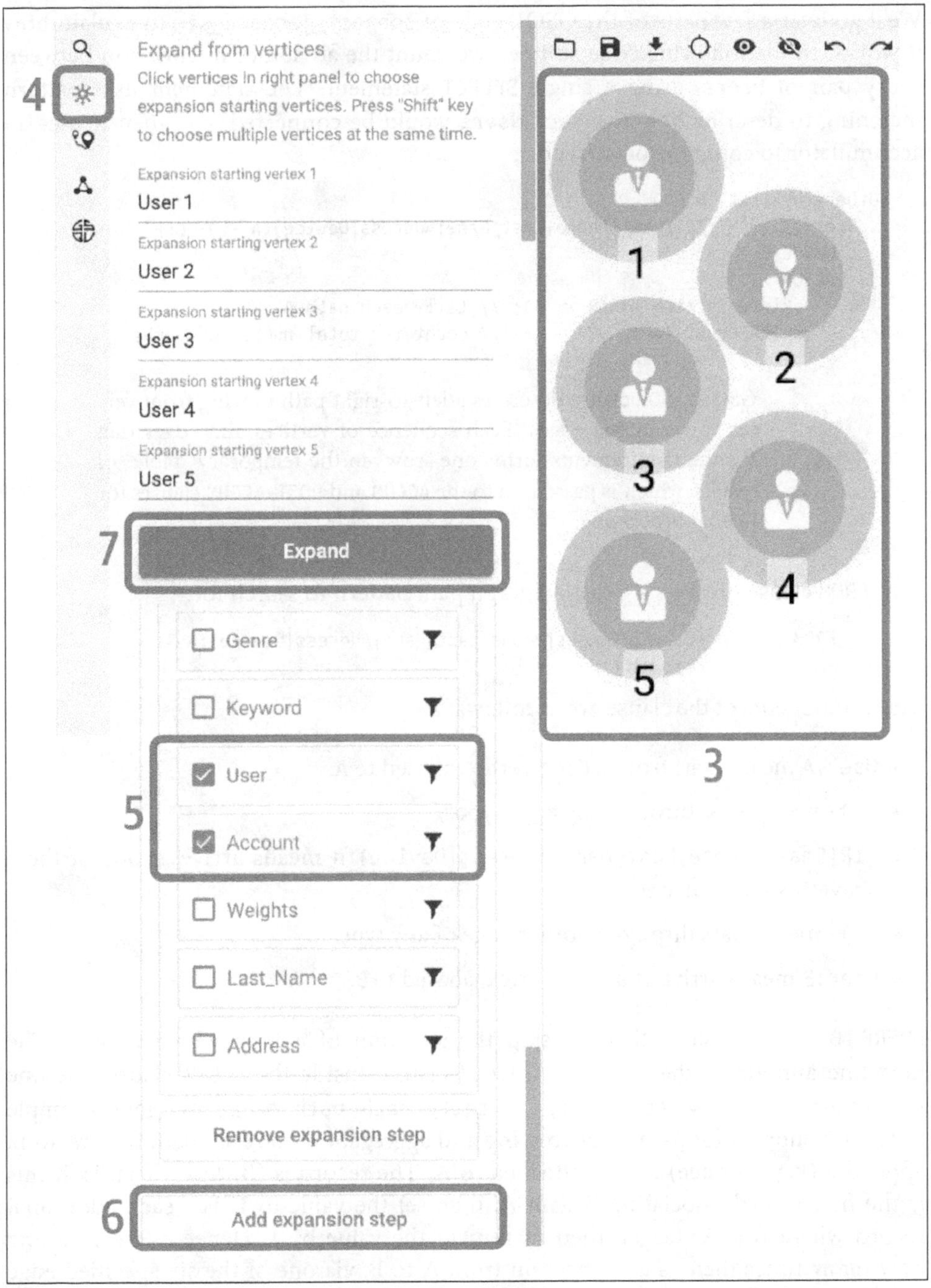

Figure 11-7. Expanding from vertices on the Explore Graph page

We'll go over a few parts of the GSQL code of `connect_jaccard_sim` to explain how it works. In the following code snippet, we count the attributes in common between every pair of **Users**, using a single SELECT statement. The statement uses pattern matching to describe how two such **Users** would be connected, and then it uses an accumulator to count the occurrences:

```
Others = SELECT B FROM
  Start:A -()- (IP|Email|Phone|Last_Name|Address|Device):n -()- User:B
    WHERE B != A
    ACCUM
      A.@intersection += (B -> 1), // tally each path A->B,
      @@path_count += 1;           // count the total number of paths
```

 GSQL's FROM clause describes a left-to-right path moving from vertex to vertex via edges. Each sequence of vertices and edges that fits the requirements forms one "row" in the temporary "table" of results, which is passed on to the ACCUM and POST-ACCUM clauses for further processing.

This FROM clause presents a two-hop graph path pattern to search for:

```
FROM User:A -()- (IP|Email|Phone|Last_Name|Address|Device):n
            -()- User:B
```

The components of the clause are as follows:

- User:A means start from a **User** vertex, aliased to A.

- -()- means pass through any edge type.

- (IP|Email|Phone|Last_Name|Address|Device):n means arrive at one of these six vertex types, aliased to n.

- -()- means pass through another edge of any type.

- User:B means arrive at a **User** vertex, aliased to B.

WHERE B != A ensures that we skip the situation of a loop where A = B. The next line announces the start of an ACCUM clause. Inside the ACCUM clause, the line (A.@intersection += (B -> 1), // tally each path A->B) is a good example of GSQL's support for parallel processing and aggregation: for each path from A to B, append a (key → value) record attached to A. The record is (B, +=1). That is, if this is the first record associating B with A, then set the value to 1. For each additional record where B is A's target, then increment the value by 1. Hence, we're counting how many times there is a connection from A to B, via one of the six specified edge types. This line ends with a comma, so the next line @@path_count += 1 is still part of the ACCUM clause. For bookkeeping purposes, @@path_count counts how many of these paths we find.

Let's look at one more code block—the final computation of Jaccard similarity and creation of connections between **Users**:

```
Result = SELECT A FROM User:A
  ACCUM FOREACH (B, overlap) IN A.@intersection DO
    FLOAT score = overlap*1.0/(@@deg.get(A) + @@deg.get(B) - overlap),
    IF score > threshold THEN
      INSERT INTO EDGE SameAs VALUES (A, B, score), // FOR Entity Res
      @@insert_count += 1,
      IF score != 1 THEN
        @@jaccard_heap += SimilarityTuple(A,B,score)
      END
    END
END;
```

This **SELECT** block does the following:

1. For each **User** A, iterate over its set of records of similar **Users** B, along with B's number of common neighbors, aliased to `overlap`.

2. For each such pair (A, B), compute the Jaccard score, using `overlap` as well as the number of qualified neighbors of A and B (`@@deg.get(A)` and `@@deg.get(B)`), computed earlier.

3. If the score is greater than the threshold, insert a **SameAs** edge between A and B.

4. `@@insert_count` and `@@jaccard_heap` are for reporting statistics.

Merging

In our third and last stage, we merge the connected communities of **User** vertices that we created in the previous step. For each community, we will select one vertex to be the survivor or lead. The remaining members will be deleted; all of the edges from an **Account** to a nonlead will be redirected to point to the lead **User**.

Do: Run the `merge_connected_users` query. The value of the threshold parameter should always be the same as the value used for `connect_jaccard_sim`.

Look at the JSON output. Note whether it says `converged = TRUE` or `FALSE`. Figure 11-8 displays the user communities for Accounts 1, 2, 3, 4, and 5. Each user community has been reduced to a single **User** (real person). Each of those **Users** links to one or more **Accounts** (digital identities). We've achieved our entity resolution.

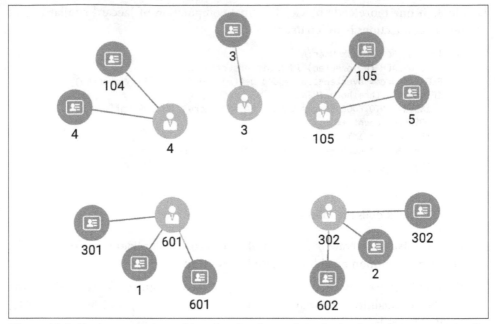

Figure 11-8. Entity resolution achieved, using Jaccard similarity (see a larger version of this figure at https://oreil.ly/gpam1108)

The merge_connected_users algorithm has three stages:

1. In each component, select a lead **User**.

2. In each component, redirect the attribute connections from other **Users** to the lead **User**.

3. Delete the **Users** that are not the lead **User** and all of the **Same_As** edges.

Let's take a closer look at the GSQL code. For each group of similar **Users** connected by **Same_As** edges, we will choose the one that happens to have the smallest ID value as the lead **User**. We use a MinAccum called @min_user_id to compare vertices' internal ID values. Whenever you input a new value to a MinAccum, it retains the lesser of its current value and the new input value. We start by initialing every vertex's @min_user_id to itself:

```
Updated_users = SELECT s FROM Users:s
    POST-ACCUM s.@min_user_id = s;
```

Then, we iterate on the following process: for each pair of connected **Users** s → t (FROM clause), vertex t updates @min_user_id to be the lesser of the two vertices' internal IDs (ACCUM clause):

```
WHILE (Updated_users.size() > 0) DO
  Updated_users = SELECT t
    FROM Updated_users:s -(SameAs:e)- User:t
      // Propagate the internal IDs from source to target vertex
    ACCUM t.@min_user_id += s.@min_user_id // t gets the lesser of t & s ids
    HAVING t.@min_user_id != t.@min_user_id' // tick' means accum's previous val
    ;
  iteration = iteration + 1;
END;
```

The HAVING clause is a filter to decide whether this particular t should be included in the Updated_users output set. Note the tick mark (') at the end of the line; this is a modifier for the accumulator t.@min_user_id. It means "the value of the accumulator *before* the ACCUM clause was executed." For looped procedures like this WHILE loop, this syntax lets us compare the previous value to current values. If t.@min_user_id's value is the same as its previous value, then t is not included in Updated_users. When no vertices have changed their @min_user_ids, we can exit the WHILE loop.

It might seem that one pass through the three steps—initialize, connect similar entities, and merge connected entities—should be enough. The merging, however, can create a situation in which new similarities arise. Take a look at Figure 11-9, which depicts the attribute connections of User 302 after Users 2 and 602 have been merged into it. Accounts 2, 302, and 602 remain separate, so you can see how each of them contributed some attributes. Because User 302 has more attributes than before, it is now possible that it is more similar than before to some other (possibly newly merged) User. Therefore, we should run another round of similarity connection and merge. Repeat these steps until no new similarities arise.

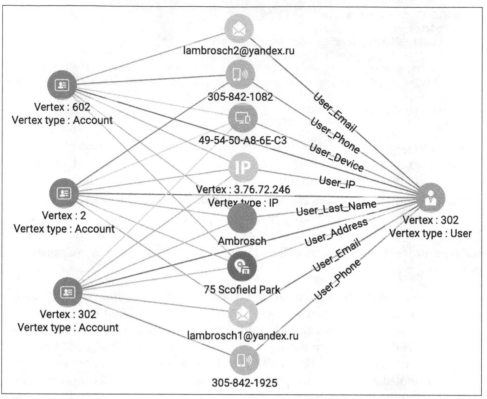

Figure 11-9. User with more attributes after entity resolution (see a larger version of this figure at https://oreil.ly/gpam1109)

As a reminder, here is the sequence of queries for simple entity resolution using Jaccard similarity:

1. Run `initialize_users`.
2. Run `connect_jaccard_sim`.
3. Run `merge_connected_users`.
4. Repeat steps 2 and 3 until the output of `merge_connected_users` says converged = TRUE.

Reset

After you've finished, or at any time, you might want to restore the database to its original state. You need to do this if you want to run the entity resolution process from the start again. The query `util_delete_users` will delete all **User** vertices and all edges connecting to them. Note that you need to change the input parameter `are_you_sure` from FALSE to TRUE. This manual effort is put in as a safety precaution.

> Deleting bulk vertices (`util_delete_users`) or creating bulk vertices (`initialize_users`) can take several seconds to take effect, even after a query says it is finished. Go to the Load Data page to check the live statistics for **User** vertices and **User**-related edges to see if the creation or deletion has finished.

Method 2: Scoring Exact and Approximate Matches

The previous section demonstrated a nice and easy graph-based entity resolution technique, but it is too basic for real-world use. It relies on exact matching of attribute values, whereas we need to allow for almost the same values, which arise from unintentional and intentional spelling variations. We also would like to make some attributes more important than others. For example, if you happen to have date-of-birth information, you might be strict about this attribute matching exactly. While persons can move and have multiple phone numbers and email addresses, they can have only one birth date. In this section, we will introduce weights to adjust the relative importance of different attributes. We will also provide a technique for approximate matches of string values.

> If you already used your starter kit to run Method 1, be sure to reset it. (See "Reset" on page 264 at the end of Method 1.)

Initialization

We are still using the same graph model with **User** vertices representing real persons and **Account** vertices representing digital accounts. So we are still using the `initialize_users` query to set up an initial set of **User** vertices.

We are adding the query `util_set_weights` as another initialization step. This query accepts weights for each of the six attributes (`IP`, `Email`, `Phone`, `Address`, `Last_Name`, and `Device`) and stores them. If this were a relational database, we would store those weights in a table. Since this is a graph, we are going to store them in a vertex. We need only one vertex, because one vertex can have multiple attributes. However, we are going to be even fancier. We are going to use a map type attribute, which will have six key → value entries. This allows us to use the map like a lookup table: tell me the name of the key (attribute name), and I'll tell you the value (weight).

If we had some ground truth training data (e.g., knowing which accounts truly belong to the same user), we could use machine learning to learn what attribute weight values are good at predicting whether two accounts belong to the same real person. Since we do not have any training data, the job of setting the best weights is left to the experience and judgment of the user.

Do: Run `initialize_users`. Check the graph statistics on the Load Data page to make sure that all 901 **User** vertices and related edges have been created. Run `util_set_weights`. The weights for the six attributes are input parameters for this query. Default weights are included, but you may change them if you wish. If you want to see the results, run `util_print_vertices`.

Scoring weighted exact matches

We are going to do our similarity comparison and linking in two phases. In phase one, we are still checking for exact matches because exact matches are more valuable than approximate matches; however, those connections will be weighted. In phase two, we will then check for approximate matches for our two attributes that have alphabetic values: `Last_Name` and `Address`.

In weighted exact matching, we create weighted connections between **Users**, where higher weights indicate stronger similarity. The net weight of a connection is the sum of the contributions from each attribute that is shared by the two **Users**. Figure 11-10 illustrates the weighted match computation. Earlier, during the initialization phase, you established weights for each of the attributes of interest. In the figure, we use the names `wt_email` and `wt_phone` for the weights associated with matching `Email` and `Phone` attributes, respectively.

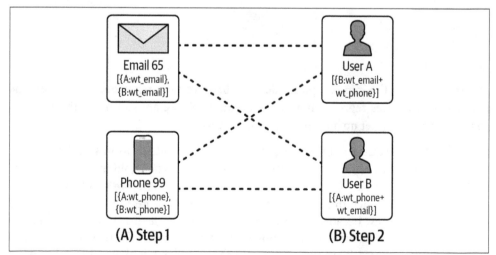

Figure 11-10. Two-phase calculation of weighted matches

The weighted match computation has two steps. In step 1, we look for connections from **Users** to **Attributes** and record a weight on each attribute for a connection to each **User**. Both User A and User B connect to Email 65, so Email 65 records A:wt_email and B:wt_email. Each **User**'s weight needs to be recorded separately. Phone 99 also connects to Users A and B so it records analogous information.

In step 2, we look for the same connections but in the other direction, with **Users** as the destinations. Both Email 65 and Phone 99 have connections to User A. User A aggregates their records from step 1. Note that some of those records refer to User A. User A ignores those, because it is not interested in connections to itself! In this example, it ends up recording B:(wt_email + wt_phone). We use this value to create a weighted **Same_As** edge between Users A and B. You can see that User B has equivalent information about User A.

Do: run the connect_weighted_match query.

Figure 11-11 shows one of the communities generated by connect_weighted_match. This particular community is the one containing User/Account 5. The figure also shows connections to two attributes, Address and Last_Name. The other attributes such as Email were used in the scoring but are not shown, to avoid clutter.

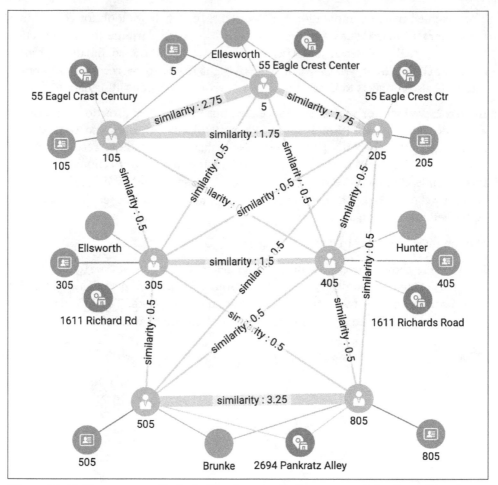

Figure 11-11. User community including Account 5 after exact weighted matching (see a larger version of this figure at https://oreil.ly/gpam1111)

The thickness of the `Same_As` edges indicates the strength of the connection. The strongest connection is between **Users** 505 and 805 at the bottom of the screen. In fact, we can see three subcommunities of **Users** among the largest community of seven members:

- Users 5, 105, and 205 at the top. The bond between Users 5 and 105 is a little stronger, for reasons not shown. All three share the same last name. They have similar addresses.

- Users 305 and 405 in the middle. Their last names and addresses are different, so some of the attributes not shown must be the cause of their similarity.

- Users 505 and 805 at the bottom. They share the same last name and address, as well as other attributes.

Scoring approximate matches

We can see in Figure 11-11 that some **Users** have similar names (Ellsworth versus Ellesworth) and similar addresses (Eagle Creek Center versus Eagle Crest Ctr). A scoring system that looks only for exact matchings gives us no credit for these near misses. An entity resolution system is ideally able to assess the similarity of two text strings and to assign a score to the situation. Do they differ by a single letter, like Ellesworth and Ellsworth? Are letters transposed, like Center and Cneter? Computer scientists like to think of the *edit distance* between two text strings: how many single-letter changes of value or position are needed to transform string X into string Y?

We are going to use Jaro-Winkler (JW) similarity[4] to measure the similarity between two strings, an enhancement of Jaro similarity. Given two strings, $s1$ and $s2$, that have m matching characters and t transformation steps between them, their Jaro similarity is defined as:

$$Jaro(s1, s2) = \frac{1}{3}\left(\frac{m}{|s1|} + \frac{m}{|s2|} + \frac{m-t}{m}\right).$$

If the strings are identical, then $m = |s1| = |s2|$, and $t = 0$, so the equation simplifies to $(1 + 1 + 1)/3 = 1$. On the other hand, if there are no letters in common, then the score is 0. JW similarity takes Jaro as a starting point and adds an additional reward if the beginnings of each string—reading from the left end—match exactly.

The net similarity score for two attribute values is their JW similarity multiplied by the weight for the attribute type. For example, if the attribute's weight is 0.5, and if the JW similarity score is 0.9, then the net score is $0.5 \times 0.9 = 0.45$.

Do: Run the `score_similar_attributes` query.

The `score_similar_attributes` query considers the **User** pairs that already are linked by a **Same_As** edge. It computes the weighted JW similarity for the `Last_Name` and the `Address` attributes, and adds those scores to the existing similarity score. We chose `Last_Name` and `Address` because they are alphabetic instead of numeric. This is an application decision rather than a technical one. Figure 11-12 shows the results after adding in the scores for the approximate matches.

---

4 Even more advanced similarity algorithms exist that are able to incorporate the semantic similarity between strings as well as the edit distance. For this example, we use a relatively simple algorithm for the sake of speed and easy illustration.

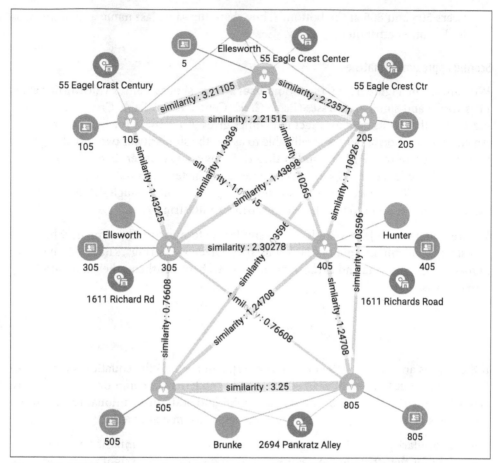

Figure 11-12. User community including Account 5 after exact and approximate weighted matching (see a larger version of this figure at https://oreil.ly/gpam1112)

Comparing Figure 11-11 and Figure 11-12, we notice the following changes:

- The connections among Users 1, 105, and 205 have strengthened due to their having similar addresses.

- User 305 is more strongly connected to the trio above due to a similar last name.

- The connection between 305 and 405 has strengthened due to their having similar addresses.

- User 405 is more strongly connected to Users 505 and 805 due to the name Hunter having some letters in common with Brunke. This last effect might be considered an unintended consequence of the JW similarity measure not being as judicious as a human evaluator would be.

Comparing two strings is a general-purpose function that does not require graph traversal, so we have implemented it as a simple string function in GSQL. Because it is not yet a built-in feature of the GSQL language, we took advantage of GSQL's ability to accept a user-supplied C++ function as a user-defined function (UDF). The UDFs for jaroDistance(s1, s2) and jaroWinklerDistance(s1, s2) are included in this starter kit. You can invoke them from within a GSQL query anywhere that you would be able to call a built-in string function. Of course, any other string comparison function could be implemented here in place of JW.

The following code snippet shows how we performed the approximate matching and scoring for the Address feature:

```
connected_users = SELECT A
    // Find all linked users, plus each user's address
    FROM Connected_users:A -(SameAs:e)- User:B,
        User:A -()- Address:A_addr,
        User:B -()- Address:B_addr
    WHERE A.id < B.id     // filter so we don't count both (A,B) & (B,A)
    ACCUM @@addr_match += 1,
    // If addresses aren't identical compute JaroWinkler * weight
      IF do_address AND A_addr.val != B_addr.val THEN
        FLOAT sim = jaroWinklerDistance(A_addr.id,B_addr.id) * addr_wt,
        @@sim_score += (A -> (B -> sim)),
        @@string_pairs += String_pair(A_addr.id, B_addr.id),
        IF sim != 0 THEN @@addr_update += 1 END
      END
```

The lines in the first FROM clause are an example of a *conjunctive path pattern*, that is, a compound pattern composed of several individual patterns, separated by commas. The commas act like Boolean AND. This conjunctive pattern means "find a User A linked to a User B, and find the Address connected to A, and find the Address connected to B." The following WHERE clause filters out the case where A = B and prevents a pair (A, B) from being processed twice.

The IF statement filters out the case where A and B are different but have identical addresses. If their addresses are the same, then we already gave them full credit when we ran connect_weighted_match. We then compute the weighted scoring, using the jaroWinklerDistance function and the weight for Address, storing the score in a FLOAT variable sim, which gets temporarily stored in a lookup table. The last two lines in the IF statement are just to record our activity, for informative output at the end.

Merging similar entities

In Method 1, we had a simple scheme for deciding whether to merge two entities: if their Jaccard score was greater than some threshold, then we created a **Same_As** edge. The decision was made to merge everything that has a **Same_As** edge. We want a more nuanced approach now. Our scoring has adjustable weights, and the **Same_As** edges record our scores. We can use another threshold score to decide which **Users** to merge.

We only need to make two small changes to `merge_connected_users` to let the user set a threshold:

1. Save a copy of `merge_connected_users` as a new query called `merge_simi lar_users`.

2. Add a threshold parameter to the query header:

   ```
   CREATE QUERY merge_similar_users(FLOAT threshold=1.0, BOOL verbose=FALSE)
   ```

3. In the SELECT block that finds connected **Users**, add a WHERE clause to check the **Same_As** edge's similarity value:

   ```
   WHILE (Updated_users.size() > 0) DO
     IF verbose THEN PRINT iteration, Updated_users.size(); END;
     Updated_users = SELECT t
       FROM Updated_users:s -(SameAs:e)- User:t
       WHERE e.similarity > threshold
         // Propagate the internal IDs from source to target vertex
       ACCUM t.@min_user_id += s.@min_user_id   // t gets the lesser of t & s ids
       HAVING t.@min_user_id != t.@min_user_id' // accum' is accum's previous val
       ;
     iteration = iteration + 1;
   END;
   ```

Run `merge_similar_users`. Pick a threshold value and see if you get the result that you expect.

For the community shown in Figure 11-12, Figure 11-13 shows the three different merging results for threshold values of 1.0, 2.5, and 3.0.

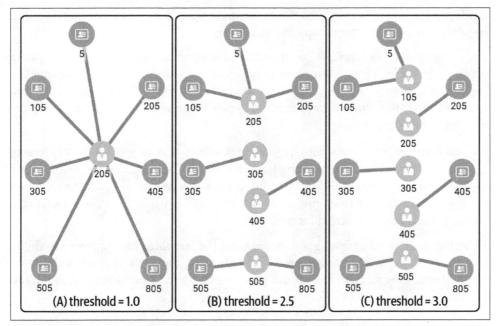

Figure 11-13. Entity resolution with different threshold levels (see a larger version of this figure at https://oreil.ly/gpam1113)

That concludes our second and more nuanced method of entity resolution.

To review, here is the sequence of queries we ran for entity resolution using weighted exact and approximate matching:

1. Run `initialize_users`.
2. Run `util_set_weights`.
3. Run `connect_weighed_match`.
4. Run `score_similar_attributes`.
5. Run `merge_similar_users`.
6. Repeat steps 3, 4 and 5 until the output of `merge_similar_users` says `converged = TRUE`.

Chapter Summary

In this chapter, we saw how graph algorithms and other graph techniques can be used for sophisticated entity resolution. Similarity algorithms and the connected component algorithm play key roles. We considered several schemes for assessing the similarity of two entities: Jaccard similarity, the weighted sum of exact matches, and Jaro-Winkler similarity for comparing text strings.

These approaches can readily be extended to supervised learning if training data becomes available. There are a number of model parameters that can be learned to improve the accuracy of the entity resolution: the scoring weights of each attribute for exact matching, tuning the scoring of approximate matches, and thresholds for merging similar **Users**.

We saw how the FROM clause in GSQL queries selects data in a graph by expressing a path or pattern. We also saw examples of the ACCUM clause and accumulators being used to compute and store information such as the common neighbors between vertices, a tally, an accumulating score, or even an evolving ID value, marking a vertex as a member of a particular community.

This chapter showed us how graph-based machine learning can improve the ability of enterprises to see the truth behind the data. In the next chapter, we'll apply graph machine learning to one of the most popular and important use cases: fraud detection.

CHAPTER 12

Improving Fraud Detection

In an earlier chapter, we took on the problem of fraud detection by designing graph queries that looked for certain patterns of behavior that could be suspicious. This chapter will apply machine learning methods to improve fraud detection. Machine learning can help us via anomaly detection or by training the software to recognize fraud based on examples of known fraud cases. In both cases, graph-structured data is a valuable asset for sensing the unusual (anomalies) or for supplying data features (to build predictive models). No method is perfect, but machine learning can often detect patterns and anomalies that humans would miss. Conventional approaches only follow the rules that experts dictate. Using machine learning on graphs, we can detect patterns within the data that were not explicitly flagged as fraud cases, which makes it more adaptive to changing fraud tactics.

After completing this chapter, you should be able to:

- Deploy and use the TigerGraph Machine Learning Workbench
- Use graph-based features to enrich the feature vector of a dataset and then compare the model accuracies with and without the graph features
- Prepare data for and train a graph neural network for node prediction—in this case, fraud prediction

Goal: Improve Fraud Detection

Fraud is the use of deception for personal enrichment. Fraudsters might sabotage a system and its users, but in the end it is for personal gain. Examples of fraudulent activities are identity theft, false or exaggerated insurance claims, and money laundering. Fraud detection is a set of activities to prevent fraudsters from carrying out such activities successfully. In many cases, fraudsters want to gain money from their effort.

Therefore fraud detection is a common practice among financial institutions, but it is also prevalent across organizations that hold valuable assets and properties, such as insurance, medical, governmental, and major retail organizations.

Fraud is a major business risk and is increasingly difficult to combat. According to a study from LexisNexis, every $1 of fraud costs $3.75 for companies within the ecommerce and retail sectors in the US, which is an increase of 19.8% since 2019.[1] These fraud costs come from fraudulent transactions due to identity fraud, which includes misuse of stolen identity or personal information. Fraud detection is becoming more challenging because of the growing channels through which fraudsters can operate. For example, an alarming trend is that fraud costs are surging via mobile smartphones. During the COVID-19 pandemic, consumers were pushed to do more digital transactions. Many of those transactions rely on smartphones, which have opened up new ways for fraudsters to mislead people.

Cryptocurrency is a popular medium of exchange for fraudsters. Instead of being issued and regulated by governments or central banks, cryptocurrencies are digital assets that are transferred between account holders, typically using an open and distributed ledger. This technology allows everyone to participate in the exchange without identification through a central authority, making money laundering, scams, and theft more appealing. In 2021, criminals stole $14 billion in cryptocurrency, and crypto-related crime rose to 79% from 2020.[2]

Solution: Use Relationships to Make a Smarter Model

Fraud can be detected if more facts about the parties and activities involved can be gathered and connected to see how they fit together. For example, suppose we find unusual transaction behavior, such as moving a high volume of money between accounts in a short period of time. Statistically, a certain percentage of such behavior is due to fraud. However, if those accounts have a connection to entities that central authorities have sanctioned, then the possibility of a fraud case becomes greater. In other words, when using transactional data in isolation, we can see a limited aspect of the case, but when we connect that data to another dataset that identifies sanctioned entities, we can take into account the path length between a party and a sanctioned entity. Using those relationships between different datasets is greater than the sum of its parts.

A graph is an excellent way to discover these relationships and patterns. In an earlier chapter, we saw how to use GSQL queries to detect particular patterns of interest.

---

1 "Discover the True Cost of Fraud," LexisNexis, accessed May 29, 2023, *https://risk.lexisnexis.com/insights-resources/research/us-ca-true-cost-of-fraud-study*.

2 MacKenzie Sigalos, "Crypto Scammers Took a Record $14 Billion in 2021," CNBC, January 6, 2022, *https://www.cnbc.com/2022/01/06/crypto-scammers-took-a-record-14-billion-in-2021-chainalysis.html*.

However, relying on the investigators to know the patterns in advance is limiting. A more powerful approach is to use machine learning to determine which patterns indicate fraud.

Most machine learning methods analyze vectors or matrices. Each vector is a list of numerical characteristics or *features* of one type of entity, such as a person. The machine learning method looks for patterns among those features. The data scientist provides the system with a representative sample of actual fraudulent (and nonfraudulent) cases for the machine learning system to analyze. The machine learning system's job is to extract a *model* that says, "When you have *these* feature values, you are likely to have fraud."

This approach has been a powerful tool in fighting fraud, but it is not perfect. One limitation is that a model is only as good as the training data provided. If our feature vectors are only describing direct characteristics of entities, then we are missing out on the deeper graph-oriented relationships that could be valuable. By combining the deeper insight that is available with graph analytics, we can enrich the input or training data, thereby producing more accurate machine learning models.

In the following hands-on example, we will use the TigerGraph Machine Learning Workbench to help us extract graph features automatically to enrich training data as well as to run a graph neural network (GNN).

Using the TigerGraph Machine Learning Workbench

For this hands-on exercise, which is focused on machine learning, we will be using the TigerGraph Machine Learning Workbench, or ML Workbench for short. Based on the open source JupyterLab IDE for Python-oriented data scientists, and including TigerGraph's Python library pyTigerGraph, the ML Workbench makes it simple to develop a machine learning pipeline that includes graph data.

Setting Up the ML Workbench

We will first obtain an instance of the ML Workbench on the TigerGraph Cloud service and then connect it to a database instance.

Create a TigerGraph Cloud ML Bundle

The easiest way to set up the ML Workbench is to deploy a TigerGraph Cloud ML Bundle, which adds the ML Workbench as one of the tools available to use with a TigerGraph Cloud database instance:

1. There is a small charge for using the ML Bundle, so you will need to set up payment information on your account.

---

2. From the Clusters screen of your TigerGraph Cloud account, click on the Create Cluster button.

3. At the top of the Create Cluster page, select the ML Bundle option on the right.

4. Select an instance size. The smallest one available is fine for this exercise.

5. We will be using a dataset and queries that are built into the ML Workbench, so it doesn't matter what use case you select here. Finish setting any other options that you wish, then click Create Cluster at the bottom of the page.

The cluster takes a few minutes to provision.

Create and copy database credentials

The ML Workbench includes a robust series of example Jupyter notebooks that use pyTigerGraph to download datasets and create graphs in your cluster. Before it can do this, it must first gain access to the TigerGraph database using credentials that you provide:

1. You should still be on the Clusters page of TigerGraph Cloud. For the cluster you just created, click Access Management.

2. Click the Database Access tab and then Add Database Users.

3. Enter a username and password. Be sure to remember both of these, since you will use them later in the ML Workbench.

4. Go to the Role Management tab next to Database Access.

5. Select the checkbox next to your new user, set the role to globaldesigner, then click Save.

6. Go to the Details tab. Copy the Domain, which ends in *i.tgcloud.io*.

Connect the ML Workbench to your graph database

1. Go to GraphStudio for this database instance.

2. In the upper right corner, click on the Tools menu icon (an icon of a 3 × 3 grid), and then select ML Workbench.

3. After the workbench opens, find *config.json* in the left-side panel and double-click to edit it.

4. Replace the URL value of host with the domain value that you copied. The resulting value should still start with *https://* and end with *i.tgcloud.io*.

5. Change the username and password values to the username and password of the new user you created.

Although this process involves several steps, once you get used to the TigerGraph Cloud and ML Workbench interfaces, it will become second nature to grant ML Workbench access to your cluster through a new database user.

Working with ML Workbench and Jupyter Notes

Double-click *README.md* in the file browser's left panel in the ML Workbench, as shown in Figure 12-1, to get an overview of the general structure and capabilities of pyTigerGraph and the ML Workbench component.

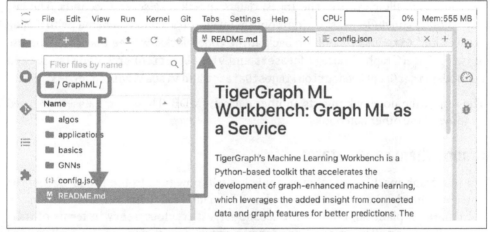

Figure 12-1. ML Workbench and the README file

You just completed the Set Up section. Scroll down to the Learn section. Here you'll see lists of tutorial and example notebooks for getting started, graph algorithms, GNNs, and end-to-end applications.

The remainder of this section walks through the *Datasets.ipynb* notebook, for users not familiar with Jupyter. If you are familiar with Jupyter, you should still go through this quickly to verify that your database connection is working.

Open the *Datasets.ipynb* notebook in the *Basics* folder. This file is a Jupyter notebook, which combines Python code snippets with explanatory comments. Python blocks are enumerated [1], [2], and so on. A thick blue bar at the left highlights the next section to be executed. Clicking the right-facing arrow at the command menu at the top will execute the next code block:

1. Click the arrow until block [1] Download dataset starts to run.

   While it is running, the number in the brackets will change to an asterisk (*). When it completes, the asterisk will change back to the number. Pay attention to any output for information or error messages.

When running an ML Workbench notebook, be sure your database is active (not paused). If it is paused, then when you try to run a block, the square brackets will contain an empty space [ ] instead of an asterisk [*].

2. Run the next three Python blocks: Create connection, Ingest data, and Visualize schema.

If you have a problem with Create connection, then you probably did not set up the *config.json* file correctly. The Ingest data step will take several seconds. The last step should conclude by showing you an image of a simple schema with **Paper** vertices and **Cite** edges. Looking back at the code blocks, we see that we made use of two pyTigerGraph libraries (`datasets` and `visualization`) and a few classes and methods: `TigerGraphConnection.ingestDataset` and `visualization.drawSchema`.

The rest of the notebook ingests another dataset, IMDB. These two datasets are used by some of the other notebooks.

Graph Schema and Dataset

For our graph machine learning example, we will now turn to the `fraud_detection` notebook inside the *applications* folder. The data used here are transactions on the Ethereum platform; Ether is the second-largest cryptocurrency in terms of market capitalization. The transactions form a graph, where vertices are wallets (i.e., accounts) on the platform, and edges are transactions between the accounts. There are 32,168 vertices and 84,088 directed edges pointing from the sending account to the receiving account. The dataset is derived from research by Liang Chen et al. in "Phishing Scams Detection in Ethereum Transaction Network,"[3] available from XBlock.[4] Having directed edges tells us how the money is moving, which is important for any financial analysis, including fraud detection.

Each account vertex has an `is_fraud` parameter. The dataset has 1,165 accounts that are labeled as fraudulent. These were reported to be accounts belonging to phishing scammers, one of the most common forms of fraud in the cryptocurrency community.

A typical phishing scam in the crypto economy occurs when the attacker sets up a site that promises to return a big reward with a small investment, usually promising that

---

3 Liang Chen et al., "Phishing Scams Detection in Ethereum Transaction Network," *ACM Transactions on Internet Technology* 21, no. 1 (February 2021): 1–16, doi: 10.1145/3398071.

4 Liang Chen et al., "Ethereum Phishing Transaction Network," XBlock, accessed May 29, 2023, *https://xblock.pro/#/dataset/13*.

the victim is getting in early on a scheme that will see huge gains. The gains never come, and the initial investment is lost forever.

Because these scammers accept many small transactions in a short amount of time and then move the money in larger chunks to other accounts, their transaction activity usually doesn't match the profile of the typical legitimate cryptocurrency user. The vertices in the dataset have seven parameters—detailed in Table 12-1—corresponding to the features described in Chen et al.

Importantly, none of these graph features are actually represented in the dataset upon loading. The dataset only contains the ID and is_fraud flag on the vertices (accounts) and the amount and timestamp on the edges (transactions). We use the given information to generate the graph features during the tutorial walkthrough.

Table 12-1. Graph-based features for the Ethereum transaction dataset

Feature	Description
FT1	Indegree, or the number of incoming transactions for an account vertex
FT2	Outdegree, or the number of outgoing transactions for an account vertex
FT3	Degree, or the total number of transactions involving an account
FT4	In-strength, or the total monetary amount of all incoming transactions
FT5	Out-strength, or the total monetary amount of all outgoing transactions
FT6	Strength, or the total monetary amount of all transactions involving an account
FT7	Number of neighbors
FT8	Inverse transaction frequency: this is the time interval between the account's first and last transaction divided by FT3

Fraudulent accounts tend to have higher values for features 4, 5, and 6 and smaller values for feature 8. Phishing attackers steal a great deal of money overall through many smaller transactions.

FT7 (number of neighbors) differs from FT3 (number of transactions) because one neighbor could be responsible for multiple transactions. When we load the data into TigerGraph, we merge all the transactions between a pair of accounts into a single edge, so we do not use FT7. Despite this simplification, we still achieve good results, as will soon be demonstrated. Additional features in a similar dataset may very well improve performance even further. While the exact graph features that a bank uses for fraud detection are both data dependent and trade secrets, it is generally believed that centrality algorithms like PageRank and community detection algorithms like Louvain have often been helpful.

Although these metrics provide a quick intuitive look at the behavior of phishing attacks, both a traditional machine learning approach and a GNN are able to figure out a more precise relationship among all of the features in order to discriminate between accounts used for phishing and accounts used legitimately. In this chapter, we'll compare the approaches and outcomes for both methods.

Check that the first code block in the fraud_detection notebook has the same connection and credentials information that you set up in *config.json* before. Run the Database Preparation steps of the fraud_detection notebook to create the graph schema and load the data.

Graph Feature Engineering

You should now be at the section entitled Graph Feature Engineering. As the notebook says, we use a pyTigerGraph featurizer object to generate features: two features from built-in algorithms (PageRank and betweenness centrality), and two from GSQL queries of our own. The Featurizer provides a high-level simplified process for generating and storing graph-based features. Algorithms in the GDS Library are automatically available to the Texturizer; users only need to specify some parameters.

We call our object f. Run code block 4 to create it:

```
[4] :     f = conn.gds.featurizer()
```

In the PageRank section, we use the tg_pagerank algorithm included in the pre-installed Featurizer algorithm set. PageRank measures the influence of vertices in a graph. If a vertex is pointed to by many other vertices that *themselves* are pointed to by many vertices, it receives a high PageRank score. Each algorithm uses a set of input parameters. You can check the documentation for the *TigerGraph GDS Library* (*https://oreil.ly/2TAhH*) to see what the parameters are for a particular algorithm. In the PageRank code block, we specify a Python dictionary of parameters and their values to pass to PageRank. Since this graph schema is so simple, the choice of vertex and edge type is made for us. We store the ranking value in each vertex under the attribute pagerank, then return the top five vertices with the highest values. There is a similar code block to generate betweenness centrality as a vertex feature. Betweenness is a slow algorithm; be patient.

Next we calculate features for the transactions based on their degree (FT3 in the feature chart) and their amount (FT6, also known as strength). These use custom queries that can be found in the *GraphML/applications/fraud_detection/gsql* folder of the notebook. Run code blocks under Degree Features and Amount Features. Each one takes about 10 to 20 seconds.

Look at the queries to check your understanding of GSQL. The amounts query sets four vertex attributes for each vertex in the graph: the minimum received, the total amount received, the minimum sent, and the total amount sent. The degrees query is even simpler, just checking the number of transactions received (the indegree) and the number sent to other vertices (the outdegree).

Now that we have a set of graph-related features on each vertex, including the ground truth of whether or not they are fraudulent accounts, we can use traditional supervised machine learning methods to try to predict fraud.

Run the next code block for FastRP[5] Embeddings. FastRP (*https://oreil.ly/PgE0O*) is a vertex embedding algorithm based on the principle of random projection (RP) to perform dimensionality reduction. FastRP is also part of the TigerGraph built-in algorithm library. For relatively small datasets like this one, it provides very good performance with reasonable resource cost.

Run the Check Labels block to check the number of fraud and normal accounts in the dataset. You should get the following statistics about the labeled accounts:

```
Fraud accounts: 1165 (3.62%%)
Normal accounts: 31003 (96.38%%)
```

In the Train/Test Split code blocks, we split the vertices using the `vertexSplitter` function into 80% training data and 20% validation data. The `vertexSplitter` function as included in the notebook assigns two Boolean features, `is_training` and `is_validation`, to each vertex, then randomly assigns each one `true` or `false` values to create the 80-20 split.

Next, we create two Vertex Loaders, which load all vertices of the graph onto the machine learning server in batches. We pass a list of attributes to include; all of these we recently created in the last few steps, except for the `is_fraud` label. We display the first five vertices in each set to make sure they were loaded in correctly.

Training Traditional Models with Graph Features

Now we are ready to train our fraud detection model. We will use XGBoost, a popular classification algorithm for tabular data. We import the `XGBClassifier` class from the `xgboost` library and create a classifier instance called `tree_model`, as shown in the Create xgboost model code block.

Next we train XGBoost models using three different sets of features so we can compare their results. For each case, we create a list consisting of the selected graph features, except for `is_fraud`. Then we use `tree_model.fit()` to say, "Using the features of our training data, try to predict the attribute `is_fraud`." After training each model, another code block evaluates each model using the `Accuracy`, `BinaryPrecision`, and `BinaryRecall` modules from the `metrics` library in pyTigerGraph.

---

[5] As graph machine learning is a rapidly developing field, the algorithms in the notebook might be updated by the time you obtain it.

Run the first case, which uses only nongraph features. Your model should achieve approximately 75% accuracy, 12% precision, and 100% recall. Remember that about 3.6% of the transactions are fraudulent. A 100% recall means our model will catch all the real cases of fraud. Since the overall accuracy is 75%, this means that the model is incorrectly classifying about 25% of the normal accounts as fraudsters.

Run the next case, which now includes PageRank and betweenness centrality. You should see that accuracy and precision go up by a few percentage points, while recall drops to about 98%. Finally, run the third case, which adds the FastRP embedding to the feature set. You should see a significant increase in accuracy and precision. Figure 12-2 compares the prediction performance of the three cases.

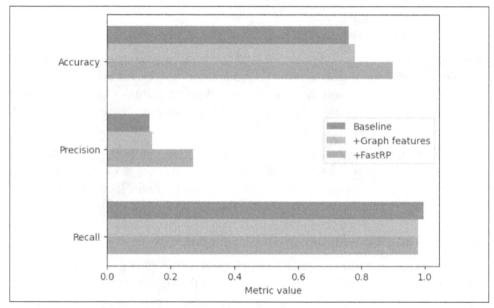

Figure 12-2. Prediction performance with and without graph features and graph embedding (see a larger version of this figure at https://oreil.ly/gpam1202)

Run the next cell under the Explain Model section to create a chart like Figure 12-3, showing the feature importance for Case 2, including the graph algorithms but not the graph embedding in our training. Note that pagerank is the second most important feature for predicting fraud, close behind the send_amount.

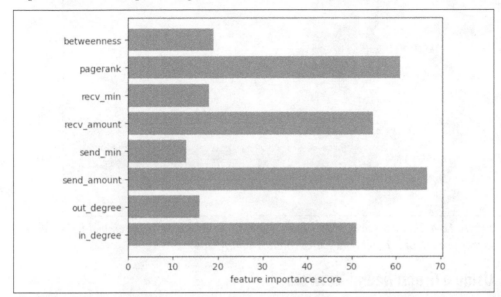

Figure 12-3. Importance of features for XGBoost model with graph algorithms (see a larger version of this figure at https://oreil.ly/gpam1203)

Next, run the subsequent cell under Explain Model to see the feature importance with the embeddings. Here, all the dimensions of the embeddings are summed into one feature importance score. Figure 12-4 shows that the embedding heavily contributes to the model's performance.

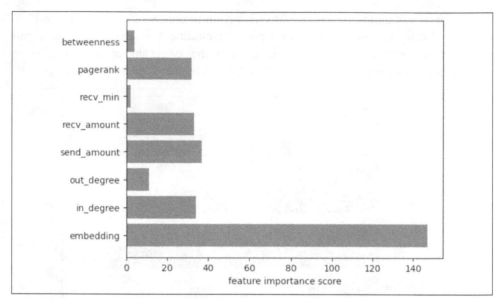

Figure 12-4. Importance of features for XGBoost model with FastRP embeddings (see a larger version of this figure at https://oreil.ly/gpam1204)

Using a Graph Neural Network

In the next section, we set up a graph neural network to try to predict fraud accounts even more accurately.

In the first block of the GNN section, we set some hyperparameters. We've already selected good hyperparameter values that produce a highly accurate result. However, fine-tuning hyperparameters is one of the arts of machine learning, so after you finish this section, come back to this stage and experiment with tweaking these values.

Just like in the last section, we set up two loaders to get the data into two big chunks: training and validation. These, however, use the neighborLoader method instead of vertexLoader. In a GNN, every vertex is influenced by its neighboring vertices. Therefore, when we load data, we load not just individual vertices but neighborhoods centered around each vertex. As you can see, the syntax for these loaders is roughly equivalent to the loaders in the xgboost section, though these loaders also incorporate some of the hyperparameters.

Now that our data is all set up, we can create and train the GNN. This notebook uses the pyTorch Geometric GDS library, which offers several GNN models. The ML Workbench is flexible enough to use any of these; it also supposes DGL and TensorFlow graph machine learning libraries. Some of the more common models are built into pyTigerGraph, for even easier use.

We will use a graph attention network (GAT in the pyTorch Geometric library), which combines the fine-grained modeling of attention models with graph neighbor convolution. We run the network for 10 epochs.

This takes slightly longer than the nongraph XGBoost model. This is partially because of the complexity of the neural network compared to the decision tree model. In the free cloud instance tier, this takes about five seconds per epoch. Enterprise-level datasets normally run on much more capable hardware, taking advantage of GPUs to speed up the process significantly more than is possible using a CPU.

The extra wait paid off, though. When the last epoch finishes, look at the returned values: we achieved greater than 90% accuracy!

Run the next several cells to get a visual look at the training over time. In the Explain Model section, we randomly select a fraudulent vertex to see what its network looks like. Since we don't have a perfectly accurate model, this cell may sometimes show vertices with few or no connections. However, if you run the cell more times, you'll probably see vertex neighborhoods closer to the one shown in Figure 12-5.

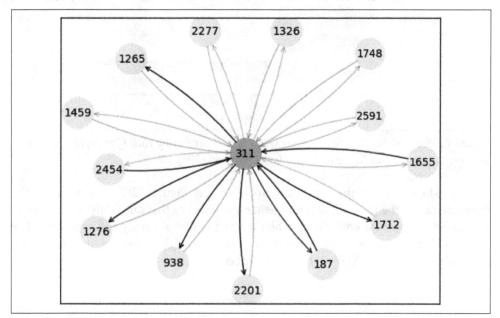

Figure 12-5. Visual explanation of prediction for vertex 311 (see a larger version of this figure at https://oreil.ly/gpam1205)

In this case, the vertex receives a high number of transactions from other vertices and then makes large transactions out to a few more. If this really is a scammer, they could be receiving many payments and then shifting their money to another set of accounts that they also have access to.

Running the last code blocks, we get another chart for importance of features, like Figure 12-6. We see that the important features in our more accurate GNN model tend to be different from the features that were identified as important in the XGBoost model. Here, PageRank is not as important for detecting fraud as amount received, amount sent, and number of incoming transactions. Remember, however, that the neighborhood convolution of the GNN model is already taking into account the effect of relationships, so graph features like PageRank might be redundant.

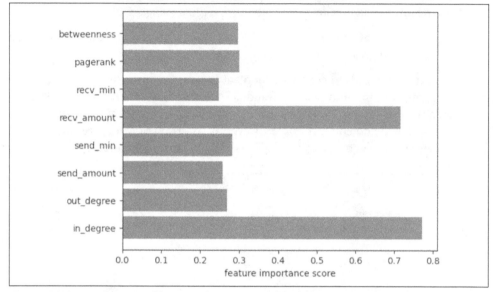

Figure 12-6. Importance of features for GNN model predicting fraud for vertex 311 (see a larger version of this figure at https://oreil.ly/gpam1206)

Finally, when running the last code block, we get Figure 12-7, which shows the performance of the three models altogether. Here we see that our GNN is even better than XGBoost and the embedding when looking at that accuracy and precision. The GNN achieves a smaller recall than the two other models. However, it is still good, especially compared to XGBoost without embeddings.

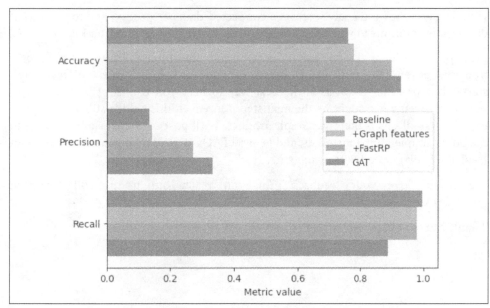

Figure 12-7. Performance of XGBoost versus XGBoost + FastRP versus GNN (see a larger version of this figure at https://oreil.ly/gpam1207)

Chapter Summary

In this chapter, we looked at a specific machine learning problem and compared three graph-enhanced approaches to solving it. Our platform was the TigerGraph ML Workbench, which includes sample notebooks and datasets ready to be used on a TigerGraph Cloud instance.

We first used a traditional decision tree machine learning library, XGBoost, to classify a dataset of Ethereum transactions into normal accounts and accounts suspected of committing fraud, using data that included graph-based features like PageRank and degree. Here, graph data, graph analytics, and even graph machine learning contributed to the data preparation phase.

We then made the same predictions using a GNN, which took graph relationships into account during the training phase, resulting in a higher precision model than was possible with XGBoost.

Connecting with You

We hope our book made a connection with you, in the form of information, insight, and even some inspiration. We love graphs and graph analytics, so we hope that love shone through. Our mission was to help you see data as connected entities, to learn to view data searches and analytics from a connected-data perspective, and to get started developing solutions to your own tasks by working with use case starter kits.

From our experience as data analysts, writers, and educators, we know that not everything makes sense the first time. Doing some hands-on exercises with the TigerGraph starter kits or other tutorials is the best way to help you connect the dots and to see for yourself what might be the next step. Moreover, this field is still growing and evolving rapidly, as is the TigerGraph product. We'll post corrections and updates to the book, supplemental materials, and general FAQs at *https://github.com/TigerGraph-DevLabs/Book-graph-powered-analytics*.

We would love your feedback. You can reach out to us collectively at *gpaml.book@gmail.com*.

Thank you, and happy exploring!

Index

columns, mapping to graph objects, 26, 30-32
Common Attack Pattern Enumerations and
    Classifications (CAPEC) initiative, 176
communities, 4
    algorithms for defining, 130-134
    finding and analyzing, 203-207
    merging connected communities, 261-264
    structure of, machine learning through, 214
    visualizing, 257
complete subgraphs, 130
Comprehensive Survey of Graph Embedding
    (Cai, Zheng, and Chang), 234
config.json file, 278, 280, 282
conjunctive path pattern, 271
connected component algorithm, 253
connected components, 130
connections, 1-2, 10
    (see also patterns)
    extracting intelligence from, 34-34
    impact on analysis, 119
    meaning derived from, 3
    questions about, addressing, 119
    searching deeply for connected information,
        35-37
connect_jaccard_sim query, 256, 260, 261, 264
connect_weighted_match query, 267, 271
convolution, 235
    (see also GCNs (graph convolutional net-
        works))
cosine similarity, 137-139
Crunchbase Starter Kit
    startup investment graph, 81
    vertices types in, 83
cryptocurrency, 276
Customer 360 (C360) graph, 43, 45-46
    (see also TigerGraph)
Customer 360 Starter Kit, 48-50
customer interaction subgraph, 57-61
customer journey query, 57, 62-63
customer journeys, 43-44
customer_interaction query, 57-59
cybersecurity
    attack detection, challenges in, 177
    cost of attacks, 175-176
    cybersecurity system requirements, 177
Cybersecurity Threat Detection Starter Kit
    event types, 179
    graph schema, 178-180
    installing and loading data, 178

queries and analytics
    alert source tracing query, 180, 188-190
    firewall bypass detection query, 181-182
    flooding detection query, 180, 184-186
    footprint detection query, 180, 187-188
    overview, 180
    suspicious IP detection query, 180,
        182-183

D

damping parameter, 158
data ambiguity, 39
data analytics, 119, 125
    (see also graph analytics)
data breaches (see cybersecurity)
data complexity, schema complexity vs., 194
data representation, evolution of, 1-2
data structure, impact on analysis, 119
data triplets, 37
Datasets.ipynb notebook, 279-280
DeepWalk algorithm, 230-233
degrees query, 282
descriptors, mapping, 26
deterministic algorithms, 123, 125
DFS (depth-first search), 25, 120-121
dimensionality reduction, 229
directed edges, 18
    advantages and disadvantages of, 27
    defined, 22
    paired with reverse directed edges, 27
display_edges parameter, 158, 198
Drug Interaction 360 Graph
    graph schema, 69
    overview, 68
    queries and analytics, 69-77
        finding similar reported cases, 70, 71-73
        most_reported_drugs_for_company
            query, 70, 73-75
        top_side_effects_for_top_drugs query,
            70, 75-77

E

edges, 2, 5, 18
    (see also directed edges; undirected edges)
    advantages of, 7
    defined, 22
    directionality in, 26
    mapping tabular data to, 26, 30-32
    multiple, 28-29

K

k-core, 130
key -> value pair, 97
key role discovery, 83, 84
Kipf, Thomas, 235
Kiselev, Dmitrii, 234
kNN (k-nearest neighbors) algorithm, 143
Knowledge Graph, 4
Kronecker delta function, 133

L

Lee, Victor E. , 141
Leiden algorithm, 214
Leskovec, Jure, 240
LIMIT clause, 94, 166, 167
linear relationship, 37
link prediction, 144
local graph features, 216
Louvain algorithm, 133, 158, 214, 281
lower(trim()) function, 85

M

machine learning (ML), 9
    (see also TigerGraph Machine Learning
        Workbench)
    extracting graph features, 244
        domain-dependent features, 222-225
        domain-independent features, 216-222
        graph embeddings, 225-234
        overview, 215-216
    graph neural networks (GNNs)
        graph convolutional networks (GCN),
            235-238
        GraphSAGE, 240-242
        overview, 235
    graph-enhanced, 9-10
    pattern discovery and feature extraction
        methods, 244
    reinforcement learning, 213
    supervised learning, 213, 216
    unsupervised learning with graph algo-
        rithms, 213-215
    use cases for machine learning tasks,
        243-243
Makarov, Ilya, 234
map type attribute, 265
MapAccum, 96, 123, 187
maps, 96

matching records, 39
matrix algebra formulation, 238
MaxAccum, 166, 188
max_change parameter, 157
max_hops parameter, 198
max_iter parameter, 157
mean deviation
    in flooding detection query, 184-186
    in footprint detection query, 187
merge_connected_users algorithm, 261, 262,
    264, 272
merging records, 40
Milgram, Stanley, 35
ML (see machine learning (ML))
modularity-based algorithms, 214
modularity-based community algorithms, 132,
    133
modules, 159
money laundering (see financial crimes)
MST (minimal spanning tree) problem, 128
multihop queries, 81
multiple edges, 28-29
multitransaction query, 105, 108-110

N

neighborhood similarity, 135
neighborLoader method, 286
Nikitinsky, Nikita, 234
Node2vec algorithm, 233-235
nodes (see vertices)
normalizing scores, 138
n_sigma parameter, 184, 187

O

one-hot encoding, 232
ORDER BY clause, 94, 166, 167
outlier detection
    in flooding detection query, 184, 186
    in footprint detection query, 187
    using machine learning, 213
output_level parameter, 159
out_degree function, 71

P

Page, Larry, 157
PageRank algorithm, 124, 157, 193, 214, 281,
    282, 284
    as centrality algorithm, 130

linked to related vertices, 29
mapping tabular data to, 26, 30-32
modeling properties as, 20
printing, 86
reaching many in few hops, 35
similarity of, 144
types in Crunchbase Starter Kit, 83
types in Cybersecurity Threat Detection
    graph model, 180
types in Fraud and Money Laundering
    Detection Starter Kit, 104
types in Healthcare Referral graph model,
    149-150
types in Recommendation Engine 2.0 graph
    model, 163
types in Salesforce Customer 360 graph
    model, 54
vertex features, 216
v_type parameter, 157, 197

W

w window parameter, 232
WCC (weakly connected component), 131
weighted relationships, 40-41

Welling, Max, 235
wf parameter, 198
WHERE clause, 93, 97, 271
Widom, Jennifer, 140
word embedding, 225
word2vec algorithm, 230
World Wide Web
    distinction from internet, 2
    effect on graphs, 3
    importance of data structure on, 2

X

XGBoost algorithm, 285, 288
XGBoost model, 283, 285, 285

Y

Y-shaped graph, 75
Y-shaped pattern, 37
Ying, Rex, 240

Z

Zheng, Vincent W. , 234

About the Authors

Victor Lee is vice president of machine learning and AI at TigerGraph. His PhD dissertation was on graph-based similarity and ranking. Dr. Lee has coauthored book chapters on decision trees and dense subgraph discovery. Teaching and training have also been central to his career journey, with activities ranging from developing training materials for chip design to writing the first version of TigerGraph's technical documentation, from teaching 12 years as a full-time or part-time classroom instructor to presenting numerous webinars and in-person workshops.

Phuc Kien Nguyen is a data scientist in anti-money laundering and terrorist financing at ABN AMRO Bank. He has engineered transaction filtering solutions and developed machine learning models to detect high-risk customers for KYC purposes for more than six years. During his academic career, he focused on information science, leading him to an MSc in information architecture from Delft University of Technology.

Alexander Thomas is a former TigerGraph technical writer with a background in linguistics and education. He loves keeping up with the latest advances in artificial intelligence and data science and always has several projects going simultaneously.

Colophon

The animal on the cover of *Graph-Powered Analytics and Machine Learning with TigerGraph* is a golden-spotted tiger beetle (*Cicindela aurulenta*). It is native to South and Southeast Asia, ranging from Nepal and southern China to Indonesia, and can often be found in sandy habitats, particularly shorelines and sand dunes. Adults grow up to 20 millimeters in length and have iridescent blue-green bodies with three large yellow spots on each elytron.

Golden-spotted tiger beetles are aggressive predators that feed on many kinds of invertebrates. They have keen eyesight and are fast for their size, running down prey and then catching and dismembering them with their powerful mandibles. Their larvae feed by lying in wait in vertical burrows, ambushing prey that wander nearby and dragging them down into their burrows.

Many of the animals on O'Reilly covers are endangered; all of them are important to the world.

The cover illustration is by Karen Montgomery, based on an antique line engraving from *Wood's Illustrated Natural History*. The cover fonts are Gilroy Semibold and Guardian Sans. The text font is Adobe Minion Pro; the heading font is Adobe Myriad Condensed; and the code font is Dalton Maag's Ubuntu Mono.

CPSIA information can be obtained
at www.ICGtesting.com
Printed in the USA
JSHW052248250723
45367JS00003B/20

9 781098 106652